A NEW DEAL FOR
YOUTH

A Da Capo Press Reprint Series

FRANKLIN D. ROOSEVELT
AND THE ERA OF THE NEW DEAL

GENERAL EDITOR: FRANK FREIDEL

Harvard University

A NEW DEAL FOR YOUTH

*The Story of
the National Youth Administration*

By Betty and Ernest K. Lindley

DA CAPO PRESS • NEW YORK • 1972

Library of Congress Cataloging in Publication Data

Lindley, Betty (Grimes) 1902-
  A new deal for youth.
  (Franklin D. Roosevelt and the era of the New Deal)
  1. U.S. National Youth Administration.
  I. Lindley, Ernest Kidder, 1899-   joint author.
  II. Title. III. Series.
  HV1431.L5   1972   331.3'4'0973   72-172867
  ISBN 0-306-70382-3

This Da Capo Press edition of *A New Deal for Youth* is an
unabridged republication of the first edition published in
New York in 1938. It is reprinted by permission from a copy
of the original edition in the collection of Case Western
Reserve University.

Published by Da Capo Press, Inc.
A Subsidiary of Plenum Publishing Corporation
227 W. 17 St., New York, New York 10011

A New Deal for

YOUTH

BY ERNEST K. LINDLEY

★

FRANKLIN D. ROOSEVELT: A CAREER IN
PROGRESSIVE DEMOCRACY

THE ROOSEVELT REVOLUTION

HALF WAY WITH ROOSEVELT

A New Deal for
YOUTH

The Story of the National Youth Administration

BETTY AND ERNEST K. LINDLEY

NEW YORK · THE VIKING PRESS · PUBLISHERS
MCMXXXVIII

First published in July 1938

To Mrs. Franklin D. Roosevelt

because in mining towns, in beet sugar villages, in mountain backwashes, in city slums, on isolated farms, in high schools, in colleges, and in universities—wherever we have been—youth speak of her as their friend.

Authors' Acknowledgments

THIS BOOK ORIGINATED IN THE DESIRE OF THE NATIONAL ADVISORY Committee of the National Youth Administration for an independent survey of the activities of the NYA. Much of the information comes from first-hand observation in the field by one of the authors during the first four months of 1938 while temporarily engaged as a consultant to the National Advisory Committee. In addition, we were granted free access to the files of the National Youth Administration and have made use of assembled data hitherto unpublished.

We are indebted, first of all, to Miss Thelma McKelvey, Director of the Division of Reports and Records of the National Youth Administration. Without the aid of her efficiency and intelligence and generous contribution of time, we could not have assembled much of the material that is in this book. She and the members of her staff—Miss Mina Gardner, Mrs. Miriam Naigles, Mrs. Anita Day, and Miss Phyllis Scully—were helpful throughout and worked overtime to compile most of the data for the Appendix.

We are indebted also to Mr. Aubrey Williams, Mr. Richard R. Brown, Mr. David R. Williams, Mr. W. Thacher Winslow, Mr. John H. Pritchard, Dr. Mary H. S. Hayes, Mrs. Mary McLeod Bethune, and other members of the national NYA staff. We found them all engagingly frank in answering our questions and helpful in many other ways. The regional directors, State directors, and many of their assistants, all of them already overburdened with work, have been extremely co-operative. We are grateful to all of them. Our thankful appreciation extends also to the hundreds of work project supervisors and the many members of the faculties of high schools and colleges who generously gave us their time and interpretations.

In this book we have attempted to give a panoramic picture of the NYA. Necessarily we have made some appraisals. They are strictly our own and should not be construed as those either of NYA officials or of any member of the National Advisory Committee.

B. L. AND E. K. L.

Washington, May 8, 1938.

Foreword

By CHARLES W. TAUSSIG

CHAIRMAN OF THE NATIONAL ADVISORY COMMITTEE
OF THE NATIONAL YOUTH ADMINISTRATION

IF WE ARE TO CONSIDER AS NORMAL THE YEARS OF THE PRESENT century prior to the Great War, the entire generation which we today call "Youth" was born into an abnormal world. Greeted by a world war or the economic aftermath, they have known only a condition of social and economic instability. Unprecedented post-war agricultural prosperity was quickly followed by collapse and dire distress. A few years of a riotous industrial boom, with all the attendant luxuries and banalities, were followed in 1929 by an economic crisis, from which we are now only hesitatingly commencing to emerge.

While we in the United States have been going through our own gyrations, our youth have seen the rest of the world torn by wars and revolutions. They have seen age-old governments crack up and be replaced by a variety of dictatorships. American youth of today never knew the norms by which we judge the passing show. It is difficult for adults to understand the point of view of young people. We draw comparisons between present-day chaos and what we called normal some years back. Youth know only chaos. With all the progress that has been made in our educational technique, much of it is still based on a world which no longer exists and which has never existed for the younger generation.

Youth, in an effort to throw off the non-essentials and inadequacies of a system that prepares them for a life they have no opportunity to live, frequently discard the fundamentals of a good life. Integrity, spirituality, and a reasonable moral code are sometimes sacrificed. On the other hand, hardship and suffering have developed in them a social consciousness that did not exist in previous generations. The amenities of life are no longer taken for granted. Today young people have once more become explorers, explorers in a world in which even their elders fail to recognize familiar landmarks, a world in which many a landfall has proved but a mirage. With some justification, youth suspect the older generation of having worshiped false gods. Rightly or wrongly, they feel we have made a "mess of things." The very system which we know as Democracy is subjected by youth to a cruel analysis. Vendors of gilt substitutes find willing converts to political and social creeds that are destructive to much that this Nation stands for.

Now, if ever, we must invoke our cardinal principles of free thought, free speech, and free education. Under the proper direction and leadership, our youth can and will develop a more definite and hopeful philosophy of life. Unless we educate the youth of today to function intelligently in a modern Democracy, democratic government is doomed. Who can view the political, social, and economic changes in the world without looking to our own Democracy, even with its acknowledged shortcomings, as a haven of hope? To reinforce and perfect our system of government, we will require a leadership and an electorate far more intelligent and responsive than we have had in the past. We must remember that in less than a decade the group which we now designate as "youth" will control the destiny of this Nation.

Youth are dissatisfied, and with much justification. They are sentient, restless, and explosive. Unless we can give them the opportunities which they demand, they will seek a way for themselves that may endanger the very fundamentals of our liberties. Their demands are not unreasonable. They desire an opportunity to earn a living; to marry at mating age; to attain education; to understand the principles and functions of our government. They ask only a willingness on our part to consider them fellow-citizens of a great Democracy.

This in broad terms is what is called "the youth problem." In my judgment the following specific deficiencies in our national life have created this problem:

(1) There are not jobs enough to take care of the youth who need them and want them.

(2) Our educational system is not adequate, in size or character, to prepare multitudes of youth for the work opportunities that are available.

(3) Nationally speaking, there is not equal opportunity for education. Vast areas of the United States have inadequate educational systems. There are not enough free schools to take care of the youth population, and millions of youth and children are too poor to attend free schools and colleges even where they exist.

(4) There is a gap measured in years between the time a youth leaves school and the time he finds a job. During this period society completely abandons him. Most of our criminals are to be found in this social no-man's land.

The National Youth Administration was created in an attempt to find a solution or a partial solution for these four shortcomings in our social and economic life.

It is of importance that the reader of this book keep in mind the basic philosophy of our American approach to this problem. The problem is not unique to the United States. It exists in most countries throughout the world. But an American solution must be predicated on the maintenance and reinforcement of the family unit. In totalitarian states, by contrast, the community and family are subordinated to a regimented nationalism.

Our American philosophy neither prevents a national approach to the problem nor puts undue emphasis on sectionalism at the expense of national purpose and national unity. On the contrary, equalizing opportunities within our communities and bolstering the more backward communities strengthen the Nation as a whole in the only way it can be strengthened in a Democracy.

On August 15, 1935, the National Advisory Committee of the National Youth Administration held its first meeting. Mr. Harry Hopkins, Administrator of the Works Progress Administration, within which organization the National Youth Administration functions, addressed the conference. A few excerpts from his talk will illustrate the official point of view at the commencement of this new adventure in applied Democracy:

It is awfully easy to make a speech about youth; how they have been neglected and the difficulties and disadvantages which have come to them through unemployment. When you try to put some body to this and to be specific, definite, and precise as to what we are going to do, then it gets a little complicated. Our other student aid things are pretty simple. You say to the University President: "Pick out the boys and girls who are broke. Put them to work and give them a benefit." That is easy. But, when you get to some of these other problems on a national basis, it isn't so simple. I have given this a great deal of thought and I have nothing on my mind to offer as a solution to our problems, and I know of no one else who has anything to offer resembling a satisfactory program for young people. I want to assure you that the government is looking for ideas, that this program is not fixed and set, that we are not afraid of exploring anything within the law.

On the same occasion, Mr. Aubrey Williams, the Director of the National Youth Administration, spoke along the same lines. He said:

We have no answers already written to the problems of young people. Those answers that we have are obviously meager and do not provide any general solution. . . . I do not know that there are any answers we can write or put into effect. To do very much about this situation may be beyond any group of people, no matter how sincere and how earnest they are. Certainly it reaches out and has implications for the whole growing concern of the Nation.

I quote these two leaders to indicate the humility with which the National Youth Administration approached this great problem. No one person and no small group knew the answer. The answer to the problem, and I think we have more than an inkling now as to what that answer really is, lay in the hearts of the tens of thousands of communities scattered throughout the United States. Every individual connected with the now vast Youth Administration organization, from the President of the United States down to the individual youth beneficiary in the most remote sections of our country, is contributing to its solution. Whether we are on the right course, the reader will have to judge for himself.

Having close personal knowledge of the task attempted, I feel that this book accurately and vividly portrays the achievements of the National Youth Administration. I doubt if, in the annals of governments, there has ever been an official organization comparable in peacetime activity to NYA. Enthusiasm, training, competency, humanity, and unceasing labor permeate the entire organization. Every field of social work is represented in its paid or volunteer personnel. Educators, social workers, religious leaders, labor leaders, farming experts, industrialists, doctors, nurses, all play their part. Not the least valuable contributors are the many leaders of private youth organizations, who have participated in our work actively or in an advisory capacity.

The entire Youth Administration, but particularly the National Advisory Committee, endeavors to work closely and sympathetically with various so-called youth movements and organizations of youth, irrespective of whether the ideas of these organizations are wholly approved of. At a recent conference of the National Advisory Committee, the question of continuing to work with organizations of youth, some of which are popularly termed "radical," was discussed. The following significant statements were made by two members of the Advisory Committee and the thoughts therein contained were unanimously approved by the Committee:

I feel definitely that, if we hold ourselves aloof, we are stultifying and sacrificing our own opportunity to be helpful. And certainly what we did yesterday in having representatives of youth organizations join in with us in our discussions was just exactly the sort of thing we ought to do. For if we are really in contact with these people, we will accomplish a great deal more than if we set ourselves up on heights and refuse to listen to any idea or contribution they have. I think our experience has been that if we let them see we are receptive and sympathetic, we will find they are in turn responsive, and then, when we have suggestions to make, we will find them a great deal more receptive sometimes to checks or brakes that we might wish to put on their activities than they would be if we set ourselves apart.[1]

I am interested in youth unemployed, whatever the formula by which they express themselves. When we have an acute unemployment situation, we cannot expect that every movement will express itself in reasonable and sane terms. We probably need to listen to them all the more because they are rather emotional and rather unusual in their terminology. But wherever they have actual elemental facts to point to, that points to our need to deal with those facts. In the second place, it is clear to me that we may overestimate the significance of the radical formulæ used by youth today. When they get emotionally interested, they are naturally going to seek out the most favorable form for protest they can find. Youth rejoices in being able to state a thing in a manner rather painful to his adults and it does not indicate at all that he is a revolutionary person getting ready to put a bomb under the American government. I think we would make a very great mistake to keep out of touch with these matters. Thirdly, in proportion as we deal effec-

---

[1] The Reverend Edward R. Moore, Catholic Charities of the Archdiocese of New York, New York City.

tively with these people, even their use of the formulæ will tend to disappear. You cannot sustain formulæ on just language and if we can take the sting out of an unbearable situation, then radical formulæ are gone.[2]

It is this broad, tolerant, democratic approach to the problems of youth which I believe has made so effective the methods used by the National Youth Administration.

I think there are five outstanding accomplishments that might be credited to the National Youth Administration, which are dramatically related in this book:

(1) That the Youth Administration has made an excellent start toward filling the gap between leaving school and finding a job.

(2) That a new technique in education is in the process of being developed: that is, education through work. The inclusion of related studies to actual work on a project has been an outstanding success.

(3) The exceptionally large percentage of youth trained on National Youth Administration projects who, after three to six months' combined work and education, have been able to find employment in private enterprise.

(4) That there has been found much socially useful work within the various communities that unemployed youth can be given, which will enrich the community as well as the lives of the erstwhile unemployed youth.

(5) That an average of over $50,000,000 per year was spent by the government on this work at an administrative overhead of less than 5 per cent.

I cannot, in this short introduction, name the hundreds of individuals who have contributed so largely to the success of the National Youth Administration. Yet, I cannot fail to mention one outstanding personality who, though having no offi-

---

[2] Dr. Mordecai Johnson, President of Howard University, Washington, D. C.

cial connection with the NYA, is recognized by acclamation as its spiritual leader. I refer to Mrs. Franklin D. Roosevelt. Mrs. Roosevelt happens to hold a great position, but this is merely a coincidence in her relation to the National Youth Administration. She is by training and practice a social worker and a teacher but, above all, a great humanitarian. Months before the National Youth Administration was created, Mrs. Roosevelt spent considerable time meeting with a group of representative underprivileged youth in New York City. This group, numbering about thirty, represented a cross-section of urban young people. On several occasions, I had the privilege of attending these conferences at her home in New York. They were very informal. She had a graceful way of making these youth forget that she was the wife of the President of the United States and regard her only as a puzzled friend looking for a means of alleviating their condition. I doubt if the young people knew that many details of these conferences were related by Mrs. Roosevelt to the President. When the President decided to create the National Youth Administration, he was acting not merely on his own considerable knowledge of the problem, but partly on a factual representation of the plight of youth conveyed directly to him by youth themselves through a sympathetic and wise messenger. Since the formation of the NYA, Mrs. Roosevelt has kept in close and active touch with its work. I question whether any individual has visited as many projects scattered throughout the entire United States as has Mrs. Roosevelt. Her wise criticism has on many occasions saved the National Youth Administration from making mistakes. Some of the projects enumerated or discussed here were conceived by her.

It is, therefore, fitting that this book should be dedicated to Mrs. Franklin D. Roosevelt, not as First Lady, but as a woman of vision, intuition, and great love.

CHARLES W. TAUSSIG.

Contents

FOREWORD BY CHARLES W. TAUSSIG   vii

I. A NEW DEAL FOR YOUTH   3

II. YOUTH INHERITS THE DEPRESSION   6
First Aids to Youth. Creation of NYA.

III. OUT OF SCHOOL AND OUT OF WORK   17
Who Are the NYA Project Workers? What Does NYA
Offer Them? The Evolution of NYA Work Projects. The
NYA Work Program Today. Boys Can Build. Boys in Work-
shops. Boys and Girls in Public Service. Girls in Home Eco-
nomics. The Community Youth Center Emerges.

IV. SPARE TIME PUT TO USE   68
WPA Co-operates. General and Vocational Schools Help.
Training for Health. Leisure-Time Recreation. Vocational In-
formation.

V. CO-OPERATING FOR AN EDUCATION   86
NYA Resident Centers.

VI. FINDING THE FIRST JOB   109
Junior Guidance and Placement.

VII. THESE ARE THEIR STORIES   122
Supervisors Tell about NYA Youth. NYA Youth Speak for
Themselves.

VIII. A NEW DEMOCRACY IN EDUCATION   156
College Aid Work Projects. Caliber of NYA Students.
School Aid.

IX. CHALLENGE TO EDUCATION   192
The Unequal Distribution of Education. Why Are Many
Boys and Girls Averse to School? The White-Collar Com-
plex. NYA and the Educational System.

X. THE BALANCE SHEET FOR NYA   202
NYA Youth and Health. Engineers' Report on NYA Work
Program. NYA and Organized Labor. Administrative Person-
nel. How Much Does It Cost? The Future of NYA.

CONTENTS OF APPENDIX

I. 1. Members of National Administrative Staff, National Advisory
    Committee, and Executive Committee of NYA   219
   2. Administrative Chart of NYA   222
II. Examples of Co-sponsoring Agencies   223
III. Types of Work Activity   225
IV. Types of Work Performed on a Single Project   228
V. Resident Projects in Operation, March 31, 1938, by States   231
VI. Junior Placement Offices Started in Co-operation with State Employment Services   238
VII. Industrial and Occupational Studies Prepared by NYA in Different States   239
VIII. Median Weekly Wage of Youth Placed by Junior Placement Offices   241
IX. Approved Student Aid Applicants
    Table 1. Per Cent. Distribution of Approved Applicants for NYA Student Aid by Yearly Family Income   242
    Table 2. Per Cent. Distribution of Approved Applicants for NYA Student Aid by Size of Family   243
    Table 3. Distribution of Approved Applicants for NYA Student Aid by Occupation of Family Heads   244
X. Institutions Participating in the Student Aid Program
    Table 4. Number of Institutions Participating in NYA Student Aid Program by Types of Institutions (Monthly Totals from September 1935 through March 1938)   245
    Table 5. Number of Students Assisted under NYA Student Aid Program by Types of Institutions (Monthly Totals from September 1935 through March 1938)   247
XI. Employment on Work Projects
    Table 6. Employment on NYA Work Projects by Sex and by Relief Status (Monthly Totals from January 1936 through March 1938)   248
    Table 7. Total Employment on NYA Work Projects by Type of Work, Relief Status, and Sex   249
    Table 8. Total Employment (Relief and Non-Relief) on NYA Work Projects by Type of Project and by State   250
XII. Fund Allocations and Employment Nationally and by States
    Table 9. Fund Allocations for NYA Work Projects Program and Student Aid Program for Fiscal Year Ending June 30, 1938, by States   254
    Table 10. (A) Grand Total of State Tables Showing Fund Allocations and Employment for March 1938   256
    (B) State by State Summary Tables of NYA Program Giving Total Fund Allocations by Year, and Employment on Work Projects Program and Student Aid Program for March 1938 (Arranged Alphabetically by States)   257
INDEX   311

A New Deal for

YOUTH

CHAPTER I

A New Deal for Youth

"JUST WHAT IS NYA?"

"I heard about a boy at college who gets some sort of Government scholarship."

"Isn't it the same as the CCC?"

With few exceptions, these were the comments we heard from our friends, from educators, bishops, business men, even from Government people, when we told them: "We are planning to write a book about the National Youth Administration."

We didn't know much about the NYA, ourselves, but we had heard enough to stimulate our curiosity about this new and interesting development on the American scene.

We knew, for example, that on June 26, 1935, by executive order of the President, the National Youth Administration was set up with $50,000,000 of relief funds earmarked for its use.

This was the President's declaration, in establishing the NYA:

I have determined that we shall do something for the Nation's unemployed youth, because we can ill afford to lose the skill and energy of these young men and women. They must have their chance in school, their turn as apprentices, and their opportunity for jobs—a chance to work and earn for themselves.

It is recognized that the final solution of this whole problem of unemployed youth will not be attained until there is resumption of normal business activities and opportunities for private employment on a wide scale. I believe that the National Youth Program will serve the most pressing and immediate needs of that portion of unemployed youth most seriously affected at the present time.

It is my sincere hope that all public and private agencies, groups, and organizations, as well as educators, recreational leaders, employers, and labor leaders, will co-operate wholeheartedly with the National and State Youth Administrations in the furtherance of this National Youth Program.

The yield on this investment should be high.

We collected reports of NYA activities, State by State, from all parts of the United States. We pored over columns of figures. But they didn't give a picture of the 327,000 high school and college boys and girls who are earning from $6 to $40 a month by work planned in their own educational institutions and paid for by the Federal Government. Still less did these reports give us a comprehension of the program for 155,000 boys and girls from relief families who are earning by part-time work from $10 to $25 a month, and many of whom on their own volunteer time are receiving related training under the impetus of NYA.

So, with a suitcase in one hand and a notebook and typewriter in the other, we set out to see NYA in action. In our trips, we tried to see as many projects as possible, talk with NYA youth themselves, meet the NYA personnel, visit junior employment services (another NYA activity), get the reactions of local people to the NYA program, and talk with employers who have ex-NYA boys and girls on their pay-rolls at the present time.

It occurred to us that perhaps the best possible introduction to NYA might be through pictures. As the program varies greatly from State to State and even from locality to locality, it is impossible to show all phases in photographs. The pictures on the following pages illustrate activities of NYA girls and boys. Except the high school students, who form a separate and younger group, these young people are from 18 to 24 years old and average less than 20 years of age. Most of them had never held regular jobs before going to work for NYA.

Fifty-two NYA boys converted this swamp and unsightly dump in Fort Morgan, Colorado, into a public recreation ground with 40 acres of grass, shrubs, and trees, and a new 5-acre swimming pool. Boys built bath houses, picnic tables and benches, and recreational equipment. The city of Fort Morgan furnished $9763 in materials and supervision, and NYA spent $2918.79 for youth labor and supervision.

An NYA boy at Gloucester, Massachusetts, removes lobster eggs for restocking at a Government fish hatchery. This lobster yielded 30,000 eggs.

An Indian youth on the Onondaga Reservation, in New York, shapes a log for a summer camp which he and other NYA boys are building for the children on this reservation.

Southern boys whose parents are tenant farmers and sharecroppers are learning new ways to farm at NYA Resident Centers. By half-time work they earn
their subsistence and a small cash surplus. The other half of their time is
devoted to studies related to the work they are doing. Boys in one group are
learning how to raise flowers for commercial markets.

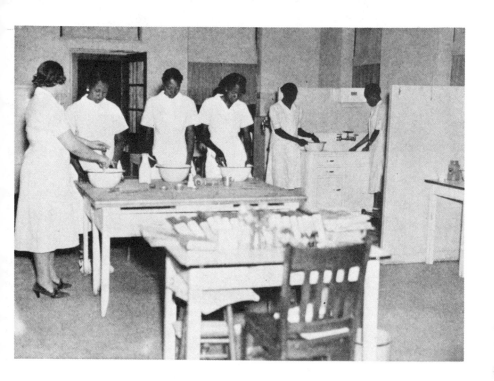

At the Fort Valley (Georgia) Normal and Industrial School, Negro boys and girls, most of whom never finished grade school, are earning their way by NYA work while they receive special training in agriculture, trades, and homemaking. The boys are developing the only Negro recreational camp in the State. Here they are working on a dam for an 18-acre lake. At night they study. NYA girls at this Resident Center learn how to sew, garden, cook and prepare meals, and do household cleaning. Both boys and girls are taught high standards of cleanliness and neatness.

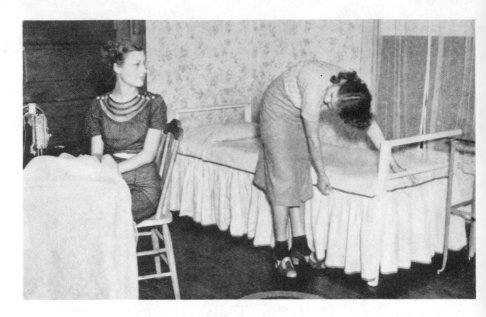

Girls from relief families get their chance to "go away to school" at NYA Resident Centers. They work part-time for public agencies, earning enough to meet their co-operative living costs and to have a small cash balance left. NYA Resident girls plan, prepare, and serve their own meals, take care of their own quarters, and have normal, youthful good times, which their over-crowded, impoverished homes have often denied them.

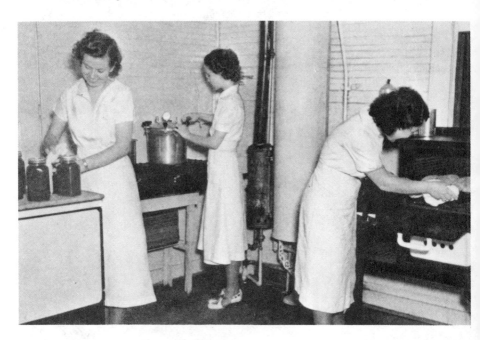

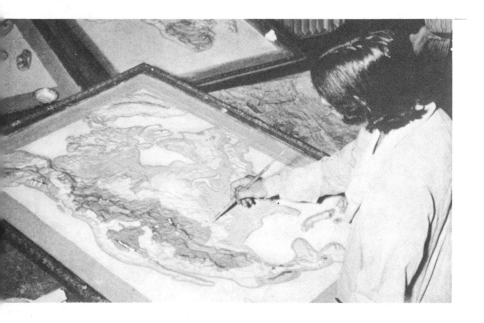

These NYA girls are making maps and globes for public schools. Several thousand NYA girls and boys are employed in making visual-aid materials for schools and libraries and constructing exhibits for agricultural demonstrations.

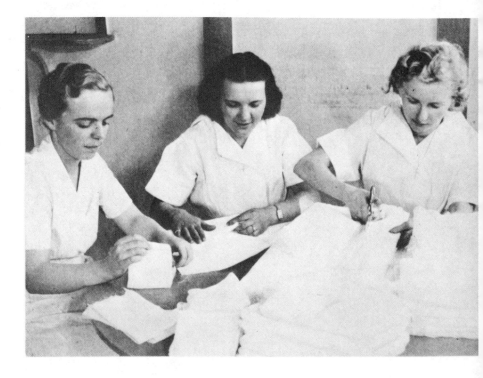

NYA out-of-school girls assist in public agencies in every State. The girl repairing a book is one of thousands who work part-time in public libraries. NYA girls help in day nurseries, WPA nursery schools, and public kindergartens, where they learn the proper feeding, care, and play activities of young children. Many work as nurse aides in public hospitals.

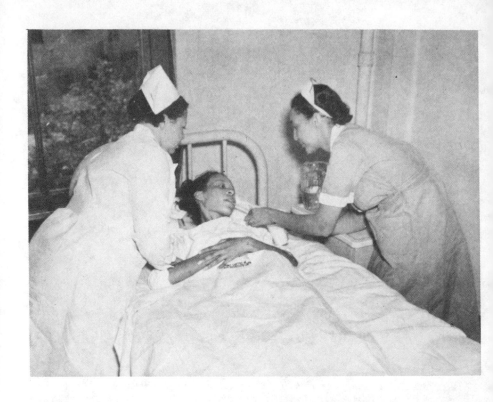

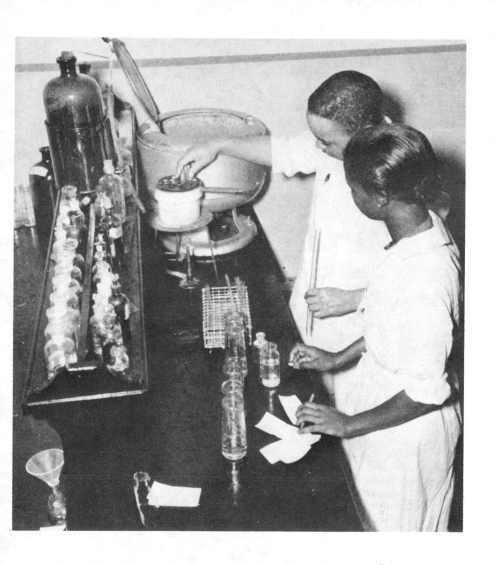

Negro NYA girls assist the regular nursing and maintenance staff in every department of Flint-Goodridge Hospital, New Orleans. Their work is supplemented by classroom study. Some find jobs as practical nurses, others as children's nurses or household workers. The health information which they acquire is of special value in this community, where the Negro death rate is a little more than twice as high as the average for the whole population of the United States.

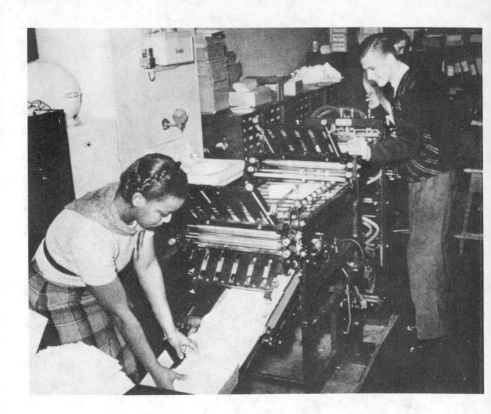

While augmenting the regular services of the New York Department of Health, in Albany, these NYA young people prepare themselves for civil service examinations for office-machine operators. Throughout the country many thousand NYA youth from relief families are working as junior clerks and stenographers in State, county, and municipal offices.

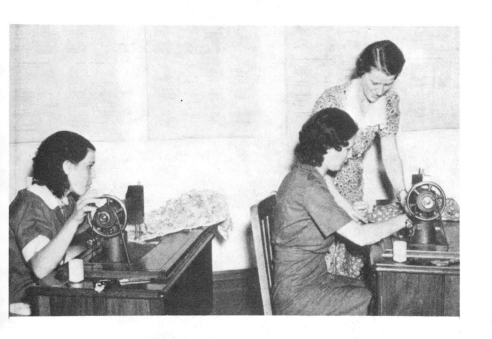

All over the country, NYA girls sew for public institutions. County and municipal boards of welfare distribute their products. After working hours, girls often stay for additional training in the use of patterns and fabrics and for other related information. On their own time they often use NYA sewing rooms to make and repair clothing for themselves and their families.

One hundred thousand young people are working their way through college with the aid of NYA jobs. They receive an average of $12 a month. An NYA biology student assembles the bones of a chimpanzee, to be used for classroom demonstration; an NYA girl operates a photo-record camera to copy valuable reference material. Eleven NYA students at the University of Nebraska constructed this observatory in four months' time. NYA is also helping more than 200,000 boys and girls to remain in high school by part-time jobs.

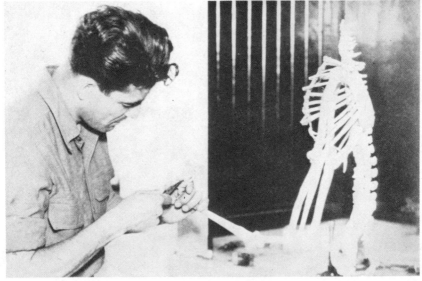

NYA boys have built six cabins for self-supporting students at the University of Maine. Each cabin houses four boys. They cut their own fuel on timberland owned by the university, do all their own housework and cook their own meals, and so reduce materially the high cost of going to college.

In New Orleans, a group of NYA boys stays "overtime" to learn how to bore an automobile block.

NYA teaches the rudiments of auto mechanics to many jobless out-of-school boys. The three boys assembling a motor are at Quoddy Village, Maine, where 175 boys from New England and New York State relief families are working and studying in 30 different occupations.

This Minnesota NYA youth was placed as an assistant mechanic in a Naval Training Station.

These NYA boys are getting their first experience in welding at the municipal garage in Rochester, New York.

Thousands of NYA out-of-school boys are engaged in conservation work. They plant trees and shrubs to arrest soil erosion, build feeders and shelters for game birds, construct and maintain fish-breeding and -rearing ponds, clean and restock lakes and streams. Many of them under expert supervision learn how to care for and repair trees.

In Lincoln, Nebraska, NYA out-of-school youths are landscaping a 40-acre addition to a city park.

In Minnesota, under the direction of the State Highway Department, NYA boys build roadside parks and picnic equipment. In the winter, they do masonry work under portable shelters. In many States park-improvement work is a major NYA activity.

In several States, NYA boys make isolation huts which public health agencies distribute to tubercular patients who cannot afford to leave their homes and for whom no other facilities are available.

The loss of one-half million school days annually because children could not cross swollen creeks has been eliminated by two hundred steel pipe footbridges built by NYA out-of-school boys in West Virginia. Some of the bridges are built chiefly from materials salvaged from abandoned pipelines.

In Morgan County, Kentucky, WPA built a new consolidated school. NYA boys made laboratory tables, cabinets, tablet armchairs, and hundreds of other articles for use by these mountain children. Above, a Morgan County youth making a chair in an NYA workshop.

In New Mexico, Spanish-American boys from relief families have revived their heritage of handicraft by making furniture like this in NYA workshops. After becoming skilled craftsmen, many have left NYA to go into business for themselves. NYA girls wove the curtains and rugs and Colcha-embroidered the bedspread shown. The lighting fixtures also are NYA-made.

In NYA workshops tens of thousands of pieces of school furniture have been repaired and built.

These NYA boys are building furniture and equipment for the Gunnison, Colorado, Community Center, a $100,000 adobe brick structure entirely NYA-built.

The boy with the plane acquired enough experience in an NYA carpentry shop in Minnesota to get a job in a sash and door firm.

This dreary, dilapidated structure was where the Negro children of Clarksville, Arkansas, went to school until NYA youth built them this new school with a light, airy interior. Both Negro and white parent teacher associations raised money for materials and equipment.

After working on an NYA building repair job, three boys from a southern rural relief family became dissatisfied with their dark, rickety home.

So they tore it down, and moved their family temporarily into two sheds shown in picture. Using the old materials plus a small quantity of new lumber, they completely rebuilt their home, adding windows and enlarging the porch. After rebuilding, the boys stained it a dark green.

More than 300 Wisconsin boys from rural relief families work part-time on public property while receiving special agricultural or trade training at vocational schools. By living co-operatively and doing their own cooking and laundry they pay all their expenses from their NYA earnings of $24.85 a month each.

Leisure-time study for NYA boys in the farm dormitory, Ruston Polytechnic Institute, Ruston, Louisiana.

The boy with the meat-saw wanted to learn to be a butcher, so he was assigned to work in the kitchen of the co-operative dormitory (Southwestern Institute, Lafayette, Louisiana).

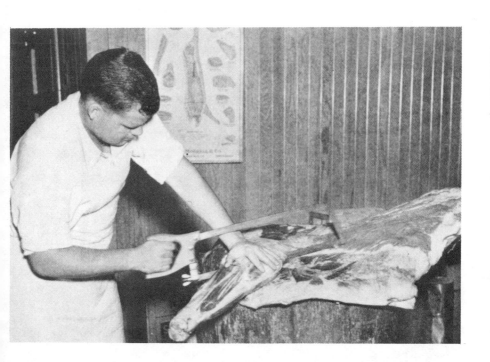

Murray City, Utah, furnished materials and expert supervision for this new municipally owned Diesel-operated power plant, built by NYA out-of-school boys. Under the direction of engineers, NYA youth also installed the equipment.

In many communities NYA out-of-school boys have built Youth Centers, where young people may work, study, and find recreation. This one is at Shawnee, Oklahoma.

NYA out-of-school boys in Nashua, New Hampshire, make and letter street signs.

In a Los Angeles NYA workshop, discarded toys are repaired for distribution to underprivileged children.

This NYA youth from a relief family is repairing a radio which a social agency will give to a "shut-in."

In the Kentucky mountains, an NYA supervisor travels by mule and on foot to invite isolated families to a "listening post," where many of them hear a radio for the first time. They listen to entertainment and information broadcast especially for them by the University of Kentucky.

Most of these pictures were taken by NYA supervisors or by photographers for the Works Progress Administration. They give an idea not only of the scope of the NYA program but of the types of young people who are employed on it, which means the types of young people who today are unable to find jobs in private employment or to continue their education without NYA part-time work.

The ensuing chapters will tell more about the NYA program and the hundreds of thousands of young people it touches. They will report also a few of the things about which some of these young people are thinking.

CHAPTER II

Youth Inherits the Depression

BOYS AND GIRLS 16 TO 24 YEARS OLD MAKE UP ONE-SIXTH OF the population of the United States. How these youth, approximately 21,200,000 in number,[1] are occupied is not accurately known. The best available data indicate that in November 1937:

5,200,000 were attending schools and colleges;[2]

3,200,000—nearly all girls—were engaged in homemaking or, for other reasons, were neither in educational institutions nor available for gainful work;

7,100,000 were employed;[3]

1,800,000 were employed part-time;

3,900,000 were unemployed—that is, able to work, and seeking work, but unable to find it in private industry.

Of these youth who could find no jobs, nearly 2,400,000 were boys. More than 1,000,000 were boys in their late teens and the others were 20 to 24 years old. More than 1,500,000 were girls, about half in their teens and half from 20 to 24. The boys alone outnumbered the entire American expeditionary force to France during 1917–18. Boys and girls to-

---

[1] Based on Census Bureau's Estimate of Population for October 1, 1937.

[2] Estimate based on attendance in colleges and last two years of secondary schools during 1935–36, with percentages added for increased enrollments since then and for retarded pupils.

[3] Includes those temporarily absent from regular jobs. These figures on full- and part-time employment and unemployment are estimates based on the enumerative test census of November–December 1937. This was taken on 1600 postal routes, representing 1½ per cent. of the entire population, as a check on the voluntary unemployment registration of November 16–20.

gether were almost equal in number to the entire United States Army during the World War.

During the most prosperous months of the last eight years, the roster of idle youth may have dropped to 3,000,000 or less. During the worst months it may have risen to 7,000,000 or more—equal to the total population of Canada 16 years of age or older. The removal of 3,900,000 young people from the list of unemployed would not require 3,900,000 jobs. If more young men could find jobs at adequate wages, more girls would give up work, or looking for it, and devote themselves exclusively to homemaking. If more fathers were employed, more youth might remain in school longer and more of the girls might stay at home while awaiting marriage. On the other hand, from 250,000 to 350,000 more youth would be in the labor market if the Federal Government, through the National Youth Administration, were not helping them to stay in high schools and colleges. In addition, many—probably most—of the 1,800,000 youth who are employed part-time want regular full-time jobs. And many who have full-time jobs do not earn enough to live independently or establish their own homes. Some of them are working for no pay.[4]

The waiting-lines of unemployed youth are not stationary. Every year 2,250,000 boys and girls leave schools and colleges (some before they are 16). Perhaps 2,000,000 join the queues of job-seekers. A few are employed immediately. Others have to wait—sometimes for years. Girls have had a relatively easier time than boys in finding jobs during the depression years. Work in retail stores, offices, restaurants, hotels, domestic service, teaching, the textile and clothing industries, and other fields in which large numbers of women are employed has been more stable than employment in construction, mining, heavy manufacturing, and other fields which employ men

---

[4] Homer P. Rainey and others: *How Fare American Youth?* Pp. 32–33, D. Appleton-Century Company, 1937.

almost exclusively. Moreover, it is customary to pay women lower wages than men. In November 1937 only 56 out of every 100 young men 20 to 24 years old were employed full-time, and only 68 out of every 100 were employed full- or part-time, compared with 90 out of every 100 in 1930. The employment of boys 18 and 19 years old probably has declined even more sharply.

The employment of youth less than 18 years old had been dropping for a generation prior to the great depression. Between 1920 and 1930, the number of 16-year-olds gainfully employed decreased by more than 35 per cent. Among 17-year-olds, the drop was about 25 per cent. During the depression years, more youth in their teens have stayed in school longer. Although it may be considered desirable that all youth remain in school until they reach the age of 18, the cold fact remains that during these depression years many hundreds of thousands of boys and girls of less than 18 have been both out of school and out of work.

Youth 16 to 24 years old account for one-third of all the unemployed in the United States. The percentage of unemployment is higher in this age-range than in any other. The Federal Census of Unemployment and Partial Unemployment in November 1937 showed that in some States as many as 39 per cent. of the totally unemployed were 15 to 24 years old. While a few industries favor the young—and consider men superannuated when they reach 40 or 45—in a majority of occupations youth is at a disadvantage. A test survey of rural youth in Iowa in 1934 disclosed that among more than 1000 who had been out of school an average of three and one-quarter years, 56 per cent. had never held any regular positions. Test surveys in Connecticut, Pennsylvania, and Massachusetts showed that among job-seeking youth 16 and 17 years of age, from 56 to 69 per cent. were unemployed.[5]

---

[5] Ibid., p. 36.

The United States Employment Service has found the greatest difficulty in obtaining jobs for young men under 25:

> In general the reason is that in a period . . . when labor is plentiful in most lines, employers insist on getting an experienced worker where one is available. Where qualified experienced workers over 25 years of age are available, few employers can be expected to hire and train young persons whose capacities and efficiencies are yet to be demonstrated.[6]

Depression unemployment among youth is not peculiar to the United States. In 1931, 30 per cent. of all the unemployed in Great Britain were 14 to 24 years old. In November 1933, 34 per cent. of all the unemployed in Sweden were 16 to 25 years of age. In 1932, 41 per cent. of all the unemployed in Italy were 15 to 25 years of age. In June 1933, 26 per cent. of all the unemployed in Germany were 24 years of age or less.[7]

In some countries compulsory military service takes up part of the slack. In some, frustrated youth have flocked into the shirted private armies of dictators, actual or aspiring. The United States so far has been spared both of these alternatives. But whether it takes the form of apathy and broken morale or of resentment and revolt (either individual or collective), there must be a price to pay for maintaining a horde of frustrated youth in idleness.

FIRST AIDS TO YOUTH

The first new Federal agency created under the Roosevelt Administration was for the benefit of unemployed youth. The Civilian Conservation Corps, set up in April 1933, put 250,000 unmarried young men between the ages of 18 and 25, from

---

[6] *Who Are the Job Seekers?* P. 41. Government Printing Office, 1937.

[7] W. Thacher Winslow: *Youth, A World Problem.* P. 101. National Youth Administration. Government Printing Office, 1937.

families on public relief rolls, to work in forestry, park, and soil-erosion camps throughout the country. Almost instantly this program won general public approval. To these young men were added some 28,000 war veterans, 14,800 Indians, and nearly 25,000 older men from relief rolls in areas near CCC camps. In 1935 the age limits were spread to include young people from 17 to 28. In August 1935 the CCC reached its peak of 505,782 enrollees, from which it has dropped gradually to approximately 300,000.

Successful as it has been, the CCC inherently can be only one element in a program designed to help the mass of unemployed youth. At the outset, it was thought of primarily as a conservation and relief program; little attention was given to the general education or occupational training of CCC enrollees. However, it was discovered that 84 per cent. of them had not completed high school, 44 per cent. had not completed the elementary grades, and some were illiterate. Almost half of them had never had any regular employment. The educational program of the CCC has been greatly expanded, although, owing to various difficulties, it has not, in the opinion of the Advisory Committee on Education, realized its full potentialities.[8] The cost of the CCC—approximately $1200 annually for each enrollee—put a financial limit on its expansion. Moreover, it reached none of the girls.

Beginning in 1932, college attendance dropped for the first time since the World War. Many parents who ordinarily would have sent their children to college found themselves financially unable to do so. The opportunities for young people to earn their way through college had shrunk. Various educators proposed that the Federal Government make available a small amount of money for the assistance of promising but needy college students. In the fall of 1933, the Federal Emer-

---

[8] *Report of the Advisory Committee on Education.* P. 119. Government Printing Office, 1938.

gency Relief Administration established experimentally at the University of Minnesota a student-aid program. In February 1934 this form of aid was extended throughout the country to non-profit-making and tax-exempt institutions of higher education. Some 75,000 students were permitted to earn an average of $15 a month on work projects developed by the colleges. This program met with such approval that it was resumed by FERA on a slightly larger scale during the college year 1934–35.

In the summer of 1934, FERA set up several educational camps for unemployed women. This experiment grew, under FERA, to encompass 47 camps with an enrollment of 3000 women, most of them 20 to 25 years of age. For periods of from one to four months each, they were given elementary training in home economics, care of health, simple types of work, such as book-repairing and the preparation of hospital and household supplies, and various creative arts.

As economic recovery set in, it became evident that there was a shortage of skilled workers in many lines. President Roosevelt created, in June 1934, a Federal Committee on Apprentice Training to help the States to "inaugurate or continue programs in accordance with basic standards for apprentice training."

During the pit-depression period of 1932 and early 1933, the plight of youth had been dramatized by the thousands of boys and girls who had taken to "bumming" their way around the country. The transient camps established by FERA temporarily took care of many of these youth on the road—in May 1935, when we were well above the depression bottom, 54,000 youth were in transient camps. Others were drawn into the CCC and other Federal programs for the unemployed, or perhaps found private employment.

Some older youth found temporary work on the emergency program of FERA, the Civil Works Administration, and the Works Progress Administration. FERA grants kept schools open in many rural communities that had exhausted their resources. Through FERA, CWA, WPA, and PWA, Federal money was used to improve, repair, and enlarge school buildings and related educational facilities throughout the country.

CREATION OF NYA

The various direct and indirect aids to youth provided during the first two years of the Roosevelt Administration cost considerable money and effort. It soon became evident that they were inadequate. Some of them sank scalpels far enough into the social organism to expose to view conditions far worse than most people had suspected. In May 1935 there were 2,877,000 youth, 16 to 24 years old, on relief (and these did not include youth in CCC camps or on other special Federal programs). More than 1,250,000 of them were seeking work but could not find it. In the urban areas less than half, and in the rural areas less than one-fourth, of all youth on relief had gone to school beyond the eighth grade.[9] A great majority of them had no skills. Millions of youth on the margin of relief or a few levels above it faced similar difficulties with similar handicaps.

Destructive as enforced idleness may be at any age, it is likely to be most devastating to youth. Older people usually have formed habits of work. If their work habits and self-respect decay, they at least have less long to live than the oncoming generation. Youth who have not learned to work at all, much less how to do any particular kind of work, may be a deadweight on the nation for half a century to come.

The Federal Government was trying to preserve the morale and skills of the heads of indigent families by creating emer-

---

[9] See Works Progress Administration: *Youth on Relief*, 1936, and *Rural Youth on Relief*, 1937. Government Printing Office.

gency work. For the millions of younger children in relief families, food, clothing, shelter, and schooling were the essential guarantees against the degeneration of the human assets of the nation. But youth mired between school and self-support obviously required something more. Most of all they needed activity, preferably regular work, and some sense of being wanted.

As the magnitude and long-term social hazards of the idle youth problem became more apparent in 1933 and 1934, many persons urged that the Federal Government try to deal with it more comprehensively. Among them probably the most influential were Mrs. Roosevelt, Mr. Charles W. Taussig, President of the American Molasses Company, and Mr. Harry L. Hopkins, FERA Administrator, and other officials of FERA, the Children's Bureau, and the Office of Education.[10]

Although sympathetic to their suggestions, President Roosevelt at first demurred at spending more money for youth. He apparently considered that, in view of other imperative needs, the CCC, in which he felt an inventor's legitimate pride, college student aid, and the various incidental aids already provided were taking as much of the total emergency expenditures as he was justified in earmarking for youth. He also expressed concern that a special Federal youth agency, as such, might be misconstrued as a step toward the political organization or regimentation of youth. In the late spring of 1935, however, following the appropriation of $4,880,000,000 for work relief, he decided to take this risk. On June 26, 1935, he established by executive order the National Youth Administration and tentatively allotted for its use during the ensuing fiscal year $50,000,000.

---

[10] See Department of Labor: *Employment for Graduates of Educational Institutions;* and Committee on Youth Problems of the Office of Education: *Nation-Wide Community Youth Program,* issued in March and April 1935, respectively. Government Printing Office.

Each of four Government agencies wished to administer this program. The competition was especially spirited between the Office of Education and the relief officials. The President finally settled this contest in favor of the latter by designating Mr. Aubrey Williams, Deputy WPA Administrator, as Executive Director of NYA. To give other groups a voice in the drafting of the program he created two committees. The first was an Executive Committee of departmental officials under the chairmanship of Miss Josephine Roche, Assistant Secretary of the Treasury. The second, under the chairmanship of Mr. Taussig, was a National Advisory Committee made up of 35 representatives of business, labor, agriculture, education, church and welfare groups, and youth.

This organization set out to do something for youth. It had a very small amount of money (about $10 per idle youth). These limited funds (and the terms of the appropriation) made it necessary first to give attention to youth in families on relief. At the outset three basic related decisions were made: that the administration of the program should be decentralized, that the fullest efforts should be made to enlist the active co-operation of all State and local agencies interested in youth, and that ample room should be left for experiment.

NYA took over from FERA the college student aid and the educational camps for unemployed young women. The educational camps were conducted for two years, during which they reached a peak enrollment of 3500 in 29 camps in the fall of 1936. NYA officials gradually arrived at the conclusion that all that was done in these camps, and more, could be done more efficiently by other methods. NYA also took over temporarily the financing and nominal supervision of the Federal Committee on Apprentice Training. On June 1, 1937, this committee was transferred to the Department of Labor, where it seemed to belong, since it was working along conventional lines in a narrow field with the close co-operation of certain trade unions and industries.

The college aid plan, inherited from FERA, formed the nucleus of the first division of the NYA program. Student aid was expanded in two directions: to include a few graduate students and a large number of needy high school students. Three other main divisions were set up: part-time work for out-of-school and out-of-work youth in families on relief, related training and the encouragement of constructive leisure-time activity for these youth, and vocational guidance and placement for all unemployed youth. From these four divisions (and the discarded camps for unemployed women) a fifth has recently been emerging: a novel experiment in education known as the Resident Program.

At the top of the administrative framework of NYA is a small national office with Mr. Richard R. Brown, assistant executive director under Mr. Williams, in active charge. For each State, for New York City, and for the District of Columbia, there is an NYA Youth Director, under whom, in turn, are various assistants, district and county supervisors, and project supervisors or foremen. Dovetailing into this structure are unpaid advisory committees in all States, New York City, and the District of Columbia; more than 2600 local committees; and thousands of State and local agencies and private organizations, including the colleges and high schools that administer student aid.

More youth are enrolled on NYA programs than in the CCC. Yet for three years NYA has flourished with scant national publicity. NYA youth wear no uniforms, no distinguishing insignia. The NYA work programs are made up of thousands of small units—a boy here and a girl there, 15 boys here and 20 girls there, rarely as many as 100 working in the same place at the same task. Shaped by a multitude of local and individual needs and facilities and by the imagination and ingenuity of State directors, local organizations, and individual private citizens, including the young people themselves, these units are diverse in character. Moreover, their patterns change from month to month and from week to week.

It is precisely because this program for youth in need is so varied, changing from State to State and from town to town, and from rural area to city, that it is so absorbing to try to picture and comprehend it. Its drama comes from the accumulation of small incidents rather than from the fanfare of youth on parade. NYA does not pretend to offer a basic solution for the immense social and economic problems which today affect youth as well as the rest of the population. It tries to help young people in the crisis of unemployment and poverty to be a little more self-sufficient, to spend some of their time and energies in making themselves better equipped to meet the realities of work, learning, and leisure time. The next chapters show the various ways in which NYA is approaching these needs for the less privileged youth of this country.

CHAPTER III

Out of School and Out of Work

"WHERE HAVE YOU WORKED BEFORE?"

"How long did you go to school?"

These are the two eternal questions asked the young man or woman looking for a job. One 18-year-old boy with whom we talked summed up his own experiences by saying:

"I had to quit school when I was in the eighth grade because my old man didn't have a job and he said I'd have to get out and do something. I've been trying to do something ever since. . . . Once in a while I get some handbills to throw out. When there's a chance for a job, and that don't come but once in a blue moon, what do they ask you? 'Where did you work last?' If you haven't had a job, they don't even want to talk to you. But where you gonna get that first job? I ask you. It takes carfare to go around looking, too, and that don't grow on apple trees."

The work program of the NYA, started in January 1936, has been developed to meet the needs of the lowest-income group of boys and girls who have grown up in the depression. In April 1938, 180,000 unmarried young people from 18 to 24 years old were employed part-time on a wide variety of NYA work projects.

WHO ARE THE NYA PROJECT WORKERS?

Ninety-five per cent. of them come from families certified as in need of public relief. Most of these families are unusually large; more than one-third of them have seven or more to feed, clothe, and shelter; 29 per cent. more are families numbering five and six to a household; 28 per cent. are families of four. Only 9 per cent. are families of three (with one child).[1]

It is not hard to imagine the difficult home situations these young people face. Their parents have fully expected that they would be self-supporting by the time they were 18, if not sooner; undoubtedly many have anticipated that their sons, at least, would contribute something to the family income. Instead, the jobless young people have been a further drain on already incredibly meager family incomes.

Although the NYA work program may employ unmarried youth 18 to 24 years old, the average age of project workers today is slightly under 20.[2] They are divided almost equally between the sexes. Racially, their distribution among whites, Negroes, Indians, and other racial minorities is in proportion to the general population.

Perhaps the most arresting data about this large cross-section of underprivileged youth are on their educational background. The United States spends more than any other nation in the world on its educational system, but a study of 35,638 youth on NYA work projects[3] reveals that we have a considerable group who have not had a fair share in this education. Only half of these NYA boys and girls ever went to school a day beyond the eighth grade. About 47 per cent. of them left school between the ninth and twelfth grades, and only about 3 per cent. attended college at all. This study included no States in the deep South, where the educational level is still lower. In

---

[1] From a sample research of 19,306 youth on NYA work projects in California, Kentucky, Nebraska, Ohio, and New York City.

[2] From a sampling of 6697 project youth in California, Nebraska, and Ohio. Also Youth Directors in nine States other than the above three report average age of project youth as between 19 and 20.

[3] From a sample research of 35,638 project youth in Kansas, Minnesota, Nebraska, California, Ohio, West Virginia, Kentucky, New Hampshire, and New York City.

Louisiana, the school attendance of white boys and girls on the NYA work program averages six years; of Negro youth, one year more.[4] In Colorado, youth on the NYA work program have spent an average of only six years in school. Arkansas relief youth, on the average, left their school books behind them between the sixth and seventh grades—and the majority of rural schools in Arkansas are open only six months a year. On one work project that we visited in the mountains of Kentucky, 17 of the 26 boys could neither read nor write when they became NYA workers, and we were told that they were typical of the relief youth in that area.

In an attempt to discover why so many of these young people left school at such an early age, a sample questionnaire was sent to 13,547 of them.[5] Financial difficulties accounted for about 47 per cent.; discouragement and lack of interest were the reasons given by 25 per cent.

If these young people have not been in school, what have they been doing? We asked a number of them this very question. "I lie around and look for work," and "Oh, I don't know, what is there to do?" are typical answers. A study of almost 20,000 project youth[6] shows that before NYA employment one-third had never had any kind of job at all; one-sixth had done some work as unskilled laborers; one-eighth reported

---

[4] We inquired into the reasons for the slightly longer school attendance of Negro youth in this group. Most frequently we were told that in these families of very low income, many Negro women seek and obtain some work as domestic servants, whereas white women rarely do, with the result that Negro children sometimes can remain in school a little longer. However, it should be noted that, owing to the generally lower standards in Negro schools, the education of Negroes who have been in school seven years may be poorer than that of white children who have been in school only six years.

[5] From a sampling of 13,547 youth on work projects in California, Kentucky, Minnesota, and Ohio.

[6] In California, Kentucky, Michigan, Minnesota, Ohio, and West Virginia. Youth directors in most of the States we have visited, other than these six, estimate a much higher percentage of youth with no work experience whatsoever. The lowest estimate we have had from these directors is 50 per cent. and the highest is 95 per cent.

some employment as domestics; one-tenth had at some time found a little work as farm hands; another tenth had been employed in factories or workshops. The remaining 17.5 per cent. had held odd jobs in a variety of fields. Without question, the great majority of NYA youth who reported some work experience have had only temporary jobs. For example, the one-tenth who had been farm hands had gone into the harvest fields for a few weeks a year. Many of those in domestic work had done odd jobs around a household or cared for children for a few hours a week. Christmas and other seasonal or sporadic employment probably accounts for large numbers more. It seems conservative to conclude that the great majority of youth now working on NYA projects have never had regular jobs.

WHAT DOES NYA OFFER THEM?

The work program gives this group of young people an average of 44.5 hours' work a month with an average monthly pay of $15.73.[7]

We can gather the meaning of these hours of work and these dollars of pay only by the observations we have made and the comments we have heard as we have traveled over the country, seeing projects and youth and talking with supervisors and members of communities who have watched the development of the NYA work program. We have seen and heard abundant indications that the great majority of young people on relief are eager to work. For years, to most of them, a job has been a fabulous unreality. Here is at least part-time

---

[7] Official WPA regulations state that the maximum hours of work for NYA project youth shall be 8 hours a day, 40 hours a week, and 70 hours a month. Earnings range from a minimum of $10 to a maximum of $25 a month, based on wage rates established in accordance with prevailing local wage standards. Administrative Order No. 60 of the Works Progress Administration.

work on which they can depend. Someone wants their efforts.

In every State in which we asked: "What do NYA workers do with their money?" we got the same answers. First, they help at home; overnight, they have placed themselves on the asset side of the family ledger; instead of being another person to share limited family food supplies, each can contribute something to the family expenses. The value of this shedding of the feeling of guilt and defeat, which this contribution to the family means, cannot be computed. This is one boy's description of what his NYA job has meant to him:

"Maybe you don't know what it's like to come home and have everyone looking at you, and you know they're thinking, even if they don't say it, 'He didn't find a job.' It gets terrible. You just don't want to come home. . . . But a guy's gotta eat some place and you gotta sleep some place. . . . I tell you, the first time I walked in the front door with my pay-check, I was somebody!"

After they have helped out at home, we were told, most of these young workers buy themselves some clothes; for years they have worn hand-me-downs.

"Usually, after about the second pay-check," an NYA super-visor said, "a boy will come to work with a new pair of trousers. They probably cost him two or three dollars, but they're his and he bought them with his own money. Maybe on his next wages he'll get a pair of shoes. The girl will blossom out in a $2.95 dress. You can't possibly know what it means to her. We notice that she keeps herself cleaner, that her hair isn't straggling all over the place. You can actually see shoulders straightened up when these boys and girls appear with their new clothes."

If they have any money left, there is a little chance for entertainment—a movie, taking a girl for an ice cream soda, going to a dance, riding in a bus. One boy with whom we talked must be typical of many.

"It makes you feel like a man to have some money jingling in your pocket," he said.

THE EVOLUTION OF NYA WORK PROJECTS

When funds amounting to $30,000,000 a year were first made available for youth work projects in the fall of 1935, the newly formed National Youth Administration in Washington was firm in its stand for a decentralized program. The specific needs of youth in New York City, for example, were totally different in character from the wants of the Kentucky mountaineers or of the Arkansas sharecroppers. A Youth Director for each State was appointed, and he, in turn, divided his State into districts, with supervisory personnel for each. State organizations began to plan a host of projects. Boys and girls were to be put to work in January 1936. This general picture of these first days of NYA by one State director is typical of what we heard also from several others:

"We were told we had so much money allotted to us, and that we could put as many relief boys and girls to work as possible with that money, within the general regulations about wages and hours of work. When we asked Washington: 'What kind of work?' we were told: 'That's up to you. Plan the best projects you can. Get them sponsored by public agencies in your own communities. Go to it.' We did. But we didn't know, we couldn't possibly have known, what kind of work these youth wanted and needed. We planned it the best we could. We wanted good sponsors who would provide us with places for work projects, money for materials, and help with supervision. They were hard to get then, because many of them thought these young people were only loafers. Well, it seemed at that time that the quickest way to get our boys and girls to work was to put them in obvious jobs, like helping to supervise young children on public playgrounds. It didn't take us very long to find out that work like that was for only a very few of our youth. The rest were wasting time. Then we got clerical jobs for a lot of them—too many of them—in city and county and State offices. Only a certain number belonged there. We realized that we had to have other kinds of work, many other kinds. We formed State and local advisory committees of men and women with fundamental interests in youth and we asked them to help us to plan honest and real work. We talked with the youth and they had good ideas. We found out that we needed a great variety of work, because young people don't fit into any one or two—or six—grooves."

THE NYA WORK PROGRAM TODAY

Today there are hundreds of different types of NYA projects. Standards have evolved by which State directors evaluate their programs. First, the work must be real work. Second, it should add to the employability of young people by giving them experience in work routine, and, wherever possible, definite job experience in fields in which they are interested and capable. Third, the work should be of genuine benefit to the community—preferably to the youth of the community.

During the fiscal year ending June 30, 1938, $35,800,000 of Federal money has been spent on the NYA work program. Of this amount, 75 per cent. has gone for actual wages to youth;[8] the remaining 25 per cent. has been spent for supervision and materials.

Although the NYA may be the sole sponsor of its own projects, most of them today are co-sponsored by public or

---

[8] This is in accordance with official regulation, which states: "At least seventy-five per cent. of the funds allocated to the State for NYA work projects shall be expended for the wages of young people certified as eligible for relief." NYA Bulletin No. 11.

quasi-public agencies. A sampling of 130 representative work projects discloses 73 different co-sponsoring agencies.[9]

Co-sponsors help to plan work projects, contribute money for materials, often pay for supervision, and generally advise and assist in the maintenance of the projects.

At the start of the work program, some sponsors were skeptical of the efficiency of relief youth labor. Now it seems conclusive that most NYA boys and girls have proved themselves willing and capable workers, and that, within the limits of sponsors' abilities to contribute to the program, there is excellent co-operation with State and local agencies. Up to December 1, 1937, these co-sponsors furnished funds amounting to more than $3,500,000 for materials and supervision for NYA projects.

Because the work program is decentralized under State administrations, which further decentralize their own programs according to the needs of youth and communities, projects cannot be classified rigidly. In a sampling of 150 projects, 169 different work activities were engaged in by youth.[10]

We tried to see as much as we could of NYA in action during three months. Obviously, it was impossible to visit every State or to cover every community in which NYA functions in the States we did visit. We have selected for description specific projects which illustrate the range of the NYA work program in its present development.

Boys Can Build

Construction is the dominant trend in the work program; two years ago it played only a minor role. It is specifically required that NYA shall undertake no construction work which

---

[9] For list, see Appendix II.
[10] For list of these various activities, see Appendix III.

would be provided for out of State or local budgets, so that displacement of adult workers by youth labor is avoided.

The construction program has the roots of its growth in small jobs done for public agencies. They were the proving ground. Thousands of these small jobs continue to be done wherever they are needed, but NYA today engages also in a wide range of larger construction work. From a wealth of examples we have chosen some that illustrate the evolution of the building program, starting with minor work, progressing into repair and remodeling of buildings, and culminating in the construction of schoolhouses, community centers, and other good-sized buildings.

New York: Nineteen hundred NYA boys are working as youth laborers in the dramatic development of New York City's public parks under Commissioner Robert Moses. Each boy works five 8-hour days a month under WPA superintendents and NYA foremen, who are responsible to the City Department of Parks.

The first job to which NYA youth were assigned in New York City was at Owls Head Park, a 38-acre private estate that had been deeded to the city. Crews of youth spread 8500 cubic yards of top-soil, planted 3000 pounds of clover and grass seed, laid 30,000 square feet of sod, put in two acres of rip-rapping, laid 8750 linear feet of drainage and water lines, set 60 man-holes and catch-basins in brick and cement, and built several miles of concrete, flagstone, and Colprovia paths and walks.

Now in Van Cortlandt Park, Inwood Park, and Prospect Park youth are doing even more extensive construction and landscaping work, assisting in the building of retaining walls, stone fireplaces, culverts, and fences.

Colorado: The city and county of Denver own 1789 acres

of land, situated about five miles outside the present city limits. The city is expanding in this direction. There were not adequate funds either to develop this land or to halt severe wind and soil erosion. The city and county agreed to sponsor an NYA project to conserve and develop this park area. In this instance, sponsorship includes the furnishing of transportation for NYA workers, materials for their work, and pay for supervisors. NYA hires one expert chief supervisor.

Ninety boys are working part-time in developing this park. About 80 of them are Mexican and Spanish-American youth whose only work experience has been in the beet fields of Colorado.

As we drove through this large area of neglected land, we saw groups of boys building roads, culverts, and curbings; others were busy planting, transplanting, and caring for trees and shrubbery; many were shaping grounds to halt soil erosion; some were building fireplaces for picnic and camp use. In a workshop situated on the project, boys were building picnic tables, incinerators, and other park equipment. One group of boys with a supervisor was off in the mountains cutting timber to be dressed and used in the shop. After every day's work, the boys gather in the shop, on their own time, and the supervisor conducts an informal hour of study and discussion of the actual work they have been doing that day.

When a boy is assigned to this project, he is given a chance to do many different kinds of work so that he may find what his aptitudes and interests are. Then he may concentrate on types of work for which he is most suited. The community will have a park which otherwise would not have been developed, and many boys are getting a start in landscaping, conservation, road construction, and the fundamentals of carpentry and cement and brick masonry.

South Dakota: Working under the supervision of the City

Engineer of Redfield, South Dakota, 14 NYA boys have landscaped the new artificial lake built for this town by WPA. These NYA boys also built a 200-foot boardwalk, a 16-foot pier, two rafts, two diving towers, a safety line of buoys made from barrels, and a guard rail and seats for spectators. The city of Redfield sponsored the work and furnished $500 for materials.

West Virginia: Two years ago it was estimated that about 3000 of the 5000 rural schools in this State had unusable playgrounds. We saw many of these schools, built in pockets on the hillsides; children stepped from schoolrooms into seas of mud. Out-of-school NYA boys already have put more than 1000 of these playgrounds in good condition. Usually this work calls for grading, filling, drainage, and the building of stone retaining walls. A large number of school bus shelters have also been built in this State. We saw school athletic grounds that had either been entirely constructed or materially improved by NYA work. At the Parkersburg Junior High School athletic field, NYA boys have built an 8-foot brick wall, 197 feet long, with two brick ticket booths. Here they also dug a one-quarter-mile track, put in a 14-inch stone base with a 5-inch cinder top, and built a steel rail around the track. In addition 240 yards of cement curbing and a press box in the stadium were completed when we visited this project. Plans for further work here include the building of shops and vocational classrooms for industrial and trade training in the space under the stadium, and the construction of a garage for 25 school busses.

Minnesota: About 1000 NYA boys in this State, under the sponsorship of the State Highway Department, are developing roadside parks with recreational facilities for Minnesota's own people and for the large number of summer tourists who flock to its lakes and woods. In some of these developments, log cabins for campers are built on public property.

One roadside park that we visited at Stillwater extends for two miles along the St. Croix River. Groups of NYA boys had changed a mass of weeds and general debris into an area that hikers and motorists can enjoy for many years. First, the land was cleared, graded, and planted with grass and shrubbery. Then the boys built side roads with cement curbings and stone-walled overlooks giving motorists and pedestrians long vistas up and down the river. We saw trails and paths, stone steps leading to the river, a stone and log bridge across a creek, stone fireplaces and ovens, picnic tables and benches—all built by NYA youth. One fireplace was encircled by a stone council ring, seating 40 to 50 people. We were told that many Minnesota NYA-built parks have these council rings, and that they are popular with girls' and boys' clubs as well as with adults who gather around the fire for cooking, singing, story-telling, and games.

The State Highway Department furnishes all materials, equipment, and supervision for this NYA roadside park work. In the winter months the boys do the masonry under portable shelters which they have built for themselves and for which they have made stoves from discarded metal oil barrels.

Economically these roadside parks are valuable to a State that considers summer tourist trade an important source of income. The boys who build the parks secure sound experience in roadmaking, landscaping, carpentry, masonry, and the operation of roadbuilding machinery.

Rhode Island: Last summer, 30 NYA boys, working part-time, undertook to put the Pawtucket Boys' Club building in good shape. This club serves underprivileged children of the community. Mr. Phillip G. Geiger, Director of the Club, submitted a list itemizing 93 different jobs done by the NYA youth in their thorough renovation of the building and its equipment.[11]

North Dakota: In the drought-stricken western part of this State, NYA boys and girls have repaired and renovated school buildings. Because of very limited school funds, this work could not have been done otherwise. Last summer in Antelope four boys and one girl shingled the roof of the rural school, calcimined the walls, washed and repaired windows, cleaned the chimney and stovepipes, scrubbed and waxed the floors, repaired and varnished desks and woodwork, renovated outbuildings, slated blackboards, and painted the exterior.

Kansas: At Topeka, we saw 17 powdered blue-shale tennis courts constructed by NYA boys under the sponsorship of the City School Board, which furnished $2733.33 for materials.

To build these courts, boys, under a skilled supervisor, leveled and terraced the ground, laid water pipes and connections, erected 350 yards of fencing, quarried, crushed, sifted, and spread the shale. They also built backstops, an upkeep house, and a stone drinking fountain. NYA girls made the tennis nets. These courts are open to the general public at all times. We were told that the only similar courts in Kansas are at Fort Leavenworth, where each cost $1500. The unit cost for each NYA court at Topeka, including all materials, labor, and supervision, was $1076.

In many sections of Kansas, there are few camping facilities for children or adults, and, consequently, camping has been an impossible luxury for families who could not afford travel to such distant places as Colorado or the northern lake country. We saw several camping sites that NYA is developing in Kansas for less privileged people. In Shawnee County, we looked over

---

[11] For list of these specific jobs, typical of many NYA projects, see Appendix IV.

a 22-acre camp site which the County Commissioners made available to the Organized Boys and Girls Agencies, whose members are the Girl Scouts, the Boy Scouts, the YMCA, the YWCA, the 4-H Clubs, and the Campfire Girls. This land adjoins a 400-acre area which WPA is making into an artificial lake. Neither the county nor these organizations had sufficient funds for improvements, but they agreed to co-operate with NYA in a work project on this property. Service clubs such as Kiwanis and Rotary joined in. NYA youth are now clearing this land, building roads, developing recreational facilities, and installing sanitary sewage and water supply systems. From lumber salvaged from transient camps and from new materials bought by the co-sponsors, these boys are building shower houses, quarters for a camp cook, nurse, and other camp officers, and a lodge, 55 by 52 feet, with a kitchen and storage, dining, and recreational rooms. Under skilled supervisors, the boys do all the labor, which includes quarrying native limestone for roads, foundations, and fireplaces. They are learning carpentry, masonry, plumbing, roadbuilding, and landscaping; and the county of Shawnee will have a camping area which would not otherwise have been developed for many years.

Louisiana: NYA was offered the abandoned third floor of the old Criminal Court Building on Tulane Avenue, in New Orleans. Space was urgently needed for district offices and for homemaking projects. Mr. A. J. Sarré, State NYA Director, described his first impression of these 25,000 feet of space:

"It looked hopeless. The roof leaked. Plaster had crumbled and was falling off. The place was filthy and unpainted. It hadn't been used for years. But there was a lot of room and the light was good. So we took it and put 110 boys to work, under craft supervisors paid by us."

For three months, working 70 hours a month each, these boys plastered, repaired windows, rewired, put in plumbing, laid new floors, put up new partitions, painted, and put this waste space into first-class condition. The city furnished most of the materials, and now contributes light, heat, water, and elevator service for the NYA offices, sewing and cooking rooms, library repair shop, bookkeeping and stenographic projects.

In New Orleans, NYA also fell heir to an abandoned police station. Crews of boys reconditioned the building and installed electricity and plumbing. It is now used as an automobile mechanics' shop, where NYA youth repair publicly owned cars and trucks. On city property in the rear of this building, we saw NYA boys working on a new frame building, 63 by 26 feet, which they will use as a mill shop.

Kentucky: NYA out-of-school boys have repaired, repainted, and generally improved more than 1500 rural schools. We saw more than 20 of them. In Morgan County, Mr. Ova Haney, Superintendent of Schools, told us:

"Some of these school buildings that NYA has repaired never have had a coat of paint and I know lots of them that hadn't been painted or repaired for at least 15 years. Our county is just too poor to do this work, and, if it hadn't been for NYA, it never would have been done."

In this same rural county, at a consolidated school in a small town called Ezel, we saw a science building that 18 NYA boys had remodeled from an old residence. The town people told us how the boys excavated and cemented a basement 10 feet deep and 40 feet square. The foundation was also rebuilt and new windows installed. Partitions were removed, plaster repaired, woodwork refinished, and an enclosed porch added. The interior and exterior of the building were painted. Boys also laid the sewer line to the street and built cement sidewalks. At this school, NYA had in addition constructed a bus garage, swings, teeters, and a combination basketball and tennis court.

"I don't think most of these boys ever even had a hammer in their hands before they started this work," the Superintendent of Schools told us as we left Ezel.

Arizona: During 1936, deaths from tuberculosis in Arizona increased 11.8 per cent. A considerable number of these deaths occurred in families too poor to take advantage of sanitariums or to provide isolation for ill members of the family.

NYA boys are building portable tuberculosis isolation huts for the State Board of Health. They are little seven-by-nine-foot cottages with three-foot screened openings extending around the walls at bed height. There is room inside for a bed and a small chair and dresser. The huts are doubly insulated to protect the patient from summer heat. Space is allowed for a small stove for winter use. Canvas curtains protect the patient in rainy weather.

When the Department of Health has a case of tuberculosis in a communicable stage, and when the family cannot provide adequate care for the patient or protection for other members of the family, the hut is hauled to this home and the sick person isolated. In his private hut he can have fresh air and sunshine.

The State Board of Health furnishes the materials for these cottages and NYA supplies the labor. The total average cost of one hut is $146.28.

Similar tuberculosis isolation huts are built in several other States by NYA boys. In Arkansas, we saw one constructed as a trailer.

Georgia: Every Future Farmers of America club in this State pledged $3.00 for each of its members, who number 6000, so that a State FFA camp might be developed. With this money, a 150-acre camp site was purchased on Jackson Lake in central Georgia. Under the sponsorship and direction of the State

Division of Vocational Education, 125 NYA boys are clearing the land, much of which is jungle-like in undergrowth, and quarrying native granite, which they are using to erect a large recreation building and a dining hall with kitchens and storage rooms. These boys have completed five cabins, each housing 12 to 20 occupants, and a seven-room house for the camp director.

Florida: At Campbellton, the Negro school burned down. The children were herded into a small church and all eight grades were taught in one poorly lighted, badly ventilated room. The County Board of Public Instruction could not supply funds for a new school, but agreed to furnish $650 for materials and supervision, provided NYA youth would undertake the construction work.

Final plans were made for two frame buildings, each 20 by 60 feet, with limestone flues and foundations. On January 1, 1937, 32 part-time NYA workers began the job, and it was finished in three and one-half months. Besides actually constructing the buildings, the boys installed blackboards, made 78 school desks, 4 benches, and 10 tables. The total NYA cost for this work was $800. So, for less than $1500, the Negro children of Campbellton have an adequate school, and 32 NYA boys have learned some of the fundamentals of construction work and cabinet-making.

Colorado: In five Colorado communities, youth are not only constructing buildings but are also making the adobe or sun-dried earthen bricks that are used for the walls. The chief advantage of adobe is its cheapness; in addition it has good insulating qualities against both heat and cold and is fire-resistant.

This is the production record of seven NYA boys in their first seven days of adobe brick construction:

First day	—	370 bricks[12]
Second day	—	740 bricks
Third day	—	1040 bricks
Fourth day	—	1000 bricks
Fifth day	—	1300 bricks
Sixth day	—	1250 bricks
Seventh day	—	1000 bricks

In Gunnison, a small mountain town, NYA boys are finishing an adobe Community and Youth Center to provide educational, social, and recreational facilities for children, youth, and adults of the town and the surrounding country.

The building (120 by 60 feet in dimension, with 12,520 square feet of floor space) contains a large general assembly room; classrooms for community education, home hygiene, and health courses; recreational rooms, including a pool room, a ping-pong room, and game rooms; club rooms for girls and boys; a modern kitchen; a banquet hall for all community gatherings, with space for dancing and other forms of community recreation; a county library room; and office space for the director of the community hall. Any group in the county may engage the social rooms at no cost.

In workshops, NYA boys have made most of the furniture and equipment for this center. The town of Gunnison contributed the land and more than $18,000 for construction and equipment materials. Mayor John P. McDonough has appointed a committee of Gunnison citizens to serve as the directing agency of the center. The town of Gunnison has assumed responsibility for the maintenance of the building as well as for the organization and administration of a well-rounded community program.

Utah: On February 1, 1938, 100 NYA boys in the town of Sandy started to construct a $150,000 Industrial Arts Trade

---

[12] Each about 50 pounds in weight.

Building which public-school youth and out-of-school NYA boys and girls will use. This concrete and steel building, one and one-half stories high, 312 feet long by 69 feet wide, will house trade shops and home economics units, class and discussion rooms, a library, and social rooms. The Jordan School District of Utah is furnishing materials and craft supervision.

West Virginia: The first large NYA construction project we saw was a community center, 70 by 135 feet, in New Haven, an unincorporated village of about 700 people on the bank of the Ohio River.

"Did NYA boys build this whole thing?" we asked, as we looked at the glazed hollow tile and brick exterior.

"Yes, except possibly for one part," we were told. "You see, when the boys began to pour the concrete floors, we had a rush job on. Seventy-five men who lived around here, most of them farmers, turned up to give the boys a hand. Working with the boys, it didn't take them long."

Boys were finishing the interior as we went through the building. About one-half of the basement space houses lockers, showers, and dressing rooms. The other half has been scientifically planned as storage quarters for a farmers' co-operative; the rent that the co-operative has agreed to pay will cover the major cost of upkeep for the building. On the first floor, an auditorium with a collapsible stage may be used also as a gymnasium. Here, too, are a kitchen, storage rooms, and a large, light workshop. On the second floor we saw the space for a community library, a social room, and for girls' homemaking activities.

This building is planned for the use of the entire community. Youth may work, study, and play here; adult education classes, social groups, and community organizations will have access to these facilities.

The people of the village and countryside seemed to be

enthusiastic about this center. The co-sponsors are the Municipal Council and the Men's Civic Club of New Haven (this lively village has both). They have contributed over $16,000 in materials and supervision.

We met and talked with one of the members of the Men's Civic Club, Dr. Roscoe Floyd Bryan. He gave $5000 of his own money for materials. We asked how Dr. Bryan had first become interested in NYA. We were told that he had watched a group of project boys at work improving a school building and grounds ten miles away and had decided that something practical and effective was being done for young people by giving them work and training.

"Do you think this NYA work has meant something here?" we asked Dr. Bryan.

"It's the greatest single thing that's happened to this part of the country," he answered. "See that house over there?" He pointed to a small frame building in the distance. "Three brothers from that home have been sentenced to life in the State Penitentiary. Why, this whole NYA building won't cost what the State's going to spend on those three boys. I tell you, it used to be so around here that you couldn't leave your car for a second without having the gas and tires stolen. Petty thieving was everywhere. We just haven't had any of it since we started this NYA building. Boys need to be busy."

About 100 different boys have worked part-time on this building. When inexperienced boys came on the job, they were asked what they would like to learn. Some knew and others did not. They were given a chance to do a variety of work and, when they discovered their aptitudes, they were encouraged to develop them.

We heard of several boys who left this project for private employment. One had a construction job at $175 a month, another at $160, and a third at $140. Two had become carpenters' helpers; and four others had found good jobs on construction work. Without the experience and training they received in building this community center, they could not have obtained these jobs.

Boys in Workshops

Next to construction, workshops are the biggest development in the out-of-school program. NYA supervisors canvass the possibilities for placement in municipal workshops, such as city waterworks, fire departments, and general maintenance shops. Since there is an NYA policy that these youth workers are not to displace any regular employees, only a small number of boys can be employed in this type of shop. A large number of them show mechanical ability and keen interest in carpentry, cabinet-making, automobile mechanics, and other manual skills. So NYA has set up its own workshops where boys may learn as they repair and produce equipment for public institutions.

In the early days, many of these shops were limited in the variety and value of their output. Often only hand tools were available, and boys did wood-carving, built bird houses for city parks and light recreational equipment for schools, and repaired toys for community agencies. There was something wrong with this picture; neither were the boys getting fundamental training and work experience nor were communities deriving important benefits from the work of youth.

Today the standards for NYA workshops are high. We have seen many that are well equipped both with hand tools and with modern power machines. It has become the usual practice to employ skilled workers as NYA shop foremen. Their duties are twofold—to teach the boys the fundamentals of shop work and to train them to meet standards of work habits required in private industry.

We have selected for description several that illustrate the present trends in this phase of the NYA program.

Massachusetts: Twenty-four out-of-school boys with mechanical aptitudes and interests are working as helpers in the maintenance shops of the Boston Fire Department. Under the regular supervisory staff of the department, these boys are assisting in the repair and painting of fire trucks, the rebuilding and repair of batteries, the repair of fire hose and upholstery, and in the machine shop. One boy works in the bookkeeping office, where he helps in keeping the department's inventory. Some of these boys will undoubtedly find regular employment with municipal fire departments, and others are gaining experience that can lead to jobs in privately owned shops.

California: San Diego has a system of city shops well equipped with up-to-date machinery. In these shops the Department of Public Works is giving 16 out-of-school NYA boys a chance to get enough work experience to qualify them as apprentices in a variety of trades. These boys are helpers to skilled city employees in these different municipal shops:

> Automotive-electric shop (for general motor repair, wheel aligning, axle straightening, etc., for all city-owned vehicles);
> Brake shop (repairs, adjustments, and relining);
> Automobile paint and upholstery shops;
> Machine shop (lathing, drilling, reboring, tool-making, etc.);
> Radio shop (installation, repairing, and maintaining of shortwave radios in police cars and motorcycles);
> Print shop (this shop prints all city publications);
> Carpentry and blacksmith shop;
> Meter and automatic signal shop (repair and adjustment of water and gas meters, and the repair and maintenance of automotive traffic signals).

The 16 boys working in these shops are getting a start in definite trades, and the city is benefiting from the extended services it can provide because of the work the boys are doing.

Missouri: In Kansas City we visited a workshop sponsored by the public schools, in which 80 NYA boys work in three shifts. The shop has excellent light power equipment, including a sander, planer, joiner, band saw, cut-off saw, jig saw, and emery wheels.

The school board sends orders for school furniture and equipment to this shop. When we were there, the boys had just completed 50 individual blackboard easels for primary grades. We saw several other examples of their products: book shelves, chairs, and ping-pong paddles and other recreational equipment for public schools.

One NYA boy was in charge of the hand-tool room. It was his job to check in and out the hundreds of tools in use. Another boy served as timekeeper. The NYA supervisor of this project was a skilled carpenter.

"Most of these boys learn fast," he told us. "That's because they're interested. You know, this is the first time lots of them have ever had a chance to work. We start them out with hand tools, and, when they've learned how to use them, they graduate to the machines. We work here just like in any shop. If work doesn't come up to scratch, the boys do it over. Some learn faster than others, and that's only natural. Lots of these boys come back on their own time and make things for themselves. I encourage them to do it, because the more they work the more they'll learn."

Tennessee: In the winter of 1936–37, the disastrous flood waters of the Mississippi inundated more than 20 schools in Dyer County. When the waters receded, it was found that these buildings had suffered serious structural damage and that chairs, desks, tables, bookcases, and other equipment that had stood several feet deep in mud and water could no longer be used. The county did not have enough money to repair either the buildings or the furniture.

Early in the summer of 1937, 15 boys in the NYA workshop in Dyersburg began to renovate the buildings and equipment. Some of the schoolhouses were leveled up on their foundations, repaired, and repainted. More than 500 student desks were rebuilt; where the wood was completely spoiled, the iron was salvaged and the boys constructed new desks. NYA boys also reclaimed teachers' desks, tables, and other damaged equipment. The county furnished needed materials and some supervision.

West Virginia: Fires in the Central Junior High School and the Third Ward Elementary School of Elkins put more than 1800 pieces of school furniture out of commission.

While the buildings were being repaired by the county, 21 NYA boys moved this damaged furniture to their workshop. Seventeen hundred school desks and 110 armchairs were refinished. This work required the removing of paint and varnish, straightening, planing, sanding, staining, shellacking, varnishing, and repainting. Besides this repair, these boys built the following new school equipment: 13 bookcases, 10 typewriting tables, 8 reading tables, a desk, a drawing table, and a 21-drawer filing cabinet.

The county Board of Education supplied $925 for materials and the pay of a skilled foreman; NYA spent $425 in wages to youth and $125 for supervision. For a little less than $1500, these two schools were re-equipped for use.

Kentucky: We took a trip through some of the eastern mountain counties to see what NYA was doing for the poverty-stricken youth in this stranded-population area. We had read the report of a study of 1676 NYA boys and girls from these pauper counties. They had an average of six years of schooling;[13] they usually came from families of more than seven members; 1316 of them had never held any kind of job, temporary or permanent, before NYA work; only 18 had ever had any kind of vocational training either in school or as apprentices.

Well-organized workshops have been one of NYA's answers to these appalling conditions in which youth are living in the Kentucky mountains. Because schools are poorly equipped, there is a desperate need for all types of furniture, which these destitute counties cannot afford to buy.

We visited an NYA workshop at West Liberty, in Morgan County. It is situated on the grounds of a new consolidated school which WPA built of native stone. We were told many times that this school is the finest in the whole mountain region of Kentucky. The building it replaced is still standing; in any developed community in the country this dilapidated structure would have been condemned many years ago. Morgan County had no money to equip its new school. Enrollment increased from slightly over 200 pupils to 450. Forty-three NYA boys in the West Liberty workshop have equipped this building; they made not only tablet armchairs, primary school chairs, pupils' and teachers' desks, bookcases, reading tables, waste paper baskets, filing cabinets, science laboratory tables with gas and electric outlets, and home economics equipment, but also ventilating grilles, lockers, panels for girls' and boys' lavatories, and shower partitions.

The boys in this shop also make and repair furniture for the rural schools of the county. They have built retaining walls, sidewalks, cisterns, and sanitary toilets for schools. Playgrounds have been improved and equipped with apparatus made in the shop.

The school board furnishes the materials with which the

[13] As the school terms are short and attendance is very irregular, six years of schooling in this region are not equivalent to six years in a good common school.

boys work. NYA employs a skilled supervisor, in this instance a man with a background of carpentry and teaching.

"Many of the boys in this shop walk ten to fifteen miles to work here," he said. "That's what these jobs mean to them. And do they change! You wouldn't recognize them for the same boys after they've been on the job awhile. Of course, there's a few ornery ones, but maybe you'd be ornery too, if you'd had as little to eat as they've had for a long time. I'll say most of these boys work hard and want to learn all they can. There's a lot of them that work on their own time, too. I don't know any of them that ever saw a lathe before they started here."

Arkansas: NYA workshops here produce school furniture, street signs, concrete park benches, fire ladders, music racks, and mailbox posts. When we were in Arkansas in January 1938, the first baby incubator had been built and was being tested. The rate of premature births (and consequently of infant mortality) is extremely high in some of the rural sections of this State, where hospital facilities are practically non-existent. Since many of these rural homes do not have electricity, NYA boys were experimenting in heating this incubator by brick, sand, or hot water bottles. We have heard that since our visit this unique workshop product has been perfected, and more are being built for county health agents to use. The cost of materials for the incubator is $6.50.

Boys and Girls in Public Service

A large group of work projects is set up with these two purposes in view: to extend the services of existing public agencies and to give boys and girls beginners' jobs in the varied activities of these agencies. For example, library facilities in many parts of the country are curtailed because of lack of funds for personnel; valuable conservation work is left undone because States cannot afford to hire workers; public hospitals cannot widen their services to patients because their budgets do not permit sufficient staffs; many municipal, county, and State bureaus need more clerical help if they are to extend their services to greater numbers of people. NYA has placed many boys and girls as assistants in these various positions of socially useful work. A decided effort is made to fit individual youths in jobs for which they are suited so that their work experiences may be of value to them in their search for permanent employment.

It is impossible to describe all the types of projects coming under this public service category; we have chosen examples from among those in which the largest numbers of youth are employed.

Public Libraries: The out-of-school program of NYA has provided many public libraries in every State with young workers. These are usually boys and girls with educational backgrounds better than the average of other young people on relief. It is probably true that most of these boys and girls will not find employment in the library field, but their experience in filing, classifying, issuing books, repairing books and periodicals, and all the other routines in library work adds to their employability.

In the City Library of Greeley, Colorado, we saw NYA girls working as assistants to the general library staff. In the basement, we visited the central organization unit of the Weld County Library, a venture organized in 1930 by public-minded citizens to provide library facilities for small towns and rural areas in this county. Five thousand books had been collected and small branches established in private homes, stores, and filling stations.

In July 1936, NYA agreed to help in the development of this county library. In the first 18 months of NYA co-operation, the number of books for circulation to the branch libraries was increased to 15,000. These books were obtained by drives for donations both of books and of money for the purchase of new volumes. NYA girls rebound and repaired books, and catalogued, classified, carded, pocketed, slipped, stenciled, and shellacked them for rotating distribution. They also classified, mounted, and filed 20,000 pictures for use as visual-aid material for rural school teachers.

NYA girls are in complete charge of ten of these rural branch libraries, and assist in nine more. Communities have co-operated by providing empty schoolrooms to house the libraries. In Grover, Colorado, a village of 300 people, club women obtained an empty office building and cleaned, re-decorated, and shelved it for the NYA library. In the small mountain town of Sulphur Springs, the vestibule of the church was turned into a library.

NYA employs one expert supervisor for this project. She travels from branch to branch, transferring books so that each community may always have fresh reading matter. She also trains the NYA girls in library techniques.

Here is an example of a Weld County NYA branch library. It is in a schoolroom in Gill, a village of 150 people. There has never been a library here before. One NYA girl, a high school graduate, checks books in and out, holds story hours for children, and, in her spare time, makes visual-aid materials. In 18 months, users of this new library took out 24,669 books.

In connection with this county-wide project, 10 NYA boys work in a Greeley shop to make library furniture and equipment. Their products include typing tables, bindery tables, reading tables for adults and children, card-index cabinets of two- to thirty-drawer units, bookcases, magazine racks, storage cabinets, circulation desks, footstools, step stools, waste paper baskets, bulletin boards, picture file boxes, and placard holders. We were told by city librarians in Greeley that the finished products of these boys are equal in quality to the finest available library equipment, which, of course, none of these branch libraries could have afforded to purchase.

Mesick is a village of 306 people, in rural Wexford County, Michigan. Last summer Mr. W. E. Baker, the superintendent of the consolidated school, made the school bus available for an NYA traveling library. Five hundred books were obtained from the Central State Teachers College, and the county agricultural agent supplied agricultural bulletins. NYA youth drove this library from farm to farm, covering the school bus route. Regular stops were made at each farm at two-week intervals, so that patrons might exchange their books and bulletins. This project met with such approval from its users that it is being repeated again this summer.

Clerical and Stenographic Work: When NYA boys and girls have had training in commercial work either in high school or in business college, or when they show specific clerical or stenographic interest and ability, they are given jobs in State, county, or municipal offices, provided their work will extend the services of these offices. Small numbers of NYA youths are also employed in quasi-public offices such as those of the Red Cross, settlement houses, and other agencies recognized by local Community Chests.

In Albany, New York, 16 NYA girls assist the State Department of Health in its work of distributing health information and bulletins. These girls are getting valuable training and experience in the use of calculating, tabulating, and addressograph machines, and the New York State Department of Health is able to extend its services to a wider range of citizens. Most of the NYA workers on this project are preparing themselves to take State civil service examinations as office-machine operators.

At the Kent County Court House in Dover, Delaware, six NYA girls with clerical training are transcribing from books of original entry records of all property and real estate transactions over a period of 100 years. This new accessible file should prove valuable to citizens needing information for abstracts and deeds.

In Bridgeport, Connecticut, the clerk of the Fairfield County Superior Court supervises 18 part-time NYA workers who are typing and checking judgments to bring up to date court records which were more than a year behind. NYA workers are making a useful contribution to the efficiency of this court, and are maintaining and improving their skills.

In New York City, Chicago, Philadelphia, Boston, and Hartford, 745 NYA youth are employed part-time as aides to the United States Bureau of Immigration and Naturalization. They assist in the regular clerical and stenographic routines of the bureau, and check and bring up to date records which are helpful in the establishment of citizenship. Young men and women employed in these bureaus are receiving a high type of training in office work, and the services of the bureaus are extended through this work, which their normal budgets do not cover.

We visited the Milwaukee County Court House in Milwaukee, Wisconsin, where 120 NYA boys and girls, all high school graduates with commercial training, are working part-time in 18 different county offices. Their work varies from running switchboards, typing, taking dictation, filing, indexing, and recording, to the operation of office machines. We talked with Mrs. Theresa Kraus, the NYA supervisor of this project.

"These boys and girls have never had a chance to apply their training," she told us, "until they got these jobs. They work under the regular office managers. We arrange their work in half-day units. The other half-days they take additional commercial work in the Milwaukee Vocational School. Seventeen from this project have found what I would call very good jobs in private employment. I am sure these jobs are a direct result of the experience and the training they have had in our county offices. On their own time, all of these NYA workers consult with me. One wants to know how to prepare for a State or Federal civil service examination. Another brings me an application blank for a job in some business office. From my experience with these young people, I know they're eager for work. I think we're helping some of them to be able to find it."

Nursery School Aides: Thirty-eight hundred girls earn their NYA wages as assistants in WPA nursery schools, established for pre-school children from relief families. NYA aides assist in the regular routines of the nursery schools, which include care of the children, preparation of meals, and educational and play programs for these two-to-five-year-olds. Out-of-school girls who show a marked interest in children are assigned to this work. Knowledge of proper care and feeding of children can add to their employability in the field of domestic service. It is also a sound training for better family life.

School Lunches: Two thousand NYA out-of-school girls are employed to assist in the preparation and serving of school lunches to undernourished children. These are two representative projects:

In the high school at Wicomico Church, Virginia, four NYA girls, working under the supervision of the home economics teacher, buy, prepare, and serve meals to underweight pupils whose families are in need. During the summer, boys in the Future Farmers of America raised vegetables which the

NYA girls stored and canned for school lunch use. NYA girls check the gains in weight and height of children using the lunchroom.

In Sedalia, Missouri, 10 NYA girls, under the direction of the school nurse, help to prepare and serve hot lunches to an average of 350 undernourished children daily in five public schools.

Hospital and Health Aides: We visited half a dozen public hospitals in which NYA girls are serving as nurse aides. Most public hospitals cannot afford a large enough staff to take care of the greatest possible number of patients. NYA girls working in hospitals supplement the regular staff and receive in return training for practical nursing or for jobs in doctors' or dentists' offices.

In New Orleans we went through Flint-Goodridge Hospital, a model unit of Dillard University. Twenty Negro NYA girls work in all departments of this hospital—at the switchboard, in the diet kitchens, in the out-patient clinic, in the operating and delivery rooms, in the nursery. We saw four NYA girls making bandages and swabs. One Negro girl, a college graduate, works in the pathological laboratory; when the chief technician took her vacation, this girl was able to take full charge of the laboratory. She has been promised a position as an assistant to a private pathologist in New Orleans. In October 1937, 17 Negro boys were assigned to this hospital as orderlies. In four months' time, six had received private employment, three as regular hospital orderlies. Mr. Albert W. Dent, Superintendent of Flint-Goodridge Hospital, told us that all boys from this project would find jobs readily, as this is the only training of this type available in New Orleans.

"NYA has helped us in this Hospital to serve our people better," Mr. Dent said. "And when you realize that the Negro death rate in New Orleans is a little more than twice as high as the average for the whole population of the United States you know that this training is of inestimable value."

Zanesville, Ohio, has a progressive health program. Two doctors are employed part-time by the city; one treats patients at the city clinic, and the other visits public schools. All first-grade children receive general physical examinations. Zanesville also employs two full-time city nurses and one full-time school nurse. Five NYA girls are working as assistants in the city clinic and in the schools. At the clinic these girls sterilize instruments, apply dressings, give medicines, type letters, answer telephones, and schedule appointments. In the schools, NYA girls prepare children for physical examinations, write to parents concerning the examinations, and assist in giving eye, ear, teeth, heart, lung, tuberculosis, and Schick tests. The work is supervised by the city doctors and nurses. It has been estimated that the city has been able to triple its health services because of the assistance of these five NYA workers.

Recreational Assistance: Ten thousand NYA youth are assisting in recreational programs on city and school playgrounds, in settlement houses, and in neighborhood clubs. These youth work under the direction of teachers, playground supervisors, WPA recreational directors, and settlement house workers. Recreational assistance does not give the definite job training that many other out-of-school projects do, but it does fill vital community needs in rural and city slums where underprivileged children have little chance for healthy play.

Three thousand out-of-school youth in New York City are expanding the programs in the city's well-organized settlement houses.

A typical small recreational program is in Cheyenne, Wyoming, where four NYA girls work under the direction of adult playground supervisors in three school and city parks. These girls organize and supervise games, teach handicrafts, and guard the physical safety of the 650 children who play daily in these parks.

In Birmingham, Alabama, NYA co-operated in establishing a boys' club for Negro children living in a congested district where the streets and alleys were the only play areas. A building to house this club was donated by a local citizen, and Negroes raised $1000 to repair the structure and equip it for boys' activities. More than 500 boys, eight to fourteen years old, now use this building. Twenty-five NYA youth working part-time and one full-time NYA supervisor carry on a program of athletic games, study classes, choral groups, manual training and art classes, physical education classes, and Sunday discussion groups. A library has been established in the building and is run by NYA workers. Without NYA help, this development could not have taken place. The Juvenile Court of Birmingham has endorsed the enterprise as conducive to a lowering of juvenile delinquency.

Conservation: In the two years ending with the spring of 1938, several thousand NYA boys have worked on a large variety of land and wild-life conservation projects. In Texas, out-of-school youth, working under the direction of the Agricultural Extension Service, have surveyed 706,816 acres of land for terraces, which includes the location of terrace lines and outlets. Under the direction of county agricultural agents, NYA boys have conducted soil-conservation demonstrations in 45 counties.

In one dust-bowl district in Kansas, NYA boys assisted in running contour lines on 4000 acres of pasture land and 15,000 acres of crop land.

In Wisconsin, in 1937, 400 NYA boys, working under county conservation organizations, built thousands of feeders and shelters for game birds, constructed and maintained fish-breeding and -rearing ponds, cleaned and restocked polluted lakes and streams, built dams and planted willows at the head-waters of trout streams to prevent loss of fish in high-water periods, and planted several hundreds of thousands of trees on public property. In 1935 in one county alone, these boys laid out 20 seed beds and planted 90,000 white, Norway, and Scotch pine seeds. They raised the seedlings, and this year are transplanting them to school grounds and other public property as a demonstration of reforestation.

In Melrose, Massachusetts, 20 NYA boys assist the City Engineer and Superintendent of Public Works in spraying, trimming, and transplanting shade trees. NYA has employed an expert tree surgeon to supervise this project. Under his direction boys are learning cavity-repair, fertilization, pruning, and the prevention and treatment of tree diseases.

The Inspector of Orchards in Manistee County, Michigan, supervises five NYA boys who are cutting and burning diseased fruit trees. This work is of great economic value in a community which depends largely on its cherry and apple crops for income.

In Tennessee, NYA boys have built fish-rearing ponds for the State Department of Conservation, which is trying to re-stock depleted streams.

In New Mexico five out-of-school boys are assigned to United States Forest Rangers, whom they assist in patrolling recreational areas and in the protection and care of public forest lands.

In the summer of 1937, in Pennsylvania, five NYA youth, under supervision of the State Department of Agriculture, distributed and cared for 600 Japanese beetle traps. Twice a week, these boys made the rounds of the traps, emptied and rebaited them, and mailed reports of captures of this injurious pest. At the end of the season, they also dismantled the traps.

Agricultural Demonstration: Two thousand NYA boys

and girls are working as assistants to county agricultural agents. Some are added to clerical staffs so that greater service can be extended to farmers through the increased distribution of bulletins. Others assist in agricultural exhibits and the testing of soil, seeds, livestock, and produce.

GIRLS IN HOME ECONOMICS

Perhaps the most complicated and most discussed question that has faced NYA in the out-of-school program is: "What are the best types of work that can be planned for girls from families on relief?"

Studies were made; conferences were held. These facts stood out blatantly: there are few employment outlets for girls with sixth, seventh, and eighth grade educations. There are thousands of NYA girls in this group. Fourteen per cent. of the women employed in the United States are in professional occupations, which are a sealed door to these girls. Eighteen per cent. of employed women work as typists, stenographers, file clerks, bookkeepers, and cashiers; these jobs demand skills for which the background of most NYA girls inadequately prepares them. Almost 10 per cent. work in what the census terms "trades," which include the work of saleswomen and clerks in stores. Any department store employment office will testify that the girl without a high school diploma has small chance of getting a job. Factory work and domestic and personal service are the chief job opportunities for unskilled girls with poor educational backgrounds.

While many girls work for a few years, the labor of American women today is still basically that of homemaking; and NYA has met the question of the employment of girls in a realistic way. When girls can compete for clerical or semi-professional jobs, they are given work experience and training in those fields. For the rest—the majority of NYA girls—work projects are planned which will give them opportunities to be better homemakers. Sewing is the most common occupation. There is a decided movement to expand NYA sewing room activities. Many projects now offer related work in marketing, meal planning, cooking, hygiene, first aid and home care of the sick, and child care and training.

Kentucky: Cannel City is a run-down rural village in the Kentucky mountains. There is an NYA sewing room here, to which 25 girls from relief families from miles around come to work 50 hours a month for $10. We talked with several of these girls, whose earnings are the sole cash income for their impoverished families. Every two weeks, they work three six-hour days and one seven-hour day. Because many of the girls walk from eight to fifteen miles for this work, their days in the sewing room are arranged consecutively, and they stay with relatives or friends at night until they have worked their four days.

We took a mule trip up the creek beds to where many of these girls live. There are no roads except the main county highway. Large families exist on the food they can raise on two or three acres of poor land; five bushels of corn is a rather good yield for this worn-out mountain soil. The woods have been depleted of timber and game. A few mountaineers raise scrub pigs and chickens. A cow is a rarity; the land cannot produce food sufficient for a family, much less feed for cattle. On its land a family raises corn, beans, oats, and potatoes. In dilapidated cabin after cabin we found that the typical food for the day was oats for breakfast; potatoes, beans, and pork at noon; potatoes, beans, and pork at night. When the pork gives out, potatoes, beans, and oats must suffice. We met one woman who had just walked ten miles to "swap" three eggs for some salt.

The NYA sewing room is a new world to girls from these mountain families. In Cannel City, the sewing project is housed in a room in an abandoned hotel. NYA boys renovated this room. There are five good sewing machines for the girls to use. They make children's garments for distribution to youngsters who do not have enough clothing to go to school. In January these girls completed 130 articles of children's clothing, including underwear, coats, suits, dresses, shirts, and overalls. NYA boys have made a loom for this workshop and girls are reviving a traditional craft of the mountains. One paid full-time NYA supervisor is in charge.

We were very humble before the girls' pride in this sewing room, as they showed us the machine covers they had made, the rag rugs they had woven on the loom, and the curtains they had designed and sewn.

Wisconsin: One of the best-organized and best-equipped sewing rooms we have seen is in Milwaukee, where 250 girls in shifts of 70 work ten half-days a month. Milwaukee County has furnished this workroom with 61 portable electric and 22 treadle sewing machines. The county pays the salary of one chief supervisor and NYA employs five assistants.

Last year over 40,000 articles of clothing were finished in this sewing room and delivered to Milwaukee County institutions and to needy children in public schools. The institutions and schools provide all materials. We saw warm, well-tailored women's winter coats and children's snow suits made there. We watched girls working on an order of 600 dresses for the Milwaukee Home for Dependent Children.

NYA girls in this sewing room learn every process in the making of garments—from cutting, basting, sewing, and fitting, to finishing. Many were acquiring skills of value in factory as well as home occupations. When a new, totally unskilled girl comes to this sewing room, she is usually started on infants' layettes, for which there are always orders. From simple hemming she progresses to more skilled sewing.

A weaving department has been installed on this project as an educational rather than as a production asset; during the year, 44 rugs and 168 yards of upholstery material have been woven on two looms lent by the Wisconsin Workshop for the Blind.

If girls are incompetent, they are dropped. All the 250 NYA workers in this sewing room, we were told, are studying either in the Milwaukee Vocational School or in social centers. In October, a check-up revealed that the 191 girls then working on this project were enrolled in 258 different study courses.

Many of these girls, on their own time, make clothing for themselves, and rugs, curtains, pillows, table runners, and luncheon sets for their homes.

Louisiana: In New Orleans we spent a morning with 60 NYA girls who are learning the essentials of homemaking.

"A study of New Orleans girls of this background shows that the great majority will be married and running their own homes within three to five years," a supervisor told us. "Many of them who come from large families are now responsible for a good share of the cooking, cleaning, laundering, and care of younger children. Our work here is planned to give these girls knowledge and practice which will be of value in their jobs as homemakers."

First, we visited a large, airy, well-equipped sewing room where 40 girls were working on hospital supplies, and sewing, repairing, and remodeling clothing for children's institutions of the city. One girl, who told us that she had never sewed before, was hemming towels.

"After I learn to do this kind of sewing, I'm going to learn how to use patterns," she told us.

Other girls were cutting children's dresses. Several were working on tailored surgeons' coats. Each girl learns every phase of sewing. In three and one-half months the following articles were completed in this sewing room:

82	doctors' coats, long	
398	doctors' middies	
45	doctors' pants	
1873	mouth pieces	
70	sheets	
45	pillow cases	
100	terry towel quilted pads	
130	abdominal binders	
130	breast binders	
760	linen towels	
1374	ring towels	
130	brown linen towels	
175	quilted bed pads	
138	hot water bottle covers	
15	track suits (shirts and pants)	
88	aprons	
166	gym suits	
266	track pants	
272	pr. trousers repaired	
12	night shirts	
18	outing night gowns	
12	cotton night gowns	
707	hospital shirts	
133	bed pan covers	
38	O. B. socks	
101	scarfs	
50	napkins	
12	caps	
12	aprons	
256	baby gowns	
24	curtains for project	
69	children's dresses	
21	Hoover dress aprons	
45	khaki trousers repaired	
45	khaki shirts repaired	
100	gym suits remodeled	
200	Mammy dolls for Christmas presents	

Each week eight girls who are doing hand-sewing in a small, separate room discuss with the supervisor a wide range of subjects as they sew. Grammar and pronunciation are corrected. Some of the topics the girls most frequently ask to have discussed are "Hygiene and Grooming," "Table Service and Setting," "Should Wives Work?" "Ought I to Marry?" and "Learning to Live Together."

Under a home economics supervisor, 12 girls plan, market, prepare, and serve daily lunches for all the girls on the project. Each girl pays five cents for her lunch. This covers the cost of the food. We talked with several girls who were serving on the lunch "squad" that week.

"I've learned to cook a lot of different things than we have at home," one girl said. "Then I go home and try them out on the family."

Another girl who had marketed for that day's lunch explained to us: "You know, you just don't go and buy anything. You've got to know when string beans are good. Say, there's a lot to know about buying."

All the girls on the project receive instruction in first aid and home care of the sick. They also rotate as assistants in nurseries in the city where they receive training and experience in the care and feeding of young children.

Although the principal aim of this comprehensive project is to give NYA girls sound training for better homemaking, employment possibilities are carefully watched, and several girls have found work in restaurants, lunchrooms, and drug stores. Their experience on this project has equipped them for these jobs.

Arkansas: We visited an NYA "Home Arts Practice House" in Prescott. Here girls from relief families are working part-time, learning the skills of homemaking.

NYA boys made most of the furniture for this six-room house. The city furnishes water and electricity, and the Prescott Chamber of Commerce pays the rent. Local churches and clubs donated kitchen equipment and fabrics, which the girls have made into curtains and linens. The girls clean, cook, and launder. Under a paid NYA supervisor, they study meal-planning and family-budgeting. As their work project, they conduct a day nursery for the underprivileged children of the community. They have planted and are caring for a large garden, and in the fall will can fruits and vegetables for use throughout the winter. A county health nurse gives talks and leads discussions on health subjects and first aid and home care of the sick. The supervisor of this project keeps a record of each girl's progress, and when a girl shows that she is competent to hold a job as a domestic worker, efforts are made to place her.

"We're a hundred per cent. behind NYA," we were told by the secretary of the Prescott Chamber of Commerce. "It's important for boys to learn how to be good farmers or good carpenters or good masons. And it's just as important for girls to know how to be good homemakers. That's what they're learning here. These girls are going to have better homes, better children, and the whole community will benefit because of their training in this practice home."

Virginia: The city of Hopewell provided a six-room cottage for an NYA Homemaking Center, and 18 girls from relief families were assigned to this demonstration home for work and training. These girls refinished the floors, painted the walls and woodwork, repaired, refinished, and upholstered old furniture, which had been donated, built bookcases and shelves, and made curtains and household linens for this demonstration home.

To earn their salaries, these NYA workers make children's and adults' clothing, sheets and pillow cases, and, in the summer and fall, they can fruits and vegetables, all of which are distributed by the County Welfare Department.

There is one paid NYA supervisor. City and school authorities have co-operated in teaching home economics, home hygiene, and the fundamentals of good health practices. The supervisor recently made this report:

"Already these girls are applying the practical training received at the Center. All have made clothing for members of their families; several have upholstered furniture at home; a number have made new curtains; and all have applied their new knowledge of foods at home. In a number of cases parents have been to the Center to learn more of the constructive work their daughters are doing. From the work and the training received these girls will be equipped to be better homemakers in the community."

North Carolina: In the summer of 1937, in Brevard, the County Board of Education furnished one and one-half acres of land, seeds, fertilizers, and gardening tools to two NYA boys, who raised vegetables for distribution to local families in need of food. Twelve NYA girls canned the surplus vegetables and also some fruit which the county provided. This is a résumé of costs and products through August:

Cost to Board of Education		*Cost to NYA*		*Total*
Rental of 1½ acres land	$15.00	Labor	$183.00	
Seeds	4.60	Jars	92.00	
Tomato and potato plants	4.00			
Fertilizer	12.00			
Tools and equipment	15.00			
	$50.60		$275.00	$325.60

Value	
Canned vegetables—531 half-gallon jars @ 50c	265.50
Beans—8 bushels @ $1.25	10.00
Cabbage—300 pounds @ 1½c	4.50
Okra—75 pounds @ 6c	4.50
Rhubarb—600 pounds @ 3c	18.00
Beets—12 bushels @ $2.00	24.00
Squash—16 bushels @ $1.50	24.00
Carrots—8½ bushels @ $2.00	17.00
Tomatoes—4 bushels @ $2.00	8.00
Huckleberries—8 gallons @ 40c	3.20
Apples—12 bushels @ 75c	9.00
Blackberries—32 gallons @ 25c	8.00
Total cash value	$395.70

The county authorized the purchase of 2000 cans to be used for preserving fruits and vegetables which these same young people raised during the fall and winter.

The Community Youth Center Emerges

Most communities in the United States offer meager recreational facilities for young people who are out-of-school and out-of-work. And they are the very young people who need most the normal spare-time activities of youth—athletics and games, dancing, music, dramatics, hobby clubs—or just some place to meet friends. The youth who has a job can afford to pay for membership in some organization that provides these facilities; the young man or woman who has little or no work and whose parents must struggle constantly to stretch every dollar to cover basic family needs can afford neither a membership fee for a club nor a dime or a quarter for a swim, a basketball game, or a gym class. Most high schools and colleges have elaborate athletic and social programs for their students; few have opened their doors to youth whose names are not on their enrollment lists. From the beginning of the NYA work program, supervisors and State directors have tried to find or create recreational opportunities for the economically and educationally underprivileged youth in their communities. Their greatest problem was finding space.

As more vocational workshops and homemaking units developed, housing often became a major problem. A carpentry shop or a kitchen required good lighting and ventilation. Store rooms and tool rooms were in demand. Many boys and girls were eager for study classes and training closely related to the work they were doing.

From this need for workshops, study rooms, and recreational facilities have grown many and varied NYA community youth centers. In different States they are called by different names; "Youth Opportunity Center," "Occupational Development Institute," "Youth Occupational Institute," and "Youth Center" are used in four of the States we have visited. Almost every State today has some sort of youth center in which, under one roof, the young people of a community may find work and study facilities, athletic and social opportunities. Sometimes under NYA impetus already existing organizations which serve young people have been integrated or expanded. In other instances, NYA boys have reconditioned buildings to serve as youth centers. With the extension of the NYA work program into the construction field, many youth centers are being built from the ground up by NYA workers. Local governmental agencies, civic organizations, and individuals in many States are co-operating with NYA and furnishing substantial sums of money for materials and maintenance. The youth center solves one important NYA problem. It draws many groups of youth of the community together and prevents the isolation of unemployed youth. Clubs or athletic teams made up exclusively of NYA boys or girls are discouraged; they are not a group apart; they belong to the integrated life of their own communities.

We have described under the construction projects several community centers that NYA boys are building. These are a few more examples which illustrate the divergence both of physical set-up and of organization of activities:

In the Negro slums of Chicago, the South Side Boys Club had struggled for years to give Negro boys of all ages healthful outlets for their spare time. During the depression, lack of money made it necessary to stop most of the work in the club. The building deteriorated so that much of it could no longer be used. NYA agreed to rehabilitate this club as a Negro youth center. First, NYA boys renovated the structure: they laid a new concrete floor in the basement, repaired plaster, painted walls and woodwork, and reconditioned the swimming pool, gymnasium, and locker rooms. Now several thousand Negro boys of all ages use this center for athletics, clubs, classes, cultural and social activities. NYA boys have a carpentry shop in the basement and a radio repair shop on the second floor. NYA youth assist in conducting classes and supervising clubs and athletic games for younger Negro boys.

The Library Board of the city of St. Cloud, Minnesota, purchased a large granite and brick church which had been abandoned ten years before, and has rented it to NYA for a nominal sum. One hundred and twenty NYA boys worked part-time for two and one-half months to recondition this building for use as a community center. They put in new floors and window frames, repaired plaster, painted, and assisted in the installation of plumbing and electricity. We went through this completed center, where NYA boys were constructing portable bath houses for a community beach and girls were sewing for public institutions. One unusual work project in this center was a gravel-testing laboratory where five NYA youth, under a chemist supervisor, test gravel for the city, county, State, and WPA engineers. We saw the kitchen, reading, conference, lounge, and social rooms, and the auditorium, which seats 565 people. All the facilities of this building are available at no charge to community organizations such as the Boy Scouts, Girl Scouts, the St. Cloud Chorus, church groups, teachers' clubs, and farmers' associations.

In Jacksonville, Florida, 50 Negro NYA boys are working on a Youth Community Center for which the city gave the land. The Negro YWCA raised $1000 for materials and other Negro groups have collected an additional $3000. This center will house NYA workshops and home economics rooms, an auditorium for music, dramatics, lectures, and discussion groups, and social activities for all the Negro population of the community.

"Health, jobs, homemaking, citizenship, and leisure activities—those are our goal in the NYA work program in Oklahoma. Because the Youth Center provides all of these, we're building them as fast as we can," Mr. Houston A. Wright, the State Director, explained.

Seven Youth Centers in Oklahoma had been completed by NYA youth and 15 were under construction on May 1, 1938. They are community buildings for the use of children, youth, adults, and all civic organizations. Usually they have NYA vocational and homemaking shops. Girls on NYA projects make curtains, rugs, and other furnishings for these centers. Most are built of native stone, although some have brick veneer, and one at Stillwater was constructed of tamped earth blocks with a stucco finish. They vary in size according to the needs of the community. City and county governments, boards of education, civic organizations, and individuals have contributed extensively for materials with which NYA youth erect these centers.

One of the larger Youth Centers, at Paul's Valley, was finished in March 1938. The City Council of Paul's Valley voted a $5000 bond issue as its contribution to this building, and paid the salary of one construction superintendent. Additional contributions of $4500 were made by individuals of this town. NYA boys quarried native stone for this center in the Arbuckle Mountains, 36 miles south of Paul's Valley. Under the direction of two NYA foremen, they did all the concrete work, stone masonry, carpentry, plumbing, plastering, and painting. This stone Youth Center has eight rooms and an auditorium and meeting room, 60 feet by 40. There are manual training shops and homemaking rooms. Girl Scouts, Boy Scouts, the 4-H Club, all civic clubs, the Chamber of Commerce, and other organizations use this building for gatherings. It is a place where youth may feel at home to work and play and study.

"Many of the boys whose labor built this center," Mr. Wright said, "had never before done any work in construction crafts."

This is a panorama of the NYA work program today. Not all its projects measure up to these we have pictured. We saw, for example, one group of girls whose only work was knitting sweaters for destitute school children. This project, we felt, was an uneconomic use of time, as machine-knit sweaters would have met the needs of the children at far less cost, and the girls who were employed as hand-knitters were receiving little training of real worth. We saw some poorly equipped workshops and sewing rooms, with scraps of lumber or cloth as the only materials on which the youth were working. Lack of materials and efficient equipment prevents the production of useful articles and gives young people inadequate work experience. There are a few projects in which youth are employed to make puppets for use in schools and community clubs; while the making of puppets and costumes demands some fine skills, the training it affords is in far too narrow a field. In New Mexico weaving projects have economic justification, since there are reasonable earning possibilities for Indian and Spanish youth who can produce these traditional rugs and fabrics. In another State we saw girls weaving blankets for public institutions; we doubt that the training they receive in this work will prove useful to them either as homemakers or in the industrial world.

Frankly, we had expected to see more of these dubious work projects; we found them to be by far the exception rather than the rule. Some States have eliminated them entirely, and others are replacing them as rapidly as sounder new projects can be developed. Since NYA can spend only a small percentage of its funds for materials and equipment, local communities must co-operate in providing both. In most

States, this co-operation has been obtained, as evidenced by the amount of money sponsors have contributed for the establishment and maintenance of work facilities for relief youth on NYA.

Although individual States have great latitude in working out their own types of projects and their own organization of these projects, their common experiences in the two and one-half years of the work program have produced some general techniques which can be utilized in further developments of this phase of NYA.

"Rotation" is one of these techniques. Many young people have never had a chance to learn what types of work they are best fitted to do. Work projects should be so organized that the youth have an opportunity to discover their own work interests and aptitudes. NYA does not pretend to give sufficient training to produce highly skilled workers; it merely starts young people on their way to potential beginners' jobs. It is desirable that, within projects, youth learn as many phases as possible of various trades and occupations. For example, if a boy is "learning by doing" in a carpentry shop, he should have as much experience as he can in a wide range of carpentry work. For this reason, workshops must produce a variety of articles. The growth of the construction program in NYA has helped to widen the work experiences of many boys, as building demands many different skills.

All the State directors with whom we have talked agree that volunteer supervision of NYA projects is unsuccessful except in rare instances. Skilled craftsmen who have the ability to teach have proved the best foremen for work projects.

Because NYA employs youth approximately only one-third of their working time, the question of how to arrange these hours of work has arisen. It seems now generally recognized as desirable that work projects be arranged so that youth are employed on them for standard working days of seven or eight hours. This time aspect of learning the work routine is considered valuable. Thus a boy working 44 hours a month on NYA is employed for four seven-hour days and for two eight-hour days a month. Since in most cases NYA youth pay their own transportation to and from work, it is a saving to them to have their hours of work arranged so that they will spend the minimum of their small pay-checks for transportation.

Standards of work discipline on NYA projects today are generally strict: boys and girls report to work on time, take regular lunch hours, are held responsible for the materials they use. In several States we saw monthly progress records of each boy and girl. They are kept by supervisors and indicate improvements in work abilities.

The NYA work program is based on the supposition that the energies and skills of young people are going to be in demand, that our civilization will provide jobs for those who are capable of filling them. The depression and its attendant unemployment have worked hardships on large numbers of youth who in normal times of employment would have held jobs as beginners. By providing these first jobs NYA has helped large numbers of young people to fill the dangerous gap between the time that they leave school and the time when industry shall absorb them.

The NYA work program by no means pretends that it does or can solve all the problems that face young people reaching maturity during the depression. It gives part-time employment only to unmarried youth on relief rolls. There are hundreds of thousands more who want the chance to earn some money, to do some real work, and to get some training for at least a toehold in the industrial life of the country.

We have heard questions like these brought up a number of times: "Doesn't this NYA work kill ambitions in young people?" "Aren't they satisfied to work part-time and earn a little money?" "Won't we have boys and girls considering NYA as a career?" We have found little evidence to support such suspicions. We noted that young men and women enrolled in the NYA work program seldom referred to "my NYA job." Instead, we often heard: "I work at the hospital," or "I'm laying bricks at the new school," or "My job's out at the new park."

NYA youth usually take private jobs when they can find them. They go into the harvest fields, into stores at rush times, and into other temporary work which may lead to permanent employment. Some of them step directly into full-time regular jobs. In the first two and one-half years of NYA, approximately 500,000 out-of-school and out-of-work youth have been employed on NYA jobs. Complete records have not been kept of the movement of NYA youth into private industry throughout this period. But in the twelve months ending March 1, 1938, during which 150,000 boys and girls, on the average, were on the NYA work program, 60,522 of them found jobs in private employment. During four of those months, employment opportunities generally were shrinking owing to the sharp recession in business. Remembering also that most of these young people had had extremely poor educational preparation, that few of them had ever held regular jobs, that many of them had sought work in vain for several years, and that no small number of them had suffered from undernourishment and other physical deficiencies, the large number who moved from NYA rolls into private employment would seem a good indication of the value of the experience and training received on NYA work projects.

CHAPTER IV

Spare Time Put to Use

A DAY'S WORK WAS BEGINNING IN AN NYA CARPENTRY SHOP. Forty boys were making school furniture. Some were cutting lumber, some were working at the lathe, others at power saws. One boy was carefully shellacking a bookcase. We watched the foreman as he went from boy to boy, stopping here only a minute, and staying five minutes, perhaps, with the next young man.

"All these boys are working from mechanical drawings," he told us. "Three of them at a time are assigned to our drafting room, where the drawings are made for cabinets and chairs and tables or whatever we're working on. Every boy in this shop learns to read and understand plans. I spend a lot of time with them, explaining and helping them to learn, because they can't ever expect to earn their livings as carpenters or cabinet-makers if they can't read drawings."

Much training similar to this is done on the job. But NYA youth work only one-third of the usual working month. From the beginning of the out-of-school program, supervisors, State directors, and, in some cases, youth, themselves, have asked: "Why can't some way be worked out to provide additional training in this spare time?"

On many projects that we visited, boys and girls stay overtime or come back during their spare time to obtain more knowledge and additional practice in the work they are doing. On their own time boys in workshops frequently make furniture for their homes, and girls on sewing projects bring materials to make clothes for themselves and their families. We saw one girl remodeling an older brother's overcoat into a winter coat for a small brother. The overcoat was out at the elbows and generally frayed. She was salvaging enough of the material for a small child's garment. Supervisors encourage NYA youth to use the facilities of workrooms and assist them in making articles for their own use. In several sewing rooms and workshops we saw small libraries of books and bulletins on subjects related to the work the young people were doing. The supervisors reported that this informative material circulated widely among the girls.

Instruction on the job and help to individual youth who volunteer their own time have not provided sufficient off-the-job training to meet the needs of these young people who have had so little schooling. Theirs are not the homes that have books and magazines. They have had little of the practical education that employment could have given them. They cannot afford even small fees for private instruction.

There is no national NYA policy concerning this important phase of spare-time training. NYA funds do not permit the hiring of enough additional personnel for related educational work. Each State has the responsibility of devising ways, and obtaining aid from local resources, for co-ordinated training opportunities for NYA youth. The year since the spring of 1937 showed considerable growth of this part of the program. Sometimes NYA supervisors and foremen conduct classes; in a few instances, special NYA instructors are hired; WPA adult education teachers have conducted thousands of classes attended by NYA youth; public schools, especially vocational schools, have made available teachers, classrooms, and workrooms; State, county, and municipal governmental agencies, the Red Cross, churches, settlement houses, the YWCA and the YMCA, civic organizations, and individuals have helped; NYA advisory committees have worked to expand this whole field.

Training classes of hundreds of types are now conducted for NYA workers. Some are very informal. In one Kentucky mountain sewing room, the supervisor prepared a list of simple questions for discussion each day. On the day we visited this workroom, she asked a group of 16 girls to name four outstanding events of the past year. These were the answers: "It sleeted," "My grandmother died," "NYA stopped" (the number on the project had been reduced), and "The flood." No girl in the room knew who was the Governor of the State, although one hesitatingly volunteered: "Abraham Lincoln." On a boys' project in the same county, the supervisor had taught 14 to read and write. These young men stayed after their working hours for a class in the ABC's.

Supervisors of some NYA projects organize related training classes an extra hour daily or two or three times a week so that they may give the boys or girls additional information about the actual work they are doing. For example, boys are building a rural schoolhouse; after their day's work the supervisor or foreman talks with the boys about the wood, concrete, brick, or other materials they are using, explains the care and use of hand tools and machines, teaches arithmetic by giving exercises in the correct filling out of bills of material, and discusses with the boys the construction methods employed in this building. Sometimes vocational teachers from schools give extension courses at the project or business men from a local lumberyard, hardware store, planing mill, or cement plant come in to demonstrate the proper use of their merchandise.

There is a definite tendency to widen the scope of NYA sewing rooms by related training activities in the whole home-making field. In Providence, Rhode Island, each girl has a three-hour course weekly in meal-planning and serving, cooking, handicrafts, the care of electric sewing machines, advanced dressmaking, health and personal hygiene, simple English, arithmetic, home decoration, and grooming and etiquette. The girls attend these classes on their own time. At noon each day, a hot lunch is prepared by one group of girls under the direction of a WPA dietitian, and served at a cost of ten cents to all the others who wish it. Most of them stay for this meal.

"Many of our youngsters," Mr. Peter E. Donnelly, the Rhode Island Youth Director, comments, "are of Italian and Portuguese descent, and some of them have expressed their appreciation of the opportunity to learn to prepare what they call American dishes because the young men who have captured their affections are not familiar with the types of food prepared in the foreign family."

Sponsors of work projects in some cases organize spare-time educational curricula for groups of NYA young people. In hospitals where NYA girls serve as nurse aides, staff physicians, nurses, dietitians, and laboratory technicians frequently conduct courses and discussion groups to supplement the training that the girls receive from their hospital duties. When NYA girls work as library assistants, the regular library staff often gives added instruction during off-work time. We visited the Topeka, Kansas, high school, where seven NYA girls are assigned as helpers in the cafeteria, which serves several thousand students daily. This cafeteria has modern and complete equipment. After their work hours, the girls receive instruction from the cafeteria director and her assistants in all phases of commercial restaurant work so that they may qualify for employment in hotels, restaurants, lunchrooms, and drug stores. In New York, the Long Island State Park Commission supplies specialists in forestry and nursery work, painting, carpentry, and other construction trades for demonstration and discussion classes for NYA boys working in public parks. Eight youth workers in the county surveyor's office in Central City, Nebraska, attend a weekly class in which they study the use of slide rules and levels, practical mathematics and surveying calculations, land measuring and the running of contour lines. These examples could be multiplied hundreds of times from the NYA program in the different States.

Some special NYA training programs have been set up for young people who want, and show the ability for, intensive training in particular types of work. In Parkersburg, West Virginia, there was a shortage of automobile mechanics. NYA organized an automobile mechanics' training course, furnished the space, and obtained a WPA teacher. Twenty boys enrolled. Eight were dropped after a short time because they did not show promise of development in this particular trade. The remaining twelve came every evening on their own time for instruction and practical work on cars. In eleven months they rebuilt 75 cars. One evening they were so interested in the technique of automobile-door repair that they stayed until five o'clock in the morning. The automobile mechanics of local garages often came to this workshop in the evening and helped to instruct the boys. At the conclusion of the training, eleven of the twelve found jobs in garages at $18 to $26 a week.

A dictaphone company in Rochester, New York, has agreed to give 30 NYA youth who have successfully passed an English-usage test three weeks of intensive training by providing instructors and dictaphone machines.

In Cleveland, Ohio, a department store gives training to NYA boys and girls in elevator-operation, salesmanship, and the alteration and making of draperies and upholstery.

NYA sponsored a waitress training course at the Civic Center in Salt Lake City, Utah. The restaurant inspector for the City Health Department, the head of the local cooks' and waiters' union, a beautician, and other individuals who had pertinent information for the 30 girls enrolled, came in for talks; field trips were made to a local packing plant, a cash register company, and hotels and restaurants in the city, so that the girls might acquire first-hand knowledge of importance to them in getting and keeping jobs as waitresses.

The Maine Hotel Association has co-operated with NYA for the past two years in establishing an eight weeks' pre-employment training course for unemployed girls who wish work as waitresses during the busy summer hotel season but who do not know the essentials of ushering, table-setting, order-taking, the serving of various courses at breakfast, lunch, and dinner, and party- and banquet-serving. Hotels in several communities lend equipment and personnel. Girls who successfully complete the course are given certificates, and the Maine State Employment Service handles their placement in jobs. Last year more than 500 girls who had taken this training found summer work in hotels and restaurants.

WPA Co-operates

NYA boys and girls are advised about the wide range of adult education courses conducted by WPA teachers throughout the country. In some instances, WPA assigns teachers for special NYA courses related closely to the work the youth are doing.

In February 1938, in the State of Ohio, 2989 NYA boys and girls were enrolled in spare-time classes taught by WPA teachers, NYA supervisors, settlement house personnel, public and private school teachers, churches, business colleges, libraries, and individual specialists in various commercial fields. In that month, WPA courses were given in the following subjects:

Arithmetic
Art
Automobile Mechanics
Bookkeeping
Business Etiquette
Child Care
Civics and Current Events
Commercial Art
Comptometer Operation
Conservation (Agricultural)
Cooking
Dancing
Domestic Service
Dramatics
Employment Problems of Negro
    Youth
First Aid
French
Handicrafts
Health
History

Home Economics
Home Furnishings and
    Draperies
Home Management
Hygiene
Music—Piano, Other Instru-
    ments, Voice, Theory
Negro History
Pottery
Practical Nursing
Reading
Recreational Leadership
Sewing
Shorthand
Sociology
Spanish
Spelling
Spoken English
Swimming
Typing
Vocational Orientation
Writing

Many other States show proportionately large participation
by NYA young people in WPA educational courses. In Kentucky, in 1937, approximately 2000 received instruction in
elementary school subjects, home nursing, first aid, child care,
home economics, masonry, metal work, woodwork, and handicrafts. In Mississippi, 1250 girls are studying homemaking
and domestic service.

In Illinois, NYA has emphasized pre-employment training
classes, many of which are under WPA, throughout the State.
These classes are open to all youth, but are often organized
around nuclei of NYA boys and girls. During 1937 several
thousand young people attended them. In January 1938, in
Texas, 2277 NYA youth were enrolled in part-time study
courses, and 1084 of these received instruction from WPA
teachers.

In Portland, Oregon, 10 NYA girls are working 70 hours, and taking an additional 50 hours a month of related study, in a WPA home demonstration unit, designed to train young women for domestic service and to aid in setting up standards in household employment. Work and training combine to teach the girls how to prepare and serve food, upstairs and downstairs work, laundry, child care, household management, household etiquette, and improvement in personal appearance. WPA and the vocational department of the public schools of Portland furnish teachers. Each girl remains in the course until she is able to qualify for a position in domestic service. She is then referred to the Domestic Placement Department of the State Employment Office.

In Greater Boston, NYA has developed an elaborate related training program. A WPA staff member organized the classes, which are conducted by NYA supervisors and teachers from Boston University, Harvard University, and the Boston Opportunity School. Every NYA youth is expected to take two one-hour courses each week, one related to the work he is doing and the other elective. In announcing this course, Mr. Edward L. Casey, NYA State Director, stated:

"The objectives of the related training program are: (1) to increase project efficiency by providing workers with training in their specific project tasks; (2) to train NYA workers for permanent positions. In looking for positions many of the workers have been greatly handicapped by a lack of training. These courses are designed to increase your chances of getting a job; (3) to give you an opportunity to explore and try the various occupations, so that NYA authorities will be in a better position to adjust the projects in accord with your interests and abilities."

In the spring of 1938 the courses taught were:

Job Survey Course in Trades for Men
Job Survey Course in Trades for Women

Job Survey Course in Clerical and Selling Positions for
    Men
Job Survey Course in Clerical and Selling Positions for
    Women
Office Practice
Elementary Shorthand
Advanced Shorthand
Elementary Bookkeeping
Advanced Bookkeeping
Elementary Typing
Advanced Typing
Household Management
Child Care
Sewing
Handy Facts for Men (training in general handiwork around
    the house, for superintendence of buildings, etc.)
Carpentry
Landscaping
Retailing[1]

Ninety-four different sessions of these courses are offered
each week at the Boston Opportunity School, the Young
Men's Christian Union, and the Burroughs Newsboys' Foundation in Boston proper; at the Hecht House in Dorchester;
the Central Square Center in East Boston; the Norfolk House
Center in Roxbury; the East End Union in Cambridge; the
Olivia James House and the Army Base in South Boston; the
Jamaica Plains Neighborhood House in Jamaica Plains; and
the Catholic Institute in Brighton. All of them furnish space
free of charge. NYA boys and girls, one from each class, com-
pose a Related Training Council to make suggestions concerning the form and content of the courses and to evaluate
the benefits they receive from their studies. This council of
youth publishes a semi-monthly bulletin which includes information on qualifications and opportunities in various employment fields.

---

[1] Given through the co-operation of the Prince School of Store Service.

General and Vocational Schools Help

In some localities, grade schools, high schools, and colleges have either broadened their extension courses to take in NYA workers or have established extra study groups for them. Two difficulties are frequently encountered in developing training work through these schools. First, all over the country, schools are generally overcrowded and teachers are carrying such heavy classroom loads that they do not wish to add to their duties. Second, it is difficult to get NYA boys and girls back inside the ordinary schoolhouse.

"Lots of the young people who have been out of school for a long time have a definite fixation against going inside a school door again," one NYA supervisor told us.

"Out-of-school youth do not want to go back to school," another supervisor said. "The school is not the center of youth activities any more."

Nevertheless, these obstacles have been overcome in a number of communities. NYA in New Mexico has succeeded in establishing free-time study courses in many public schools. In Clovis, a group of out-of-school girls go to the home economics department of the high school two afternoons a week for instruction in cooking and sewing. A number of other public schools in New Mexico co-operate by including NYA youth in classes in simple English, arithmetic, and other elementary subjects.

The Houghton College of Mining and the Ironwood Junior College in Michigan have initiated short courses in shop work for NYA boys who want training in addition to that which they receive in their work.

At Hornell, New York, Mr. Fred Hoey of the Alfred High School conducts a class in woodworking one evening a week for NYA boys who are working in a shop. This class is also open to other youth of the community.

The greatest development in the NYA spare-time education program has come through vocational schools, especially in States that have increased their vocational teaching personnel by the use of Federal Smith-Hughes and George-Deen funds. Wisconsin has an admirable vocational education program, with splendid buildings, equipment, and teaching personnel. All over the State NYA youth spend some of their free time in the vocational schools' shops and classrooms. In Milwaukee, the NYA working schedules are arranged in half-day periods so that the boys and girls may use their other half-days in the vocational school. Before the school year opened last August, each worker consulted with his project supervisor concerning the most profitable courses he might take. In the year 1937–38, NYA youth in Milwaukee have had a monthly average of 47 hours in project work and 43 hours in school.

In Minneapolis, in 1937, 450 NYA boys and girls enrolled in the Miller Vocational High School for one year of intensive training in thirteen different trades. The Minneapolis Board of Education co-operated with NYA in providing these courses.

In Arkansas, instructors in agriculture and teachers from the State Home Economics Department and the Trades and Industries Division conduct part-time classes for NYA boys and girls all over the State.

The Colorado NYA and the State Board for Vocational Education have a co-operative plan whereby the board furnishes supervisors for work projects and for correlated vocational classroom activities. Sixty per cent. of Colorado's out-of-school youth are now receiving this beneficial training from experts.

In Missouri last year 65 per cent. of the NYA youth took part-time educational work given by vocational agriculture and home economics teachers, WPA instructors, social agency youth leaders, local advisory committee members, and project supervisors. Free-time classes were held in 32 elementary and vocational subjects.

TRAINING FOR HEALTH

In every State we have visited, health information has been given to NYA boys or girls, sometimes by WPA teachers, often by Red Cross workers, and in many cases by members of State departments of health. We have watched several groups of NYA boys and girls as they heard and discussed general problems of health, personal and home hygiene, sanitation, disease prevention, first aid, home care of the sick, and other questions affecting their own well-being. Most of these young people listened with impressive attentiveness and some were eagerly alert in their questions. Many, we felt, were getting simple new health ideas which they would use for themselves and their families.

A State health worker was talking about venereal diseases to an NYA group we visited in Chicago. She stressed the occupational handicaps resulting from these diseases. She explained and demonstrated the Wassermann test and told these young people where they and their friends could take this test at no charge. In a number of other States, NYA is assisting the Public Health Service in its campaign to bring the problems of venereal diseases out into the open so that medical knowledge can be applied to them.

Leisure-Time Recreation

Youth who are out of school and jobless need all kinds of recreation facilities during their spare time, but few have many opportunities to find them. Settlement houses have opened their doors to groups of these boys and girls who want games, athletics, craft classes, and social activities. In some instances, the YWCA and the YMCA have made special arrangements to extend the use of their commodious facilities to NYA youth. In almost every State, NYA organizes recreation programs, often open to all youth of the community, although they are especially designed for NYA boys and girls. In Nashua and Manchester, New Hampshire, hobby clubs, dancing, gym classes, an orchestra and glee club, and craft classes have been formed by NYA youth. New York State has many drama, music, and craft groups. We watched a large chorus of NYA Negro boys and girls practicing in Schenectady. A talented boy who had received a scholarship at a music school was directing them. He had a similar group of Negro singers in Albany.

The city of Waco, Texas, bought an old home and provided materials with which NYA boys renovated and landscaped it. In this house, the Domestic Science Club, an organization of Waco women, supervises a leisure-time club for 250 NYA girls. In a large room, equipped with a piano, radio, and victrola, the girls give dances. Arts and craft classes are popular. Local people have collected a library for this house. A kitchen and dining room make home economics activities possible. In the large back yard, NYA boys built an open-air fireplace where the girls may be hostesses at barbecues and picnics.

Vocational Information

"What kind of a job do I want?"

"What sort of work could I do best?"

"What are some of the kinds of work that aren't so crowded that there might be room for me?"

"What do you have to be able to do and to know to get and keep a job in a store"—or a bakery, or a textile factory, or any place else?

These are the questions many young people want answered. They want all varieties of job information. Where have they been able to get answers—answers which they can understand and use either in looking for work or in training themselves to be able to hold jobs?

NYA has tried to spread vocational information to many young people. In different States, this is done in different ways. In many States we saw simple instruction on "How to Apply for a Job" given. Boys and girls filled out application blanks and then discussed with their supervisors possible improvements in methods of filling them out.

"Let's suppose you're looking for a job in my factory," we heard one supervisor tell an NYA boy. Then he conducted a practice interview with the boy.

"I feel that many of our young people are very shy and uncertain of themselves when it comes to talking to a possible 'boss,'" he explained to us later. "They put their worst feet 'way forward. Often in spare time we have these little practice interviews. Several of the youngsters have told me that they have been helped when they went to talk to some real employer."

In Cleveland, a drama group of NYA youth put on a play

called Want-Ad, in which they demonstrated the right and wrong ways of approaching jobs.

Often NYA supervisors arrange for boys and girls to make trips through industrial plants so that they may get some understanding of the demands that specific trades make on workers. In Mississippi, these excursions have been made a regular activity. Foremen in the plants explain to the NYA youth the amount and type of training necessary for different kinds of jobs.

NYA has made use of the radio to disseminate vocational information on a large scale. In these broadcasts, the major part of the time is usually devoted to describing the ranges and requirements of the various vocations open to youth. In Wisconsin, in 1937, two radio stations provided half-hour periods daily for eight months for broadcasts to youth on work opportunities and possibilities. These were directed by Professor A. H. Edgerton of the University of Wisconsin and Dr. Jennie M. Turner of the State Department of Vocational Education. Several other Wisconsin stations broadcast NYA vocational-information programs weekly. Maine has instituted the "Vocational School of the Air." In Michigan a Detroit station co-operates with NYA in a series of job-information radio talks. Rhode Island has a new radio venture called the "Youth Radio Counselor." Every week a vocational guidance expert interviews boys and girls and gives them definite information on different occupations. At the end of each of these broadcasts the counselor takes five or six minutes to answer questions from the letters he has received.

Some States have concentrated upon the publishing of occupational studies for young people.[2] Possible job opportunities for youth in a State are explored, and research is done concerning the qualifications and training necessary or desir-

---

[2] For complete list, see Appendix VII.

able in a number of fields. These simply written studies give in detail the information that a young man or woman might like to know about various occupations. In Illinois, we visited the research project where the NYA occupational monographs are written. Nine NYA youth were assisting WPA workers in gathering, compiling, and writing these monographs. They are sent to more than 3000 schools and libraries. About 5000 briefs of each of these monographs are mimeographed for distribution to individual young people seeking vocational information.

In St. Paul, Minnesota, we went to a Youth Rally in the YMCA. Several hundred NYA young people and their friends were there. Music and other entertainment preceded a vocational talk by a representative of a local industry. He explained the types of jobs in his industry and the qualifications demanded for them.

In Kansas, every spring and fall, NYA conducts a series of career conferences in each county.

"Our purpose is twofold," Miss Anne Laughlin, State NYA Director told us. "We want to interest service clubs, schools, and individuals in local youth problems, and we want to give our young people specific vocational information."

In each county, representatives from various businesses and occupations talk with the young people. Service clubs and schools help. Whenever possible, round-table talks are arranged so that the boys and girls feel more free to ask questions and discuss problems. These conferences are open to all the young people of the various communities. In the fall of 1937, 63 career conferences were held in Kansas. They were attended by a total of 8313 young people, of whom 6016 came from NYA.

In Missouri's Occupation Development Institutes (youth centers) civic leaders give their time to discuss job opportunities with young people. In one month, 51 types of employment were explained at occupational information meetings attended by 6871 young people.

The Illinois NYA program for out-of-school youth concentrates on job-information classes. Hundreds are held every year, and all youth are welcome to attend. Last year, more than 70,000 young people heard talks and entered discussions concerning many vocations. WPA educational personnel, NYA supervisors, public school teachers, service clubs, and a large number of individuals co-operated to make these classes possible. NYA occupational briefs were distributed. Radio stations broadcast news about this vocational activity. Churches, schools, and settlement houses all joined in to promote these courses and to provide the rooms in which they were held.

The examples we have given show the diversification of the related training program. In a few States, every NYA boy and girl is taking some spare-time related training work. It may be brush-up study on typing or shorthand. It may be participation in WPA adult education classes or attendance at vocational schools. Or it may be in especially organized NYA practice or study groups, many of which are open to all the youth of the community.

"We tell our boys and girls," said the Youth Director of a State which reports a 100 per cent. participation in related training activities, "that we expect them to attend some classes or practice or discussion groups which can add to the training they receive in their project work. We try to keep our part of this agreement by making interesting, lively, meaningful courses available to them. They don't want anything that smacks of the old-fashioned schoolroom where a superior teacher ruled over inferior children. It's difficult at first to get some of them sold on the idea of related training. We've found, however, that once they start and find out that these courses are built around such realities of their lives as their work and their health, only the exceptional boy or girl fails to welcome them."

We visited several States where 60 to 70 per cent. of the NYA youth were enrolled in free-time study groups. There are no statistics as to the number of these young people throughout the country who make use of their spare time in some educational way opened to them through their NYA work. We feel that it would be safe to estimate that at least 50 per cent. of the 155,000 NYA youth on the work program in the spring of 1938 were preparing themselves for better employment possibilities through study on their own time.

CHAPTER V

Co–operating for an Education

No BERIBBONED DIPLOMAS. NO LATIN, CHAUCER, OR *Decline and Fall of the Roman Empire*. No grades. No credits.

Instead, plowing, harrowing, fertilizing land. Raising fruits, vegetables, and livestock. Running and maintaining farm machinery. Repairing and building dairy barns, feed houses, and dormitories. Making furniture. Planning and cooking meals. Studying how and why all this work is done. Earning board and keep and having a little left over for clothes or for the folks back home who need it.

What kind of school is this?

It is an NYA Resident Project for young men and women from relief families.

From the beginning of the NYA work program, rural youth have been a challenge. It is difficult to provide sound work for isolated boys and girls who have no way of getting to or from a construction job, a workshop, or a sewing room in a town 20 miles away from their farms. It is often impossible to offer related training to these young people. When boys and girls are placed as helpers in the county agricultural agent's office or with the county surveyor, or in a library, hospital, or with the highway department, supervision is good. These types of sponsors, however, can absorb only a portion of the rural youth, who, perhaps even more than boys and girls from towns and cities, desperately need work and training under competent, helpful supervision.

Southwestern Louisiana Institute, a State engineering, teachers, and agricultural college, situated at Lafayette, started a low-cost co-operative living plan whereby students could pay $1.00 a month for room and $12 or the equivalent for food —the equivalent might be meat, vegetables, or other produce which they could bring from their home farms. WPA built two $20,000 dormitories for this democratic educational development. Four hundred boys, who otherwise could not have gone to college, poured into Southwestern. They do all their own cooking, serving, cleaning, and laundry.

The agricultural department acquired a large tract of land. Developments for this department loomed large and the budget was very small. An arrangement was made with NYA for out-of-school boys to work in developing agricultural and horticultural facilities.

But the NYA boys in that district came from farms often too far away for practical transportation. The idea naturally occurred—why couldn't they have some of the educational advantages which the college teaching staff and the equipment could give them, even if they had finished only the seventh or eighth grades? Dr. J. L. Fletcher, the Dean of the Department of Agriculture, was enthusiastic about trying this experiment. In December 1936, 25 NYA out-of-school boys arrived at Southwestern, and the first co-operative NYA Resident Project was started.

We visited this college one year later. Eighty-nine young men from families on relief were living in the co-operative dormitories. They were not regular college students. The only requirement for entrance, besides relief status, was their desire to learn how to be good all-year farmers. Every boy works 50 hours a month in the horticulture department, the dairy, the swine husbandry unit, the farm shops, the automobile mechanics shop, the cabinet-making shop, in maintenance of college grounds and buildings, or in the kitchens of the co-operative. All the boys "rotate" through all these activities.

Courses of study, not the regular college courses, but especially designed for these youth, are given in subjects related to the actual work they are doing. Plans have been completed for NYA boys to build a dormitory similar to the two constructed by WPA.

At present, boys may stay in residence for six months, with the privilege of a renewal of six months provided they show that further work and study can be of benefit to them. There are no official opening or closing dates. Boys arrive throughout the year and begin their resident work and study on the day they arrive. Each boy receives $21 a month in NYA wages, and remits $13 of this to the college for maintenance.

The resident boys live in the same co-operative dormitories as the regular college students, and all the social and athletic activities of the college are open to them. A number of boys from this Resident School have found jobs as milkers on dairy farms, in commercial nurseries, and as crew cooks for oil companies.

This first co-operative resident experiment at Southwestern Louisiana proved successful; boys worked well, improved the facilities of the college, and learned eagerly.

Five hundred and thirty-five NYA boys and girls in Louisiana are now "going away to school" in nine resident projects.[1] Plans are being completed for a resident project at the Louisiana State University to be started with 50 boys. This group will build a co-operative dormitory. Fifty more boys will then come as resident students and they will build another dormitory. A final total of 200 resident NYA youth will work and study at this university in a wide range of practical fields. None will be regular college students.

We spent an evening at an NYA home economics training center in Alexandria, Louisiana, where 49 young women

[1] For list, see Appendix V.

from rural relief families spend alternate fortnights living, working, and learning in a pleasant brick house. Twenty-two girls who live in the city of Alexandria also are assigned to this project; here is an opportunity for mutual understanding between rural and urban youth.

The girls told us how different groups plan meals, market, cook, clean, launder, raise vegetables and chickens, and can foods. Every girl "rotates" through every phase of homemaking work. To earn their NYA pay-checks, they sew for the Red Cross and for public hospitals.

Girls interested in typing, shorthand, and bookkeeping may attend WPA classes, and one afternoon a week a WPA recreational leader comes for dancing, games, athletics, and the teaching of crafts. A Red Cross nurse gives regular instruction in first aid, hygiene, and home care of the sick. NYA employs one house mother, a graduate of a home economics college.

"I'm on the finance committee this week," one NYA girl said. "We make budgets and keep books, and we even help to sign the checks!"

An advisory committee of community leaders helps to plan and direct activities; one member of this committee serves as a financial adviser, and girls on the finance committee countersign checks which she writes in payment of supplies for the house.

The girls receive from $10 to $16 a month NYA pay. When the center started in November 1937, a committee of girls figured that food costs for two weeks would average $6.00 apiece. In actual practice, this has been reduced to $5.00, which each girl pays from her earnings.

We ate supper with the girls. They were proud of their simple, good food. They showed us the table linens they had made from sugar sacks and flour sacks, the curtains they had designed and sewed, the rugs they had braided from scraps.

After supper, we sat and talked. Several were learning to knit. A young man called to see one of the girls. Two asked the supervisor if they might go for a walk.

"Certainly," she said, "it's a nice evening."

"We'll be sure to be back before nine-thirty," they called, as they left.

Later, the supervisor said to us: "I think it's an advantage for our young women to come here for two weeks, then return home for two weeks, and come back again. They constantly see contrasts in diets, cleanliness, and general household management. They often tell me of applying what they have learned here at home. Their mothers and fathers are beginning to visit them, and, of course, we like that."

Arkansas has eight Resident Centers[2] with an enrollment of 445 boys and girls, most of whom are sons and daughters of tenant farmers and sharecroppers. We drove through mile after mile of rural Arkansas and saw homes such as theirs. Many had never had doors and windows; few had ever known paint. Wind, dirt, and rain sifted through open rough-board walls. These homes were shacks which the ordinary Middle-Western farmer would not tolerate as outbuildings.

The first four Arkansas Resident Centers, opened in June 1937, were planned chiefly for agricultural work. Training was given on the job. The boys and girls wanted more than this. Not all the boys wished to be farmers; some were interested in auto mechanics or forestry. The program was reorganized after the first few months and broadened in both work and educational activities. In agricultural training, more emphasis is now placed on particular fields in which boys show individual interests, such as livestock production, dairying, soil erosion, and improved farm methods. Boys are given the chance to earn and learn in woodworking, welding, auto mechanics, soil conservation, forestry, power plant operation, and business occu-

[2] For list, see Appendix V.

pations. Besides specific vocational studies, boys and girls are receiving general related instruction in English, mathematics, science, citizenship, physical education, and use of the library.

At Magnolia Agricultural and Mechanical College, one of the four Arkansas Resident Projects of which we had a glimpse, 22 NYA boys remodeled an abandoned building for a dormitory. The 22 boys who live here have their meals with the regular student body and take part in the extra-curricular activities of the college.

President Charles A. Overstreet, with whom we talked at Magnolia, said:

"You wouldn't know these boys after they've been here a month or two. In the first six weeks, most of them gain ten to twenty pounds. A lot of them never had a day's full meals before. The associations these boys get from their new environment would be worth this whole thing even if they didn't get a single other thing. But they're getting a lot more. They're learning how to make a living on a farm, which has been rare in Arkansas, as most of our farmers don't know how to make the soil produce enough for subsistence."

At Conway, Arkansas, we ate supper with a lively group of 38 boys and 30 girls who are NYA resident workers and students at the State Teachers College. It seemed incredible that these alert, clean, simply but attractively clothed youngsters came from the desolate farms that we had seen as we drove to Conway. Girls and boys eat together at tables for ten or twelve, and one girl is a hostess at each table. As part of their regular work, the girls plan, cook, and serve the meals of the whole resident group.

"Do you like it here?" I asked my table hostess.

"Yes, I do, now," she said. "At first I was kind of homesick. You know how it is when you've never been away from home at all. Not even farther than five miles. There's eight of us children at home, too. After I got acquainted, I wasn't lonesome. I was home for Christmas and I was glad to get there. And, then, I was glad to get back here."

Two of the boys at our table were playing in a basketball game that evening, and they were plainly excited.

"Have you played basketball before you came to Conway?" we asked.

"No," one answered. "We never had any place to play."

Besides cooking for the entire resident group, the girls take complete care of their own co-operative home, sew, launder, raise chickens, tend gardens, and assist the housekeepers in the regular campus dormitories. They observe and help in the WPA nursery school. In their own NYA house, they refinished all the woodwork and waxed the floors. Each week four different girls live in a small cottage in the yard of this co-operative home. Here they cook, clean, and run a model family-sized home. Each evening, they entertain four NYA boys at supper. The boys built kitchen shelves and equipment for this cottage. The State Department of Home Economics Education furnishes two full-time supervisors for this girls' resident project planned for family-life education.

NYA boys at Conway work in the city power plant, in the college heat plant, in the State Forestry Station, and in carpentry, cabinet-making, sheet metal, and auto mechanics shops. Some are also getting work experience in landscaping, farm- and soil-mapping, and soil-erosion control. Dairying, poultry-raising, and livestock-raising are the principal agricultural pursuits. Besides related training instruction in all these fields of work, they have specially planned English, mathematics, and citizenship classes.

On a rolling hilltop in Russellville, Arkansas, 31 NYA boys, resident students at Polytechnic College, are working on a complete campus for out-of-school, unemployed Arkansas youth. We saw some of these young men building dormitories and a supervisor's house. The plans call for four dormitories to house 96 youth, a recreation hall, a dining hall, athletic grounds, and, adjacent to this campus, a poultry house, barn, and machinery repair shop. The boys may also choose work and related training in auto mechanics, power plant operation, or diversified agriculture.

In these four Arkansas Resident Centers that we visited, boys and girls do NYA work 100 hours a month to earn $25 each, of which they pay $18 for board and room and 50 cents into a co-operative medical fund.

Georgia has eight Resident Centers,[3] where 517 NYA boys and girls divide their time equally between productive work and study. For their half-time work, they each earn $27.20 a month, $17.20 of which covers the cost of their board and room. We were told that many of them send home the bigger part of their remaining $10.

Five Georgia resident projects are for white youth, and three for Negro. All but one are co-educational. Girls usually sew for public agencies to earn their wages, and in addition receive well-rounded practice and training in home economics, gardening and canning, handicrafts, and child care. Rural Georgia boys who come to these resident projects seldom know how to raise anything but cotton. Their work and their training are planned to give them knowledge and understanding of diversified farming—poultry-, swine-, and cattle-raising, dairying, gardening, and soil conservation. They have a chance to learn farm mechanics, the care and repair of farm machinery; they acquire some of the fundamentals of construction so that, when they go home, they will know how to repair and how to build new farm sheds, barns, and houses.

At Fort Valley, in middle Georgia, 81 Negro boys and girls who have gone to school only four to five years are living for six months at the Fort Valley Normal and Industrial School. The 56 resident boys are completing the only Negro

[3] For list, see Appendix V.

recreational camp in the State. Largely through the generosity of Mr. A. T. Wilson, a Negro faculty member of this school, a 150-acre tract of land was obtained, and NYA boys cleared and landscaped this property. They have completed 25 cabins to house 250 campers, a large assembly and dining hall, an athletic field, and a 500-foot earth dam with two concrete spillways, which will make an 18-acre lake. The camp is available to all Negro youth groups in Georgia. Negro organizations such as the YMCA, the YWCA, and the Urban League have formed a permanent board to administer it.

As the boys build the camp, they receive from the school's . regular staff related instruction not only in the actual work they are doing but also in practical farming, health and hygiene, and elementary subjects such as reading and writing.

In the foothills of western Georgia, 48 NYA boys and girls are resident students at West Georgia College, a junior college of the State university system. Upon entering, all these youth, most of whom had no more than elementary schooling, took intelligence tests ordinarily given to the regular student body. One NYA boy had an intelligence quotient two points higher than any ever recorded in this institution.

Southern States have led in the development of the NYA Resident Program. Rural relief youth in many parts of the South have been denied even what is usually considered a minimum American education. Many of them know only one-crop farming. If the soil is to provide them a living, they must learn new, better, and diversified farming methods. Their parents have seldom known how to raise chickens, cows, or pigs. Surprisingly few Southern tenant farmers, sharecroppers, or small individual farmers know how to raise vegetables and fruit. The NYA Resident Center can open many new agricultural possibilities to Southern youth. Of course, there is no reason why every rural boy should want to be a farmer. There is a trend in the Resident Program toward giving boys not interested in farming a chance to acquire training in other fields, such as auto mechanics, conservation, or shop work.

A group of NYA resident boys from sharecropper and tenant farmer families was asked:

"How many of you want to be farmers?"

Not more than two or three hands were raised. This same group was then asked:

"If it were possible for you to buy land and simple buildings, and pay for them over a period of time at a reasonable rate of interest, how many of you would like to farm?"

The majority quickly raised their hands.

When resident projects were first established in the cotton belt, some resistance from plantation owners was expected. This has not materialized, according to the reports of NYA officials in the Southern areas. Undoubtedly the Resident Centers are introducing to these young people a new standard of living and ways of life likely to make them discontented with their former lot. But apparently many landlords believe that this training will make more valuable tenants of the youth. Some, we are informed, have expressed sympathetic interest in the possibility that the more energetic and ambitious youngsters in the families of their tenants may have opportunities in other fields opened up to them through their training in Resident Centers.

Another reason why the South leads in the resident program may be that many of its educational institutions seem to have less reluctance than has been shown in some other sections of the country to open their doors to relief youth, sometimes illiterate, usually badly dressed, often completely inexperienced in the ordinary social amenities, but in need of earning their living as they learn spelling, writing, arithmetic, farming, trades, or homemaking.

NYA Resident Centers, however, are by no means confined to Southern States. Idaho has developed five centers[4] for rural youth, who often live in isolated mountain or farm districts.

Intermountain Institute in the fertile Snake River Valley in Idaho was originally planned with just such a philosophy as underlies the agricultural NYA Resident Project—to give farm youth who cannot take advantage of regular agricultural colleges an opportunity to earn their way as they learn practical methods of scientific farming. Because of a lack of funds, Intermountain Institute was forced to disband its school in 1933, although the land was still worked and the fine herds were maintained. A campus with dormitories, vocational farm buildings, a gymnasium, and a library was idle.

In January 1938, an arrangement was completed whereby School District Number 1 of Idaho took title to Intermountain Institute, and turned over to NYA all the campus buildings, furniture, and equipment, all barns, livestock, and poultry, and 700 acres of good farming and grazing land. First NYA resident girls moved in and made curtains, bed linens, and other household supplies for a large resident group. The girls also cook, clean, launder, raise chickens, garden, and have training classes in practical academic subjects, health and hygiene, and child care.

In the latter part of April 1938, the first groups of NYA resident boys arrived. One hundred and seventy-five are to work and study here. They are raising wheat, alfalfa hay, oats, rye, corn, sugar beets, potatoes, and garden vegetables. NYA inherited a champion Holstein herd, 1500 white Leghorn chickens, and 50 Duroc red hogs. The farm equipment includes all types of machinery from a wheat combine to hoes and rakes.

Besides farm work and study, these boys maintain and repair buildings, make roads where needed, maintain and repair the

---

[4] For list, see Appendix V.

watershed of the Weiser River, from which water for this land and other farms is obtained, and work in trade shops necessary for so large a farm plant. The State Department for Vocational Education has furnished two home economics teachers for the girls, and three agricultural teacher-supervisors for the boys. The University of Idaho is interested in providing "agricultural internes," graduate students in the College of Agriculture, to assist in the supervision of practical work and classroom instruction.

The income from crops sold goes for taxes, insurance, equipment, general upkeep, and improvement of the property. Each NYA boy and girl at this Resident Center receives $25 a month pay. All live co-operatively, with committees to budget living costs, purchase foodstuffs not raised on the farm, keep books, and charge resident students according to their individual shares of the total living expenses.

Wisconsin calls its ten[5] NYA resident projects Co-operative Training Centers. The name is singularly appropriate because the 302 rural boys enrolled in these centers each pool $20 a month of their $24.85 NYA salary into a common fund from which they pay all living expenses. Boys elect their own committees to make budgets, purchase food and household supplies, in some cases rent living quarters, keep books, and pay bills. At the end of the six or seven months' training period, the co-operatives declare dividends from surplus funds. For example, at the Co-operative Training Center at the Marinette Vocational School, 27 NYA boys rent a house for $45 a month, pay for gas, light, heat, water, and food. They do their own cooking, cleaning, personal laundry, and general household maintenance. Their February 1938 per capita living cost was $16.73, leaving a co-operative dividend of $3.27 for that month. Each Wisconsin Co-operative Center has its own self-government organization and makes its own disciplinary

---

[5] For list, see Appendix V.

rules. Once a month the elected presidents of the ten co-operatives meet in Madison to discuss common problems and to act as a youth advisory board to the State NYA.

Most of the Wisconsin centers are established at State vocational schools, and, consequently, a wide variety of both work and training can be offered the resident youth. In Racine, 30 boys are building an airplane hangar and constructing school furniture; they attend some of the regular classes in the vocational school as well as separate courses designed to fit their specific needs and educational backgrounds. At Green Bay, another NYA group is developing a 120-acre wild life sanctuary. According to individual interests and aptitudes, they have choices of practical work and study in auto mechanics, woodworking, electricity, sheet metal, a machine shop, and commercial subjects. At some centers, boys are building NYA dormitories either from salvaged lumber or from materials contributed by sponsors. Boys who wish to concentrate on farming may work and study in many different agricultural fields, from plant and animal husbandry to farm mechanics and co-operative marketing. Although the Wisconsin resident boys usually live apart from the regular student body of the school, they may take part in all social and athletic activities of the sponsoring institutions.

Each year at the University of Wisconsin, about 100 NYA boys from rural relief families attend the Agricultural Short Course. They live in barracks provided by the university and work 55 hours a month each, assisting on the university farm or in the library, or making and repairing furniture for the university.

Because of Wisconsin's outstanding vocational education system, Co-operative Training Centers have been comparatively easy to establish. Vocational schools offer well-equipped shops, excellent teaching, and deep interest in the problems of economically underprivileged youth who wish more education and training but who have found the doors of academic schools closed to them. NYA provides them work with which they can earn their livings and the opportunity to continue their education and to discover and develop useful occupational skills.

UNHARNESSING YOUTH AT QUODDY

When funds for the completion of the Passamaquoddy Tidal Power Plant were cut off, the model village of Quoddy, built to house the engineering staff, was left vacant. These housing facilities were transferred to the National Youth Administration, and a committee composed of Colonel Henry M. Waitc, Cincinnati engineer and municipal expert, Mr. Walter A. Grannen, official of the International Typographical Union, Mr. Ralph Glanders, a Vermont manufacturer, and Dr. Floyd W. Reeves, the chairman of the President's Committee on Vocational Education, worked out a program to utilize the facilities of this village for the benefit of relief youth.

In June 1937, 225 boys from the five New England States and New York arrived to begin a five-month work experience and training course. Each boy had been selected in his home community by a committee consisting of representatives of industry, labor, and education. *184996*

The Quoddy NYA project is sometimes called a vocational finding school. The aim is not to turn out skilled workers but to give boys a chance through actual work experience and related training to make an intelligent choice of the occupations for which they show interest and potential ability. Each boy is allowed to choose three different occupations in which he wishes work experience, and he divides his five months' time equally among the three. The work of maintaining the village properties offers this wide range of work opportunity:

Auto Mechanics   Photography
Blue Printing   Photolithographing
Cafeteria   Pipe Fitting
Commercial   Plumbing
Commercial Art   Recreation
Electricians   Road Construction and
Grounds Maintenance   Maintenance
Lineman   Sheet Metal
Machine Shop   Steam Boiler Operating
Mechanical Drawing   Steam Fitting
Medical   Welding
Painting   Woodwork

Every boy spends half of each day from Monday to Friday in the shop or on the job, and spends the remaining half-day in classrooms where he studies subjects related to the work he is doing. For example, a boy has been working on the removal of a wooden platform and the installation of a concrete floor in a shower room. In the classroom, he studies the tools, equipment, and materials he is using, slope measurements, measurements of volumes of concrete, methods of mixing and pouring, the operation of a mixer, and the spelling and definition of terms used in the work.

Forty per cent. of the boys attending the first Quoddy session, ending in October 1937, found jobs in private industry. This remarkable showing in a period of shrinking employment opportunities must be attributed partly to the special efforts to place these boys made by the local committees who selected them.

Quoddy boys have a well-organized recreational program. They elect their own village mayor and councilors, and edit and publish a newspaper. They receive subsistence, some clothing, and wages of $20 a month. This rate of pay at Quoddy is a special administrative exemption and is far higher than at other NYA Resident Centers. This letter, which a New York

State boy at Quoddy sent to his mother, gives a graphic picture of life at Quoddy:

> Apartment 4, Kittery Apts.,
> Quoddy Village,
> Eastport, Me.,
> January 16, 1938.

Dear Mother:

It seems we are using the apartment houses instead of the dorm. And are they nice! Three rooms and bath. The third room was kitchen and dining-room, divided by little china closets or book-cases. We use the living-room for a bedroom, of course. It holds three cots, the bedroom two. Frank and I are together in the bed-room, the other three have the larger room. They keep the boys from the same towns together, and as far as possible, by State also. There are fifteen from New York, the rest are from New England. So besides us three from ——, we have a boy from Syracuse and one from Long Island.

Mr. Wilson put me in charge when we left, and in Albany, the state director put me in charge of the whole N. Y. crew! I carried the tickets, rounded them up when we had to leave, and did the talking for the bunch. Some guy, this little boy of yours!

Yesterday, we had intelligence tests. My rating was 115. Straight dope from one of the counsellors. No more of this running down my mentality! Incidentally, part of it was on mechanical ability. For some reason I was high there, too.

As this is the wrong season for landscaping or tree surgery, (the ground is harder than concrete and covered with ice that you couldn't cut with anything short of a blow-torch,) I am starting off with carpentry. It's going to be very interesting. The boys are building a new gym. A big building covered with iron sheathing. Think of the work to be done inside, the floor and all. It seems you can't learn just one particular trade here. The government can't run a trade school. It's a place for vocational guidance. You try a number of things, learn them all well enough to get a job, of course, and then you can take the one you like best and specialize in it (outside). I am also taking reproduction on account of the draw-ing and blue prints. Later when the season opens, I can swing into the landscaping. There's plenty of room for it here. They made swell buildings but didn't do much to the ground. They have a fine library with plenty of reference books on all the work they have here. There are certain hours when we have to go over to the library and study up. I should pick up quite a lot of stuff. It won't hurt me to be a carpenter or any of those things. Might keep me from starving some day.

Some of the boys who were here last period were asked to come back as Junior Leaders to help the rest of us. They're a nice bunch of fellows.

In Albany, we were served coffee and sandwiches right in the station by girls from the NYA office there. Then a photographer took pictures. I'll try to arrange to have the paper sent you. I saw "Artist and Models" night before last at the free movie we have here. Not bad. There was a dance in Eastport but none of my gang went.

Eastport likes us. People speak to us on the street and everyone is nice to us. After all, this is different. They know what the NYA is. They have some. It would take only one bad move from the boys to change that, though, I guess. Not much danger of that, however.

Eastport has its laws and Quoddy has its rules and they match nicely. The town closes at twelve and we have to be back at one. How's that for a fit? The guys don't seem anxious to pull anything, though. On the whole, I like the place, and the fellows are O. K. The counselors are very nice, all of them. We even have some women counselors, single and fairly young.

I was issued a mackinaw of sorts here, warmer than my own. The inside is blanketing and the outside a heavy khaki denim. Looks well enough, and the Maine climate can't touch it. It is quite a bit below zero now, but the cold doesn't affect anything but exposed parts, ears and nose mostly. Not even my hands, much, and I dash around all over without gloves. There is almost no snow. Haven't gone skating yet, but I will. There is a regular rink here and we have hockey games. That's not for me, I'm gonna be a figure skater!

Hopeing yu ar wel i remane yur loveing sun,

———

In May 1938, more than 100 NYA Resident Centers had been established in 22 States. Forty-five hundred young people from poverty-stricken rural homes were earning enough money to cover their living expenses and to have small cash balances left. By raising as much as possible of their own food and by doing all their own work, these young people were able to cut living costs to as low as $12 to $20 a month each.

The resident programs as we have described them in Louisiana, Arkansas, Georgia, Idaho, and Wisconsin by no means cover the entire scope of this new NYA activity. Oklahoma has 514 girls and boys working, earning, and learning in eight Resident Centers. In South Carolina 230 girls from isolated rural areas live in co-operative camps, where, under competent supervision, they combine practical work and study in home economics, crafts, beauty culture, and office work. One hundred and twenty South Carolina boys attend four agricultural Resident Centers.

In Ohio, 144 boys remodeled an abandoned CCC camp at New Philadelphia, where they are developing Schoenbrunn State Park under the Muskingum Conservancy District. They are building a slag-surfaced road a mile and a half long, quarrying rock, building bridges, creating picnic areas with stone fireplaces, shelters, benches and tables, and sanitary facilities. Trails, stone-steps, and look-outs are under construction. One group operates a saw mill. Another has planted a 10-acre tree nursery. In the spring of 1938 they set out 500,000 seedlings. The trucks and cars used in the project are maintained and repaired by boys interested in auto mechanics. All the boys in this camp attend small group classes in first aid, hygiene, and citizenship. An educational adviser arranges special classes in surveying, electricity, mechanical drawing, auto mechanics, and other related studies for youth working in various fields.

Two hundred and nine Texas boys and girls are NYA resident students at three State colleges and at the Luling Foundation Farm, a 1200-acre experimental agricultural development. At the Prairie View State Normal and Industrial

College in Waller County, Texas, 93 Negro boys and girls are receiving intensive training for domestic service. The boys are building an NYA home economics practice house, and their related training consists of practical work and instruction in the care and repair of household woodwork, auto mechanics, dry cleaning, landscaping, butler service, and machine shop practice. The girls at Prairie View assist in the preparation and serving of meals in the regular college dining room, work in the dormitories, and assist in the school laundry. Home economics instructors conduct laboratory courses in household service, cooking, care of children, household arithmetic, and household management. All the first 18 Negro girls who completed a four-month domestic work and training course at Prairie View found full-time private employment. Efforts to place these same girls prior to their resident training had been unsuccessful.

In New York State, several new Resident Centers for the training of girls for domestic service are being organized. There are two new Resident Centers in Kansas, one a homemaking unit at Kingman, and the other at Fort Hays State Teachers College, where 76 boys and girls are working and learning the fundamentals of agriculture, shop work, construction, clerical occupations, and home economics. In Mississippi, 90 white boys and 130 Negro boys and girls are resident students in five State schools. The University of New Hampshire has a new NYA Resident Center workshop. Twenty boys in Iowa are remodeling buildings at Tabor College, which recently reopened after a suspension of nine years. Alabama, California, Minnesota, Nebraska, New Mexico, North Dakota, Pennsylvania, South Dakota, Tennessee, Utah, Virginia, Washington, and West Virginia all have NYA resident units.

Fifty more Resident Centers are opening during the summer of 1938. At present, most of these centers are units of State educational institutions where youth may take advantage of already existing equipment and teaching facilities and, by their labor, expand the institutions' physical plants and facilities. Many State directors report that they are working on plans for additional Resident Centers to open in the fall of 1938 when the regular school year begins.

Resident Centers are complicated and difficult to organize. Sponsors must contribute the larger portion of the materials with which youth are to work, as well as a good share of the instruction. NYA usually employs supervisors to establish personal relationships with the resident youth and to coordinate their work and study. Some parents have been reluctant to permit their children to go away from home for six or eight months, even though the latter will probably make several visits back home during the training period. These parents, in the lowest-income group, have not had the tradition of financially more fortunate families of sending their sons and daughters away to school. More important to them is the fact that, when a relief youth goes away from home to a Resident Center, the family does not receive as large a share of his NYA earnings as it would if he were employed on a project in his home community. After paying for subsistence, the youth at a Resident Center usually has only $5.00 to $8.00 left each month. If he were working on an NYA project and living at home, his gross income would be about $15, and most of this would be turned over to his family. If he were at a CCC camp he would receive, in addition to transportation, clothing, and subsistence, a cash payment of at least $30 a month, of which $20 or $25 would be sent home to his family. Wisconsin has solved this problem: the State relief administration increases family allowances when youths go to Resident Centers. In Georgia, an average of $10 a month above subsistence costs has been allowed to resident youth so that the family does not feel deprived of his earnings. Perhaps the earnings of NYA resident youth may be increased so that they may send a little more money back home.

The Resident Program is in a fluid state. Generally the centers are not meant for boys and girls with college abilities or college ambitions. The Student Aid Program should answer their needs. Resident Centers are intended for boys and girls who have managed to finish only the sixth or seventh or eighth grade—or possibly a year or two of high school—and who have had few opportunities to learn better ways of farming or homemaking or to get a basis of experience and knowledge in a trade. Often these youth also need to catch up in such elementary studies as reading, spelling, and arithmetic. Unless a Resident Center is established in connection with a vocational school, it is desirable that special courses of study should be organized for NYA youth. Their interests, their capabilities, and their needs are not fulfilled by regular academic classes. This often means added work for the school teaching staff. In some cases, regular college students assist in the instruction of NYA resident students. The States that have expanded vocational education through Smith-Hughes and George-Deen teachers furnish much helpful instruction and supervision for NYA centers. WPA adult education teachers, Red Cross personnel, and State health service workers often contribute their time to teach resident students.

At some Resident Centers a three-month training period has been tried. This has proved too short. Six months seems to be the minimum period in which youth can adjust themselves to new ways of living and get sufficient work experience and training to be of benefit to them.

In many States, a sound health program for NYA workers on local projects, especially in rural areas, has proved difficult. Administrative funds cannot cover the costs of general medical examinations. Clinical facilities for treatment are totally inadequate in many localities. Boys and girls from relief families can seldom afford the services of private doctors and dentists. At a Resident Center, the health of young people receives careful attention. When a center is established at a school, the regular medical facilities of the school are available to the NYA youth. When centers are set up independently, a health program is considered a necessary component.

In every Resident Center that we have visited, the supervisors and often the youth themselves have emphasized the important values which youth get from their new environment.

"The changes in these young people's appearance in even a short time are amazing. They begin to be proud of clean fingernails, well-brushed hair, and good personal hygiene habits," one NYA supervisor said.

"We notice that our young people change their diet habits," another supervisor told us. "I know several farm boys and girls who never drank milk before they came here. That's not as strange as it might seem, though, because most of their families can't afford to buy cows and few of them know how to care for cattle. Not many of the young people here were accustomed to eating green vegetables."

At another center, a supervisor commented: "Our resident students are very much interested in their health classes and discussions. They haven't been aware of the value of good home sanitation in the prevention of disease or the need to isolate members of the family with communicable diseases. Many of them have never heard of diphtheria inoculations."

The social values of co-operative living are impossible to measure. Most resident NYA youth elect their own self-government councils. Each youth has responsibilities and duties to the entire group. The individual must adjust himself to the integrated work and social life of the Resident Center. All these experiences seem to offer a practical training in intelligent citizenship.

The NYA Resident Program is still too young for a full objective evaluation. It may be the beginning of an important new educational contribution to underprivileged American youth. It makes room for the boy or girl who is too old to go back to a regular school, who is often distrustful of a regular school or for whom the regular school may be unsuited, who cannot pay for trade school training (even if there were a trade school near his home), and who must earn full subsistence while preparing to make a living.

At the NYA Resident Centers which we visited there was a quiet intellectual excitement that was contagious. We had a sense of being in a research laboratory in which an experiment was developing that might throw new light on a major human problem and point new ways for its solution.

CHAPTER VI

Finding the First Job

CONNECTING THE BOY OR GIRL WITH THE JOB IS ONE OF THE
objectives of the NYA work program. Because of their lack
both of education and of work experience, young people from
relief families have even greater difficulties than other groups
of youth in finding work. Many doors are naturally closed to
the average NYA youth who can say no more to prospective
employers than that he has gone only to grade school and that
he has never held a steady job.

It is unfortunate for any young person to be out of school
and jobless; it is in many ways most critical for relief youth
because they have the least resources for the use of enforced
idle time. The girl who traditionally "helps out at home" is
less a problem than the boy who has no place to go, no money
to spend for any kind of training, few chances for simple
recreation.

We found that NYA supervisors all over the country consider it an integral part of their work to make contacts with
potential employers of youth labor, telling them about the
actual work NYA young people are doing on projects and
about the training many of them are receiving on their own
free time as well as on the job, asking that NYA youth capable
of filling beginners' jobs be given their chance even though
their records of schooling and experience may fall below pre-
conceived employment standards.

In a number of States supervisors keep progress records of
NYA workers so that the youth themselves may have a con-

crete picture of their own work and so that possible employers of youth may have a work record on which to base their selection of new employees.

In two and one-half years the NYA work program has not become widely known. Many people with whom we talked in cities either had never heard of NYA or had only some vague idea about student aid. We found employers in small communities more conversant with NYA work and consequently more willing to accept it as job experience. In some communities, NYA supervisors had thoroughly canvassed every employment opportunity for young people and constantly reminded employers of this supply of boys and girls who were receiving work experience and on-the-job training as well as additional instruction on their own time. The administrative personnel of NYA is limited. We met supervisors everywhere who not only oversee work projects, but in addition conduct free-time training classes and try to open up any possible job opportunities they can discover for relief youth.

We talked with one boy who had never held any sort of job before NYA work.

"I feel pretty sure now that I can hold a job if I get a chance," he said. "That's the most this work means to me, except, of course, the money I earn. It's easier to keep on looking for a job once you've had one."

There are undoubtedly a great number of youth who, because they have worked only a little if at all, have lost all confidence in their ability to work. We felt that many of these boys in their part-time NYA jobs gained assurance that, granted the opportunity, they could fill jobs. Many young people have become discouraged by the constant turn-downs they have met when searching for jobs. One NYA boy reported that he had made the rounds of 20 different factories in one week looking for a job. In seven instances, he was peremptorily told to get out before he had a chance to ask for work. At several other factory employment windows, he was greeted by placards saying: "No workers needed." In only a few instances did he have the chance of even talking to anyone about a job. Perhaps it is economically a waste of time for employers or their representatives to talk with job-seekers when there are no jobs; it is not difficult, however, to imagine the discouragement and frustration which youth feel when it is hard even to get the chance to ask for a job.

"Yes, some of the young people are sullen and have chips on their shoulders," an NYA foreman told us. "And lots of them change. I think that's because even with the part-time work they have on NYA they feel that there is some place in this world where their work really can be used."

One State director stated his policy on "youth and jobs" by saying:

"We can't and we don't tell NYA youth that if they only work hard and have good intentions they'll be sure to find jobs. That simply isn't true today. What we do tell them is that we believe the more skilled they are the better their chances will be to get jobs. If a girl, for example, can type only 30 words a minute, we tell her that 50 is necessary before she can compete with many others who are looking for the same kind of work she wants."

There are relief youth who, like other youth, have unrealistic approaches to employment—girls and boys, for example, who cannot spell, whose vocabularies are limited, yet who have as their immediate objective finding jobs as private secretaries, newspaper reporters, or movie scenario writers. By giving them a chance to get more accurate vocational information, NYA sometimes helps these youth to pin their hopes on less romantic and possibly more attainable work goals.

We heard in almost all parts of the country of a growing belief on the part of young people that jobs can be obtained only through pull. "You've got to know someone to get a job," is the common statement. There is no question that this feeling has some justification. Employers are besieged by relatives and friends with requests to give their sons and daughters work. Relief youth have few avenues of personal approach to sources of employment. NYA administrators help in making contacts which relief youth cannot make for themselves.

In NYA there is undoubtedly a residue of the least employable youth. Sometimes they are the physically handicapped. We noted in several States that NYA administrators definitely tried to provide project work aimed to give this group experience and training in specialized fields in which they might become economically self-sufficient. In Milwaukee, the highest amount of placement in clerical positions has been from a group of physically handicapped boys and girls. In this instance, special efforts were made by NYA supervisors to reach possible employers and to ask them not to turn down a qualified youth merely because he walked on crutches, provided that handicap would not interfere with performance of his job.

Then there is the boy or girl who gets a reputation in his community for shiftlessness or dishonesty. We heard of a number of instances in which youth in this category have done good NYA work. The supervisor has tried to help them to rehabilitate themselves in their communities. One of these "success stories" is about a boy who was certified for relief in a small Middle-Western town. The NYA supervisors assigned him to work at a school ground improvement project. The superintendent of the school objected, saying that he knew the boy, wouldn't trust him, didn't want him around. The supervisor asked that the boy be given a trial, pointing out that the youth was a member of the community, would continue to be, and that he needed this work. The boy got along without any trouble. After six months, the school superintendent recommended him for a job in a local grocery store. He has been working there more than a year now and his employer is pleased with him.

Employment in domestic service is one field that could be greatly developed. Many girls do not want to face a life of living in someone else's house, of working long, dreary, lonely hours every day. If the woman who complains that modern girls are spoiled because they will not become maids would ask herself honestly whether she would prefer to work eight hours a day in a factory or twelve or fifteen hours in a kitchen, over laundry tubs and scrubbing pails, she might understand the usual reaction. Youth cannot be censured for lack of ambition in one breath and in the next condemned for not wanting work that is dead-end.

According to the American tradition, which is still strongly felt, a maid is either a Negro or a foreigner. "A good German girl," "a strong Swedish girl," "an Irish cook," are almost all one hears in American speech describing household help. When immigrants streamed through Ellis Island, the kitchen was often their introduction to American life. There the new language and the customs of the new country could be learned. But the feeling behind this job often was "I'll work here until I can save enough to help to buy a farm"—or start a store or get some other foothold. "My children will be Americans and they will not do what I am doing." These children and their children have inherited this feeling. Can they be asked to change it? There is no getting around the fact that domestic service in the United States carries with it, whether it should or not, a social stigma which the present generation of American girls would like to avoid.

We were in several communities where, we were told, the average wage for a house-maid was as low as $1.75 or $2.00 a week. In many, $5.00 was considered an excellent wage for a servant. To most girls the lack of freedom seems to be an even greater objection to housework than the low wages in many sections of the country. The girl who works in the factory, the store, or the office can see "boy friends" in the evening when she pleases. She may actually have less cash left at the end of the week than the girl who is doing housework, but most girls seem to think that even extra cash cannot compensate for limited opportunity to meet boys, to have friends, to be able to go somewhere with them, or at least have some place in which to see them besides a kitchen corner.

Housework requires many skills, or at least semi-skills. Girls from relief families sometimes express lack of confidence in their ability to do housework. Cooking, sewing, cleaning, caring for children, laundry, innumerable varied tasks, go into the occupation of domestic service. Among the girls who will accept housework, many do not have the training for a successful pursuit of it. NYA homemaking centers can give girls who are interested in domestic service work experience which they can make use of in this field of employment. Until standards of working conditions and general social attitudes in domestic service change, however, there will be no rush of young women into household work.

NYA work projects cannot create jobs in private industry. During the 1937–38 recession, the number of young people leaving NYA for private employment declined sharply, and in most States the quotas of youth certified for relief and waiting for NYA assignments far exceeded available allotments of NYA funds. NYA work experience and training can help to give youth the background for beginners' jobs and can give depression-stymied youth confidence in their ability to hold jobs; and NYA supervisors can serve as a link between youth and employers; but the economic system must itself make room for these youth, most of whom show that they want work, before jobs and youth will balance.

Junior Guidance and Placement

In the spring of 1936, NYA, co-operating with State employment services, started to establish guidance and placement bureaus to focus attention upon the problems of young, inexperienced job-seekers. In two years, 78 Junior Divisions have been set up in connection with regular public employment offices in 32 States.[1] The services of these Junior Divisions are available to all youth, regardless of their relief status.

Two questions naturally present themselves concerning Junior Employment Divisions. First, why should they be separate units in State employment services? Second, why should they come under NYA?

The adult experienced worker looking for a job usually has definite ideas about what he can do and in what fields he has the best chances for employment. He can easily be classified under such occupational headings as "clerical," "sales," "carpenter," etc. The young person with scant work experience, often without occupational training of any sort, presents a different problem. Because he usually has vague or erroneous conceptions of the requirements of most jobs, and because he is often shy and uncertain of himself and his abilities, he needs the specialized service of an employment office.

"In a large public employment office where applicants are classified according to occupations," Dr. Mary H. S. Hayes, NYA Director of Junior Guidance and Placement, explained, "the youth worker is necessarily likely to get lost in the shuffle. He usually must find a job because of his potentialities rather than his past employment record. For that reason, the employment interviewer needs to have as much information as pos-

---

[1] For complete list, see Appendix VI.

sible about him, his school interests, his hobbies, his ambitions, and any number of factors which may be utilized in intelligent placement of beginners in the work world. In Junior Placement offices, we have what we call multiple classification, by which youths are classified in as many fields of work as possible in view of their potential abilities and their general employment characteristics."

Because NYA, through its student aid and its out-of-school work program, can reach large numbers of youth and grasp their special problems, it was given the first task of organizing and establishing Junior Placement Divisions. Eventually, if they prove their value, they are to be taken over by the State employment services as regular parts of their organizations. By April 1, 1938, this transfer had been made in nine States (California, Connecticut, Indiana, Kentucky, Massachusetts, New Hampshire, North Carolina, Texas, and Wisconsin), and definite dates for effecting it had been made by three others (Minnesota, Iowa, and West Virginia). Some of these States are expanding this type of service. No Junior Placement Division is opened unless the State NYA Director and the State Employment Director jointly request it. NYA's role is that of establishing these Junior Divisions, demonstrating their specialized functions, and then turning them over completely to the State employment services.

Just what happens typically to a young man or woman in a Junior Placement office?

First, he goes to the receptionist. If he is under the age of 21, he is automatically directed to the Junior Division for an interview with a junior employment counselor. Should this youth show that he is occupationally mature (that is, that he has held regular jobs in skilled trades or in office work), he is referred to the proper adult division for registration. In turn, when the adult employment division interviews a young person between 21 and 25 who has little or no employment history, he is turned over to the Junior Division for its individualized attention.

The young person in the Junior Division is interviewed privately and conversationally. He provides as much employment history as he can, even of a job lasting for a day or a week, explains his own interests, and states his own work ambitions. Often, he wants vocational guidance, needs information about the job resources in his own community. In what kind of work will he be most likely to find a place? How can he most advantageously prepare himself to enter some particular field? Given a chance for a certain type of job, what can he expect to earn? These are the kinds of problems which young people bring to employment counselors.

The counselor gets as full a picture of the youth as he can, acquaints him with any immediate job prospects, and invites him to return at any time for additional conferences.

From the information the youth provides, his job possibilities are enumerated, and his name is filed in multiple occupational classifications. The Junior Division also keeps what is called a "type file." Many employers of youth labor make their requests in some such manner as this: "I want a boy with a bicycle," or "I need a boy who can wear a size 36 uniform," or "I can use a big, husky boy," or "Please send me a boy who lives in the northeast section of the city." Only by keeping a record of these types of youth can the Junior Division serve most efficiently both the employer and the job-seeker.

Junior Placement Divisions constantly make contacts with employers to build up and maintain orders for youth workers.

"We definitely seek to guard against giving employers the impression that we want them to take younger workers into their organizations by discharging older workers," Dr. Hayes has stated, "but we do feel that there are certain jobs which should be reserved for younger workers."

Only large industries maintain their own employment offices

with trained personnel for the selection of employees. In general, the selection of youth for jobs is a hit-and-miss affair. Every failure in a job is an economic loss to the employer. A failure usually has a disintegrating effect on the youth. By knowing what each job entails and by making a careful scrutiny of the individual, the Junior Placement Division renders efficient service both to employer and to employee.

From March 1936 to April 1938 Junior Divisions interviewed 259,060 young people. Of these, they placed 103,881 in private industry. Contacts were made with 59,687 employers.

NYA spent a total of $335,272 for Junior Placement up to April 1, 1938. The cost of each placement was $3.23.[2]

These were the kinds of work which the 103,881 young men and women found through Junior Placement offices:

About 10 per cent. were placed as errand boys. These were usually youth between 16 and 18 years old, and the wages they received were not high.

Approximately 14 per cent. more found work classified as "labor," which includes bean-picking, spinach-cutting, beet-topping, cotton-picking, and also such jobs as those of truck-helpers and general handymen in factories and mills.

Eleven per cent. went on the pay-rolls of factories as bench-assemblers, joggers in binderies, packers and wrappers on the belt line, machine-feeders, floor girls, etc.

Twenty-two per cent. went into mercantile employment. This includes jobs such as those of salespeople in department and 5-and-10-cent stores, demonstrators, clerks in grocery stores, stock and shipping clerks, and ushers and usherettes in theaters.

Only about 4 per cent. came under the head of skilled trades. These were largely beginners' jobs.

Clerical work accounted for 14 per cent. This takes in typ-

---

[2] This is the NYA personnel cost for making the 103,881 placements, as rent, light, and heat are provided by State employment services.

ing, stenography, cashiering in stores and restaurants, business machine operation, and general office clerking.

Twenty-three per cent. were placed as household or restaurant workers. Many of these were waitresses in tea rooms, curb girls, soda jerkers, and bus boys.

Two per cent. came under the heading of professional work, and these were nearly all in semi-professional occupations such as window-trimming, beginner-accounting, and entertaining.

A study of wages received by youth workers placed by Junior Divisions in 66 cities[3] shows great variance in different parts of the country. In Little Rock, Arkansas, the median wage for white youth was $8.29 a week, while in Reno, Nevada, the median proved to be $18.29. In Negro offices in Charlotte and Durham, North Carolina, the median weekly wages were $8.03 and $8.75, respectively; Chicago stood only slightly higher at $9.49; the District of Columbia Negro Junior Division reported $12.01 as its median wage.

The Junior Division is responsible for investigating many employment offers made for youth so that violation of labor laws may be eliminated and so that youth will not be placed in jobs in which there are moral or physical hazards.

Since the services of the Junior Placement offices are available to all youth, the registration lists show a higher average of education and work experience than would be shown by relief youth alone. An analysis of 193,715 youth who applied and of 89,203 who were placed in jobs in private industry between July 1, 1936, and January 1, 1938, revealed these characteristics:

	New Applicants[4]		Placements[5]	
Under 18 years old	50,399	26%	21,957	25%
Between 18 and 21 years old	120,513	62%	53,735	60%
Between 21 and 25 years old	22,803	12%	13,453	15%

[3] For complete lists, see Appendix VIII.
[4] Complete figures not available for last four items.
[5] Complete figures not available for these items.

Eighth grade education	37,147	19%	17,919	20%
Some high school education	68,022	35%	34,190	38%
High school graduates	86,985	45%	36,547	41%
College graduates	1,561	1%	489	1%
Worked before[6]	125,740	65%	64,388	72%
Never worked	67,819	35%	24,658	28%
Certified for relief	13,046	7%	5,172	7%
Not on relief	161,852	93%	74,451	93%

Junior counselors held 531,595 interviews with these 193,715 young people and made 46,812 visits to employers in the effort to find work for them.

The Junior Division of Guidance and Placement advises and assists NYA State administrators in the preparation of occupational manuals and briefs. In 17 States, directories of training opportunities available to youth have been published. State directors report that guidance and placement counselors are aiding them in setting up free-time training classes for unemployed youth.

A special auxiliary consultation service is maintained by NYA in 10 cities. To this service are referred young people who need more intensive and more intimate assistance than Junior Placement offices can give them. Often they are youth of high general abilities who are bewildered by the complex fields of employment and wish detailed and comprehensive help vocationally. They may be youth so discouraged that they cannot make any new plans for training. The consultation bureau serves as a vocational clinic. Youth are helped to evaluate their school backgrounds and their work histories in relation to possible future training and employment. Through aptitude and skill tests, they are helped to discover possible fields of work in which they might expect to succeed. Often

---

[6] Any job of 30 days' duration is included.

these young people want advice concerning appropriate places for training and recreation in their communities. These 10 junior consultation bureaus are set up independently but in close co-operation with Junior Placement Divisions. Their purpose is to assist youth to untangle very complex vocational problems. To schools, community organizations, and to industry they demonstrate possible ways of lowering the numbers of youth who never "find themselves" vocationally and whose work abilities are consequently lost.

CHAPTER VII

These Are Their Stories

BOYS BUILDING A COUNTRY SCHOOLHOUSE. GIRLS MAKING SWABS
in a hospital. A girl in a wind-beaten prairie library. Boys
mending school furniture. Girls cooking lunch for rickety
school children. Boys laying stones for the walls of a Youth
Center.

The faces of the thousands of NYA boys and girls we have
seen, flash through our minds. What does it mean to be young
in these last, lean years of depression? What is it like to grow
up in a relief family? What kinds of homes did these boys and
girls leave in the morning when they came to work? In a few
instances, when we talked with them, they disclosed pictures
of complex, seemingly insoluble problems resting on their
young shoulders.

We wanted to know about more of them, to get some sense
of the difference their part-time NYA employment and pay-
checks might make in their uneasy lives. So we asked supervisors, men and women who work with these boys and girls
daily on projects, to send us typical stories of NYA youth.
We did not want tabulated case histories, with all the coldness
and accuracy of fact that they often present. "Just tell us about
the boy or girl," we asked. We got several thousands of these
stories. In a few cases, the young people speak for themselves.
The first names, which we use only to designate the sex of these
youth, are fictitious. Geographical localities are included only
when they have particular significance.

Supervisors Tell about NYA Youth[1]

The District Judge asked the Area Supervisor if she could "take on" another boy. He had just sentenced a high school boy to the reformatory, but hated to see him go because he had always been a good chap.

Since John came from a WPA family, he was assigned to an NYA project. He was 18 and a senior in high school when he broke into a store and stole money. The Superintendent of Schools said John was an outstanding boy.

A visit to the home revealed that a family of six, John, his mother, his stepfather, and three half-sisters, were living in one room upstairs. The stepfather felt that John should, at the very least, be taking care of himself. John had tried to get work. He was destitute of clothes and did not have money for his graduation expenses.

John worked on NYA for four months and went to night school. He was very much interested in electricity. A year ago last August, the Area Supervisor asked the Superintendent of —— Power Company to give John a trial. He was placed as assistant at the power plant about 22 miles from town. John now has charge of the plant with an assistant working under him.

Eight months ago, a surly girl in her late teens was assigned to an NYA resident homemaking project. She answered curtly when she was spoken to and never spoke otherwise. Gradually, the supervisor drew her out. She went to visit the girl's home

---

[1] For the sake of brevity, we have condensed these stories in some instances. As nearly as possible we have kept to the original accounts of supervisors, since they indicate so clearly the relationships of the supervisors to the NYA youth.

and found that the mother was a widow and this girl the oldest of a large number of children. They lived in a shack of three small rooms. Life was haphazard—no regular mealtimes. When the children became hungry, they would eat what they could find.

The girl's project work improved and she has become a responsible member of the NYA homemaking group. Recently the other girls elected her to the finance committee of NYA workers which directs the purchase of and payment for food and all supplies for the project.

On another visit to the home, the supervisor discovered that the girl had built herself a room, collecting scrap lumber and packing boxes so that she might live more "like other folks"—with privacy and order. There was a noticeable difference in the whole home—the younger children were better kept and meals for them were better planned.

Harry is the eldest son in a family of six. His father and mother have been separated many years, and he has lived with his mother.

Harry first started working with us in October 1936 at the age of 18. He was a very frail and emaciated boy. He had completed only the sixth grade in school because it was necessary for him to find work. He worked for one of the local newspapers as a carrier. It happened that he was not able to collect for the papers delivered, so he was forced to discontinue the work.

Since coming with us he has learned the operation and complete care of the mimeograph machine; he has become a fair typist and an excellent file clerk. Moreover, he is one of the most thoroughly reliable and trustworthy persons who ever worked with us.

We have been successful in finding him several temporary

jobs. He is eager to accept them in order to build up a record of experience.

From the beginning, William's record with the Bureau of Immigration, an NYA project to which he was assigned, was not particularly good. There was some question in the mind of his NYA supervisor as to whether William should be retained on the project. Then one day, in the course of a talk with the boy, his supervisor discovered that his home situation was extremely bad. William informed the supervisor that "my old man run out on us," and that he was endeavoring to support himself, his mother, and his sister, two years old, on his NYA salary.

The Institute of Family Relations obtained for the mother a position as a janitress and took care of the family's immediate pressing needs for food and clothing. The effect on the boy was almost instantly apparent. He lost his surliness and began to take an interest in his work.

The NYA Junior Consultation Service, in giving him aptitude tests, discovered that the boy's mechanical ability was extraordinarily high. This came as a considerable surprise to the boy, who had been laboring under the delusion that he was essentially stupid and untalented. Arrangements were made by the Junior Consultation Service for him to take free courses in the field of his natural aptitudes.

He was transferred to another NYA job where he could obtain experience in auto mechanics. After three months of study and work in the mechanical field the boy obtained a full-time position as an assistant garage mechanic at $22 a week, and he is now capable of supporting himself and his dependents without outside help.

Harold is an orphan who was 22 years old in the spring of

1936 when he was first brought to the attention of the NYA. He had found it necessary to beg for his food and was living in a squatter's cabin, which he had pre-empted, on the edge of a river near town.

When first interviewed, he exuded antagonism toward everyone. His personal appearance could not help but be, and was, poor.

He was assigned to a park construction project. He became interested in the work and it was soon discovered that he could be left in complete charge of the work when it was necessary for the regular foreman to be temporarily absent. The boys accepted this and worked with him easily and well. His painting ability became known and he was put in charge of the refinishing of a cabin built by WPA labor in one of the parks.

The District NYA Supervisor had arranged for several training courses at the YMCA. Harold attended these courses and was asked to take over the assistant leadership of a Scout troop.

In the spring of 1937, this youth left NYA because he had been able to secure several contracts from townspeople to paint and repaper their houses.

Robert's age is 23. He has poor health, having had diabetes for the last eight years. He graduated from high school with a grade of B-plus for his senior year. His highest grades were earned in chemistry and radio and electricity, with an average mark of A in chemistry, and an A-minus in radio and electricity.

He has a shack of his own in which he sleeps and has a small radio repair shop.

Robert is a general handyman and a good worker. He has obtained several jobs for himself, but his poor health has made it necessary for him to stay close to home as he must take insulin shots every day. His jobs have consisted mostly of helping farmers in the beet fields.

Robert has a plan for the future which NYA is helping him

realize. He has been studying radio repair for the past five or six years.

The money he receives from NYA has enabled him to buy books, supplies, and equipment. He hopes to have enough customers soon in his repair shop so that he may be self-supporting and leave NYA.

Jane's father left her mother eight years ago. The mother sews for a livelihood when she is well enough to do so. She has been ill for some time now and needs medical attention.

Jane is 24 years of age, and is of average mentality. She completed the eighth grade. She was ill a great deal during childhood. While in the fifth grade, she had St. Vitus's dance and lost the use of her right side. Later she had a nervous breakdown. She finally had to quit school and take care of the family while her mother worked.

She has six brothers, two of whom are normal, and four blind. She has one blind sister and one who has normal sight. The blindness is congenital. Operations during early childhood would have improved their condition, but they were considered too expensive and too risky, for the oldest boy lost an eye through a careless operation.

Jane wishes to be a seamstress if she can get enough training. She is at present on a sewing project and will be recommended for work in garment manufacturing as soon as there is a place open in the power machine class.

Mary is one of seven children in a fatherless home. At the time she applied for NYA work, there was an income of only $45 a month in the home, earned by the mother on WPA. The girl had been ill for several years with tuberculosis of the bones, which compelled her to quit before she finished high school, as she was unable to do the necessary walking to and from school.

When she applied for NYA work in October 1936, however, she was greatly improved and has continued to improve since that time. She was neat about her needlework, and after a few weeks of work, her confidence in herself and her initiative were restored. Through the NYA vocational lectures, she became interested in a comptometry course. With part of her NYA wage, she has paid for the course in installments, and has now nearly finished the course and is hoping for a job soon.

John Lee is a Chinese boy whose family has been known to the County Welfare since 1932. There are six children in the family, and they have had a difficult time in managing. The father was murdered in a tong war.

The mother has made the children feel it a disgrace to have to ask for aid. When they first were getting help the two older boys refused to eat anything except what they could afford to buy from their own earnings as newsboys. In May of 1936, John lost his job as a newsboy, and collapsed one day in school. After a thorough examination at the County Hospital, it was found that he suffered only from lack of food. He had not eaten in five days because the food on the table had been furnished by the County Welfare. A month later, in July 1936, he was certified for NYA.

After receipt of his first pay-check, John's attitude changed. He felt himself to be a responsible member of his household, and immediately took over the place the father had left.

During the winter 1936–37, he did clerical work at the high school. In the summer of 1937, he was given a place of leadership on the playground. He early showed an aptitude for boxing. In the winter during his spare time he practiced boxing, and achieved some renown in amateur groups. A promoter, appreciating his skill, signed a contract with him, and in the middle of February he departed with this promoter for

Florida and was dropped from NYA. Since then he has won many bouts and was last heard from in Cuba.

Rosa is an Italian girl. She is the second of fifteen children, eleven of whom are living. She entered school at the age of eight, but became sick soon thereafter and for more than eight years was confined to an invalid's chair as a paralytic. Her eyesight also failed her for a time.

When Rosa came to us, at the age of 19, she could neither read nor write, nor even tell time by the clock. She knew very little about sewing. She was dull and heavy-hearted and it was even hard for her to pronounce words.

We turned her over to a teacher who had a great deal of patience and ability in handling backward and sensitive pupils. Eleven months later Rosa was in the fourth reader. She does well in her arithmetic and uses the dictionary with ease and understanding.

At the same time she has been progressing rapidly in the sewing room. Rosa can now make her own dresses as well as sew for others in her family.

Donald seemed incapable of doing good work when he came to the NYA program. He was careless, awkward, and indifferent and when assigned to a task could not be trusted to do a finished job. He had left school after the sixth grade.

Donald worked on the NYA program about eleven months. The foreman encouraged him to do some further study in arithmetic, and it was not long before he could do any practical problem expected of the eighth grade. In a few months he became a skilled workman. He was released from the program because he was married. I had a letter from him three days ago in which he stated that he had a good job making $84 per month with a furniture company in Michigan.

This is only one case. A large number of youth, formerly employed on the NYA program in this county, are now employed in Ohio and other States in private industry. Just how much the NYA helped them to obtain their positions, it is difficult to estimate with accuracy. It is safe to say, however, that the NYA checks helped secure their transportation out of this hill country [Breathitt County] of Kentucky.

When Julia, who had been unable to attend school beyond the sixth grade, was given work on one of the NYA sewing projects in our county, she became very anxious to do anything that was given her because she needed employment.

This is a small town and there are not many places for girls to work. In September of this year I learned of a vacancy which was to be in one of the dry cleaning plants of the town. I went to the owner and told him of Julia's ability and asked that she might come over for a try-out the following Monday. He agreed, and because of her ability to take instructions and to alter and care for clothing, he gave Julia the job. She is now able to have someone care for her invalid mother while she works. The owner states that she is the most efficient help the plant has ever had. She now makes $10 per week for four days, giving her three days to devote to the duties of the home.

Andrew began work the first part of 1936 as an unskilled laborer on an NYA work project. He was next made a timekeeper and, after a few weeks' experience and instruction, became outstanding as to speed, accuracy, and neatness.

Very soon after this, a large construction company called upon our supervisory force for a timekeeper. Andrew was recommended for this position and is now receiving approximately $65 per month salary, with prospects of an immediate advance.

Before Andrew's last employment, his father was doing

manual labor far too heavy for his strength. Andrew has now induced his father to give up this heavy toil and is assisting the family by providing the necessities of life.

Andrew's employer called upon us some few weeks ago for other timekeepers, stating that Andrew was giving very efficient and satisfactory service.

Herbert's mother died when he was quite young, and his father married four times afterward. At the time Herbert was assigned to NYA, the family was living in a canvas tent, with a wood foundation around the bottom of the tent to keep out the cold air. Furniture consisted of a stove, two beds, two chairs, a table, and a safe. At the time of the boy's certification he stated that the family had been practically living on walnuts for the past two weeks.

After a few weeks' NYA work, Herbert proved to be very capable at almost any job he was given. He was an exceptionally good carpenter and could grasp instruction readily. His NYA training included setting out shrubs, painting, and carpentry, and acting as foreman.

Before his NYA job, Herbert had not been able to find employment of any kind. This, perhaps, was due partly to his father's bad reputation. All of this quite naturally had a bad effect upon the youth. When Herbert was given the job as foreman over some NYA boys, he seemed to gain a great deal of confidence in himself.

About six months ago, the NYA Project Supervisor met a towboat man who was inquiring about a carpenter's helper. He was told about Herbert, who was recommended by the supervisor as a satisfactory worker. Herbert was soon interviewed and hired for $70 per month, eight hours per day. His wages were later increased to $110 per month and he recently wrote the NYA supervisor that he is expecting an increase to $150 per month.

The family is now living in a three-room house with sufficient furnishings. Herbert pays the rent and bought all the extra furnishings.

As their father was an invalid, twin brothers, 18 years of age, were forced to quit school after they had finished the eighth grade and seek work to support the family of six. They started on our NYA work project February 18, 1936. The boys proved to be adept with tools. For more than a year they worked in the woodshop making chairs, cabinets, tables, etc. At the shop the boys were helped to make a turning lathe for their own use. In less than six weeks they had sold eighteen chairs of their own making for $2.00 each.

During April 1937, an uncle, who is a carpenter and has a trailer shop in Oregon, visited the boys' family. When he learned that the twins were interested in carpentry work and saw that they were really accomplished workers, he assisted them in building a trailer of their own. With his car and their trailer, they embarked on their journey to Oregon, where they are still gainfully employed making trailers in their uncle's shop.

When picked up by the NYA, James (a member of a family of six and a high school commercial course graduate) had practically abandoned all hope of obtaining clerical work. For one thing, he was unable to buy the clothes necessary to make the proper impression on a prospective employer. His morale was broken and he had given up all hope of bettering his lot in the future. He was assigned to an NYA project as a clerk. The clerical experience gained on the project revived his desire for permanent employment and restored his confidence. The wages received made it possible for him to improve his appearance and with the encouragement of his supervisor he resumed job-hunting.

After numerous applications he was successful in February 1937 in obtaining a position as a shipping clerk in a large factory. Since starting on this job he has received two raises in spite of the current recession. The second of these advancements resulted from a suggestion he made to his superior which brought about a marked improvement in the routing of forms in his department.

Margaret's father is an unskilled laborer and has not had steady work. Her mother has been dead ten years. There are eight in this family.

Before her NYA employment, Margaret worked for one year in a shirt factory which closed and threw her out of work. She then worked in another sweat-shop shirt factory, which she was forced to leave because of an injury to her finger. When assigned to NYA, Margaret was placed in one of the city hospitals in the laundry department, where she did fine hand-pressing and operated a mangle. She satisfactorily participated in classes offered by the WPA Adult Education Department. She was self-assured, had a pleasing personality, and a neat appearance. After nine months with NYA, her own abilities, together with the intercession of the NYA supervisor, brought Margaret a permanent job in the hospital which put her in charge of all fine laundry work.

George, age 21, was passionately fond of music. He had graduated from high school, taking academic subjects and music, but could not continue with studies because his stepfather insisted that he "get a job."

The youth applied for NYA assistance in September 1936 and was placed on a project where he was very satisfactory as a messenger and was encouraged to keep on with his studies. During this period, George attended night classes in musical composition and played a saxophone in a small orchestra. His ambition was to go to the Boston Conservatory of Music. He took every odd job that he could find, canvassing the office force for any sort of work, and whenever he had a spare moment he kept busy transcribing musical notes.

George did so well in his work in class that he was awarded a scholarship at the Boston Conservatory of Music in September 1937. He has since written asking for a work reference, stating: "But for the help of NYA I could never have made it."

Mary Lou and Emma are the eldest of a rural Negro family of eighteen, ranging in age from 21 years to twelve months and including three sets of twins. The father is dead.

The family lived in a four-room cabin so dilapidated that the owner charged no rent. In the bedroom were four beds, only one of which had on it what might have been termed a mattress. The others had quilts pieced from whatever scraps the mother had been able to get. The children took heated rocks to bed with them at night, but even these and sleeping three in a bed did not serve to keep them comfortable. The other two rooms, another bedroom and the kitchen, had no windows or doors, cracks an inch wide in the walls, and little left of the floor. Before the two girls were assigned to NYA there were many days last fall when they had nothing to eat except locusts and hickory nuts.

The mother, though illiterate, talked quite intelligently. Her greatest sorrow was that none of the children had had any chance to go to school. There used to be a school six miles from their home, she said, but by the time the children walked that distance in all kinds of weather and " 'thout no breakfast, dey couldn't learn nothin' when dey got dere."

The girls walked five miles every day to the end of the street-car line, and then rode the car to reach the NYA project on which they worked. Mary Lou had never been to town alone in her life. Both girls are learning to read and write and are teaching the younger children at home to read and write also.

Mary Lou and Emma are eager to learn and to improve themselves. They always come neatly dressed. They have mended for the other children used clothing which the supervisor was able to get for them. In cooking class they are learning how to buy more wisely with the small income the family has, and make the family meals more nutritious.

With the supervisor's encouragement, the family has moved to another section of the county near a school, so that all the children are at present going to school. This new locality is also near a white community in which Emma will probably be able to find domestic employment.

On the morning of a bright day in October 1937, a timid knock was heard on the door of the NYA area office. When no response came to the call, "Come in," the supervisor opened the door and found a bashful, cross-eyed boy about 19 years old standing there. The youth was so frightened he could hardly speak. Upon further investigation it was found that the youth lived on a tenant farm and was the second of three boys. The oldest son had part-time employment at a mill, which was the only income for the family of five.

An instructor of a local business school was very much interested in this shy lad and was anxious that he be given a chance to earn some money in order that he might finish a business course which had to be stopped because of lack of money. So, on October 20, the youth began work in the welfare office.

He has now paid the debt on his business course, and has had his eyes straightened and recently he purchased a new pair of glasses.

Elizabeth is a handicapped girl. She has a severe case of

arthritis, so serious that she has been chair- and bed-ridden since she became ill while she was in the eighth grade. Her parents died shortly after this. They had been providing her with medical treatment during the brief period before their death, and now this was discontinued. She was assigned to NYA on March 3, 1937.

It was necessary for her to work at home. We naturally thought that any work she would do would be inferior, since it is impossible for her to move around and her hands are so badly crippled. Her work has been unusually satisfactory and has improved considerably during the year. We have been giving the dresses that she has made to local welfare agencies for distribution. She has used her NYA money to buy a wheel chair and a sun lamp. She has been able to leave her home for the first time in six years.

Here was a boy who "lived across the river," a phrase which means to the natives little shacks, poor food, ragged clothes, scrawny children, and, generally, dirt everywhere.

He was certified, and his name came to the NYA office for assignment. We had to hunt him out; he was too shy and rustic to come in. He was assigned to a road project near his house. He worked willingly, although unskillfully, and spoke only when spoken to. Gradually, he became surer of himself, his work was well done and done without orders, and he began to fraternize with the other men.

Later, he was transferred to a town job. I really believe it was almost the first time he had ever been in a town. He became acquainted with more people and finally tried to get a job on his own initiative, which represented a real achievement on his part. He failed to get a job but kept right on looking.

In the meantime, he had been able to buy some clothes that were more presentable; he was better fed, and looked it; he had a little money for trips to hunt jobs. Finally he got one on a dairy farm in Wisconsin, where he is still employed.

Paul's mother and father died before he finished high school. He and five younger brothers and sisters went to live with their grandmother and grandfather in a shack out in the country. With free school transportation, Paul was able to complete high school but could not go to college, which was his ambition. Preliminary try-out experience on several kinds of NYA projects indicated that Paul, 19 years of age, was very much interested in electrical and radio work.

The —— Trades School opened in the fall of 1936 and Paul was one of the first to enroll. He would work on the NYA and go to school after project hours. Paul was then placed in the —— School Board workshop, an NYA project, where he could gain experience in wiring and in electrical work.

When the —— Electric Company called for young men to work, in December 1937, Paul went to apply for the job. He was selected and worked with the —— Electric Company until he received employment with the —— Engineering Company the last of February 1938.

Since then, Paul has moved his grandparents, brothers, and sisters into a real home.

Perry's family (Negro) consists of a mother and three children. The mother was once on a WPA sewing project, but is off now because of bad health. Perry's salary is the only income.

On being referred to the NYA, he was placed on an orderly project at the —— Hospital and very soon won the attention of those in charge by his polite manner, efficiency, and personal neatness. When a vacancy occurred on the orderly staff, he was offered the place; his salary is $8.00 per week. He says he was put on the NYA at a time when he didn't know which way to turn. When he found out that the hospital had vacancies sometimes on the orderly staff, he made up his mind to do his work so well that they would want him.

Caroline, 20 years old, a Negro girl, is the second in a family of seven children. The father has no steady employment and does odd jobs when he can find them. The mother takes in washing.

Caroline was assigned to the homemaking project and was trained for maid service. She was taught cooking, meal planning, table-setting, serving, some sewing, and all phases of housework. She is now working in a private home where the mother is employed during the day. Caroline takes full charge of the home and of two small children while the mother is at work.

Stella is a girl 19 years of age whose mother is a widow with three children younger than Stella. The family income was only $26.40 a month, which the mother received from her WPA sewing room work until Stella began working on NYA.

Stella was put to work on our Public Service Project. Each month she saved a part of her NYA money and deposited it in a savings account. After a year's time she had saved enough to make a down payment on a little home for her mother with arrangements to make monthly payments of the same amount that she had been paying for rent.

Last fall Stella entered —— College as an NYA Student Aid pupil; she is studying to become a teacher.

Pedro comes from a Mexican family of fourteen, consisting of his father, mother, and eleven brothers and sisters. Pedro was forced to drop out of school in the seventh grade to help support his family.

He was referred to the NYA work program in November 1936, and started to work on the construction of a retaining wall. The NYA foreman encouraged Pedro to learn all he could about rock work.

The foreman on this project was called on one day by an El Paso contractor to recommend a couple of youths who showed promise as rock masons. Pedro's work experience gained on his NYA job qualified him for this private employment, and he has been working steadily on rock masonry construction since that time.

Pedro's case is typical of many Mexican boys who have made excellent rock men and who have received their start in that direction from the training they received on an NYA construction project.

Thomas lives with his aged grandparents in a dilapidated, two-room frame house.

He was recommended to the NYA as a promising student, one who was very much interested in woodworking. The shop foreman recognized his willingness and his ability to learn the trade. Thomas was soon raised to sub-foreman.

Thomas has gained confidence in himself. He knew very little about woodworking when he entered the shop, but "caught on" very quickly, and is now very efficient. He is leaving the NYA and is buying some equipment to open a shop for himself.

Malcolm, 23 years old, the son of a farmer, went through the seventh grade of school, but for the last eight years the boy has had no work except farming on very poor land.

When Malcolm went to work on the NYA program he had no work experience other than farming with simple hand implements, and he was afraid to try new activities. His first NYA work was on the building of small foot bridges. He soon learned how to handle the tools and at the end of a month he could build a good bridge without supervision. His next job was the building of playground equipment, merry-go-rounds, teeters, etc. Again he was fearful of the work, but he mastered the new technique and gained a little confidence. He was then one of a crew sent to repair a building for the Department of Public Assistance. He expressed a desire to try to paint and worked for some time at painting, doing a fair piece of work.

Last week Malcolm was busy plastering a room at the county poor farm. He explained his work with pride and satisfaction. He said: "Until I came to work on the NYA I knew things were done but I had no idea that I could ever do them, so I didn't try. Now I'd try to do any kind of work."

Eileen is 19 years old and one of nine children. The health of this family is appalling. The mother is in need of an operation for a tumor, one girl has tuberculosis, another has heart trouble, and a brother is suffering with a broken back as a result of an automobile accident in 1937.

Eileen was sent to the NYA for work by a Red Cross nurse who was interested in trying to teach her some home nursing.

When Eileen appeared at the office of the NYA supervisor and asked to be put to work, she wore a pair of soiled white slacks and a tattered sweater, although the weather was cold. She did not associate with the other workers and evaded her duties in the nursery to which she was assigned whenever it was possible.

She enrolled in the Home Hygiene and Care of the Sick course but gave no indication of interest. She said that she did not wish to care for sick people, even her own brother. After two pay periods, she appeared in a skirt and sweater, and had made an attempt to improve her appearance generally. This change seemed to carry over into her work, and better reports were given of her work and attitude in class. She worked with the other girls and did not attempt to avoid her duties. By the end of two months she was intensely interested in all she did.

She passed the Home Hygiene course with the second highest grade in a group of twenty.

Quiet follow-up in this case showed that Eileen had changed in her attitude at home. She devotes much time to the care of her invalid brother and is using a part of her small NYA salary to help pay the doctor who cares for the boy.

Doris, 23 years of age, lives with her eccentric mother, two brothers, and a sister. From childhood she was brought up to think she was different from other people, appearing for work clad in garments that were the style twenty years ago—including a long, slat sunbonnet. While having lived within just a short distance of modern conveniences, she was wholly ignorant of their use, not even having talked over a telephone. She had not finished grade school.

With her ideas and appearance, she was unable to obtain private employment. Today she has overcome her inferiority complex, decided to live and act like those around her, realized her lack of education, and, by arrangement with the county Superintendent of Public Instruction, she is studying in her spare time, and on days she does not work carries two courses in high school, where she is making A's. Through her work in the sewing room she has become a good seamstress, and through her association with other young people has become a popular girl with all whom she meets. I realize that I cannot describe this case as it has really developed, but her transformation has been unusual to those of us who are associated with her.

Richard, 19 years old, who lives with his mother and two other children in a poor home, had to leave school at the end of the seventh grade. He was assigned to an NYA workshop project in April 1937. Here he gained experience in repairing school desks, varnishing seats, installing plumbing, and painting buildings. He spent all the time he could spare learning to do the various tasks in the shop, learning to use the machinery and to operate the drills, saws, etc.

His mother, sewing on a WPA project, was receiving $36.20 per month. Rent was high and Richard had to help all he could. He picked up odd jobs, but would rush back to the shop to learn more.

The foreman of the workshop of the Public School Board was in need of help and decided to give Richard the chance. He made good and is now earning $75 a month.

When Joan's family was first interviewed, they lived in a one-room tarpaper shack. Joan was a very nervous, shy, timid, but proud girl and did not wish to have her family's circumstances disclosed.

She was unable to obtain more than an eighth grade education because of her mother's illness and the family's meager resources.

In February 1936 Joan was placed by NYA in the —— County health office. At the time of her employment she was suffering from frequent attacks of epilepsy, which we were not aware of until she had started working. After she had been working for a while she was financially able to begin treatments for this disorder. We cannot say she is cured but the nervous condition is controlled and does not occur.

After this disease was controlled, there was a very noticeable change mentally and socially. She was no longer timid, and was able to meet and talk with people more readily.

Joan managed to save enough from her earnings to build an additional room on their house. She is now saving her money for the purpose of building another room.

The earlier part of Ben's life had been deficient in nutritious food, and he was therefore decidedly weak and frail. Despite apparent physical handicaps he went on through school to the eleventh grade. He then studied chemistry evenings at the —— High School.

When Ben came to us in August 1937, we attempted to place him in a State laboratory because of his ability in chemistry. This could not be done since he was not a high school graduate. He was given a temporary assignment as a clerk on the record project, and the boy planned to complete his high school work at the —— Preparatory School. We received word several times that Ben could not adjust himself to this work and that he was also seemingly not interested. His mother reported a development of "temper tantrums." We called Ben in for a physical examination, which disclosed that he had heart trouble which might have been a "toxic thyroid" condition. Because of this physical handicap we transferred him to the chemistry department of the —— Hospital, where he immediately proved a valuable assistant. He was allowed to attend operations and to assist at post-mortem examinations.

Another examination at the clinic discovered a decided thyroid condition which had resulted in a heart lesion. By this time the hospital was so interested in Ben that they arranged for his thyroidectomy without any cost to the boy. The operation has been performed, and the hospital assured Ben that as soon as he is fully recovered they will be glad to have him return to the chemistry department and after a few months more of training and some special study they will give him permanent employment.

David has no mother. He lived with his stepfather, who, he states, mistreated him, making his home life extremely unpleasant. He therefore left and went to live with his brother-in-law, sister, and their two children. (His brother-in-law was at that time earning $16 per week.)

David, a very aggressive, ill-tempered, and troublesome

youth, was familiar to the neighborhood as a "tough gorilla" with pugnacious tendencies.

Through a series of circumstances, David's behavior and activities were brought to the attention of Sergeant ——, in charge of juvenile delinquency. David confessed that he and his "gang" had been stealing cars. Although he was only a grammar school graduate, he showed an aptitude for learning that went beyond his educational background.

For the first two weeks in NYA work, the supervisor found David unmanageable. His work habits were poor and his general attitude was one of antagonism and distrust.

The next two weeks, however, brought a distinct change. His manner improved and he performed his duties with conscientious zeal. For this good behavior, he was transferred to office work, as filing clerk, where he worked for about three weeks.

A local grocery store proprietor asked the NYA supervisor to select one of the youths for a job open in his store. Seeking to rehabilitate David, the supervisor selected him as an applicant and informed the proprietor of his background.

David worked in the store for three months, and was made manager. His employer found him so completely trustworthy that he left him in charge of the store while on vacation.

Elsie applied for work on NYA in March 1936. In our interview with Elsie, we found that she was one of a family of five including a none too sympathetic stepmother. Elsie wanted to leave home to go into training as a nurse.

The NYA supervisor referred her to the —— Hospital. The hospital superintendent agreed to take Elsie as a probationer, provided she had the money to pay for her tuition and books. With the NYA supervisor, Elsie worked out a plan whereby, if she were assigned to NYA and could continue working for one year, she could save the needed amount.

In March 1937 she came into the office and announced that she had saved the required sum of money and was to be admitted to the nurses' training course on April 1. She is now in her second year at the hospital.

Lawrence is one of seven children. This large family lives on an isolated, worn-out farm in a frame house with no conveniences. Lawrence, 20 years old, has two older brothers trying to wrest a living for the large family from this plot of land. The father has rheumatism so badly that he cannot work.

Lawrence has gone to school for only two years but he managed to do the work through grade six in that period. Since he was 14 years old he has had no work except on NYA during the last year.

He is interested in becoming a carpenter and the NYA in —— County has done many pieces of work which have given experience in the building trades. Lawrence has been a very good worker, absorbing all the knowledge on building he possibly could. He has never been late or missed a day's work. He is reliable and thorough and feels that he is now capable of being a carpenter's helper, and is making an effort to find such a place.

The county in which Lawrence lives provides almost no chance for employment but Lawrence is willing to go anywhere to earn a living.

Arthur is the 20-year-old son of a tenant farmer. His four brothers and one sister, all younger than he, attend school and work on the farm after school. The father appears to be an intelligent man, who has had a hard time raising his family on a small income. Having never spent a single day in school himself, he seems especially anxious that his children be given the advantages of an education. His chief and only crops are and have always been rice, cotton, and corn. Besides that, he works as a laborer on other farms whenever possible. The family income is approximately $200 a year.

While Arthur was in high school, he worked before and after school on the farm and often missed the first six weeks of the fall session in order to help out at home. However, he was a good student and graduated in June of 1937. He was assigned to an NYA horticulture project and has shown an aptitude for floriculture and vegetable-raising. He is a tireless worker and puts in many more than the required number of hours. Arthur states that he believes that his NYA experience will enable him to make money at farming and keep him from being just another tenant farmer.

Phyllis is one of a family of fifteen. Victims of the North Dakota drought, they drifted west to Washington, where they spent the winter, eating only dried corn and potatoes because they were afraid they would be sent back to North Dakota if they applied for relief at the Welfare Department. Finally this family was brought to the attention of the Welfare Department by a church from which they had received aid.

Phyllis has been placed on the sewing project in her district and is earning $14 per month. The change in her personality since she went to work is very noticeable. She is much more talkative and seems to feel that she is more on a level with the other girls now. This is entirely different from her attitude of gloominess and hopelessness when she began.

Arnold is the oldest of four children in a tenant farmer's family. With the only school ten miles away and with no available transportation, he did not enter the first grade until he was 11. Before going to school each morning, he worked two hours on the farm. He was too fatigued to be a good pupil. He managed to finish the fifth grade at 18.

Barefoot, in dirty and ragged shirt and overalls held by a

rope around his thin middle, he slouched into the NYA office. By this time, Arnold's younger brother was old enough to help with the farm work. It was decided to send Arnold to an NYA resident agricultural project. A few persons co-operated in obtaining shirts, a sweater, a suit of clothes, and even shoes. For the first time in his life Arnold had pajamas.

Some months later Arnold was at home because of a school holiday. Here was a tall, neatly dressed youth. His shoulders, not so thin now, were erect. He spoke with interest of the training he had received in crop rotation, farm management, and animal husbandry. This was not Arnold, the hopeless, ignorant, Southern farm hand, probably destined to become another relief case. This was Arnold, the potential independent farmer.

Grace was the youngest of ten children. Her father died, and her mother was committed to the State Asylum for the Insane. All the other children married. No one wanted Grace and she was sent from one relative to another. She was placed in various private homes as a maid without any remuneration but her board. Finally she went to stay with her brother-in-law. She was unable to obtain work and the brother-in-law gave her carfare to a near-by city and told her to get out. At this time she obtained NYA employment.

Ellen was one of six children whose father had developed silicosis and was unable to work.

Ellen was employed on NYA in October of 1937. At the time she began employment she was very poorly dressed and untidy. This, I believe, was the main reason why she could not obtain private employment. Ellen proved to be a good conscientious worker. Each month she saved her money and purchased a few articles of clothing to make herself presentable. With new confidence and a good appearance, Ellen, after persistent trips to the —— Dry Goods Store seeking work, was finally employed in February 1938.

Alvin, the oldest of nine children of a Gloucester fisherman, has recently been employed on an NYA project at the Government Fisheries Station.

With a desire to follow in the footsteps of those who have made the Gloucester fishing industry famous, this boy saved enough out of the money he has been receiving for his part-time NYA work to buy a little fishing dory, for which he paid $20. The dory, containing a gas engine, had been used for many years by an older fisherman.

Alvin has already gone into business for himself and is capable of earning $7.00 per day above his expenses, and he looks forward to the time when, through careful saving, he may be able to own a larger boat.

Caleb has, since childhood, been crippled with infantile paralysis. After graduating from high school, he obtained a position in a jewelry shop in order to learn the business. He had one year of experience when, because of the depression, he was let out. He came back home and, with his father's help, was endeavoring to pick up repair jobs of any kind that he could do. With the extra help NYA furnished him, he gradually established himself in the jewelry repair business and today is making good. He has married and is a fine example of the worthwhile help NYA furnishes toward self-sufficiency.

Howard, a 24-year-old Massachusetts boy, lives with a younger brother and an uncle, his only relatives. He has been able to acquire a small farm, which he has nearly paid for out of his NYA wages. A social organization gave him a setting of goose eggs, which our supervisor is helping him to hatch in a home-made incubator.

The boy feels that he can make a living on the farm, with an occasional one or two days' work a week in the town and, as he is receiving NYA training in town work, we expect to have him prepared to go off the NYA in a few months.

NYA Youth Speak for Themselves

In a poverty-stricken Kentucky mountain county, we met a 19-year-old NYA boy who went with us to see a remodeled school building.

"This is where I helped put in the new foundation," he said as he touched the concrete blocks. "And I worked on these windows, too. . . . Here's where I put in a new floor. . . ." He showed us each part of the building on which he had worked.

"Did you ever do any of this kind of work before?" we asked him.

"No."

"Have you done any at home since you started in here?" we wanted to know.

"Well, you see, I'm living with a fellow and his wife," he said. (We subsequently learned that he was an orphan.) "And we're building us a new house. I'm showing him how. This fellow can't pay me but once in a while on account of he hasn't much work. But I get board and room."

We said we would like to see the new house, and the boy invited us to come with him. A few hundred yards away, we saw a small house nearly completed. It was the only dwelling in the town with a cistern. The wife pointed out bookshelves, which were likewise the only ones in a home in that community.

"See the electric?" the boy asked. We looked at the ceiling where there was an outlet. "We haven't got the electric yet," the boy went on, "but you know, we'll get it some day, and when you build a house you've got to make room for the electric or you have to almost rip it apart when you do get it."

(The writer of the following letter is a 22-year-old boy in a family of five children whose father has been a paralytic patient in a county hospital for several years. This boy has been a "problem" at grade school, in his home, and in his community. He was first assigned to an NYA construction project. He did poor work. He was given another chance at a Resident Training Center, and, because he said he wanted to learn how to cook, he was assigned to the kitchen.)

I am now putting my time and Interest in Getting an Education. I am studding to Be a cook. I enjoy my course very much. The exspereance is helping me a 100%. I have been interested in my cooking course for 22 years. I have allways wanted to be a good cook. Now that I have the chance to be a cook, I am going to prove that I can. I am putting all of my interest in this special course which I have longed for 22 years and now that I have the every thing in my power to Make a good cook out of my self, I can not thank the National Youth Administration enough for what they are doing for me.

I have not had much education. I finished the 8th grade in grade school and I couldn't go to High School as my Mother need my support in keeping food and fuel in the house and now I have the operatonity to go to school and learn the Trade and cours which I have allways wanted. And I am going to make a good cook out of myself!

I want to thank the National Youth Administration for there support in gitting me back to school to take the cours of study which I have allways wanted. I will prove my statement by pitching in at hitting the ball.

(The writer of this letter is a 23-year-old girl, one of ten children in a Southern sharecropper's family. The supervisor reports: "On many occasions her father has beaten her, her mother, and the other children when he came home drunk." This girl was assigned to an NYA library in a small town.)

I am the oldest child of the family so naturally I had to do without food and clothing that I really needed. . . . Now in every way I am in a better social position. Until about two months ago I payed six dollars a month for board. Now I am paying five dollars. [Supervisor reports that she contributes work for remainder of board.] . . . Two weeks ago I rode my first time on the train. I went to ——. While I was there I purchased a coat, also while I was there I rode my first time on an elevator. Since I have been working for the NYA I have learned to use a telephone. I have learned to do errands. I can say unpleasant things in a pleasant way. I can remind people of their over-due books without hurting their feelings.

(*Supervisor's Note:* This orphan girl comes from a farming town of 1100 in Southern Utah. The possibilities of her securing other than seasonal employment are remote. Were the town larger or the population wealthier, she might enter domestic service, but she is an example of a youth backed up on a farm, where further training would be impossible were it not for NYA. The library is maintained only by NYA help and is indeed an important contribution to this small community.)

I have two sisters and one brother. We try to co-operate and help each other as best we can. Some times there isn't much help we can give.

During the last part of November and the first part of December, I was employed as a waitress in a café. I worked at this place for about four weeks. I think if they needed help at this time I could get back there.

At the present time I have no connections that will help me get a job. It seems my interest lies in library work. I have enjoyed my work at the library to the fullest extent.

The money I have received from NYA has been used to a good advantage. I clothe myself and buy groceries for the home.

(The writer of this letter is a 20-year-old girl who had high marks in her commercial courses in high school.)

I am writing this letter to thank you and the NYA for helping me find a steady job and at the same time win back my self-confidence.

A year ago when I graduated from —— High School, I, like all the others, began to search for employment. I failed to find anything at all until last December when I got an NYA job two days a week at the State Employment Service. I had been trying to get in the —— Watch Company but couldn't because my neck had been deformed when I was nine years old. I became discouraged because everything looked so hopeless. Through your assistance and the NYA it was possible for me to take treatments on my neck. These have helped me beyond words. As soon as the employment authorities at the watch factory noticed the improvement they decided to hire me and I started May 17. I also do some office work there which has been made easier for me because of my office training at the State Employment Service.

(This letter was written by a 22-year-old Spanish-American boy in New Mexico. The sister of whom he speaks has four small children. The boy worked in an NYA woodworking shop while attending high school.)

As I look into the book of the past I find that I was born under great poverty, and a weakling. Misfortune was born with me, because I have been quite weak since I contracted pneumonia at the age of one. During the influenza epidemic in 1918 my mother was taken away with that terrible wave of death. Since then my oldest sister has been a mother to me. Following the death of my mother my sister took care of the whole family of six who were all young and unable to care for ourselves.

In 1920 my father married for the second time; trouble started soon after, because of misunderstandings between the two families, inequality of ideas. In 1921 my oldest sister got married, so I went to live with her. In 1930 I had completed my grade school course, and had no desire to go to high school because my father under foreign influence did not approve of higher learning. That year passed by me with great unhappiness, for I had nothing to do but pick cotton. While I was working in the fields a longing came to me to return to school.

It wasn't very long before I got a job in a boarding house earning a dollar a day and board. I continued to work for sixteen months, and all this time I was saving a little money with hopes of returning to school. Before the month of February of 1934 was ended the manager of the boarding house moved away so I lost my job. I then had to return home again, and was out of a job for the next month. In April of that year I was fortunate enough to get another job at a filling station earning twenty-five cents a day and lodging. I worked there through the summer and the manager encouraged me to return to school, and offered to give me a part-time job. When the fall came I started to go to school again. Since then I have been very fortunate in getting part-time jobs and a little outside help.

The first year of my high school career passed in great happiness. In the summer of 1934, I was taken down by sudden illness which kept me in bed for a whole month, and withdrew me from earning any money that summer. I am very grateful to my oldest sister who was so generous in taking care of me during that time and provided for the continuance of my schooling the next fall. Speaking of great people, I think that she is the greatest person I have ever known.

I was able to complete my first two high school terms, and was on my way with the third when I lost my job at the filling station, because of a change in management. I wasn't entirely out of a job then, because I still had a number of odd jobs. About the tenth of April of 1937 I enrolled under the NYA. This job has been a blessing to me because it has helped me a lot in my school work, and besides it has taught me a trade that is both beneficial and interesting to do as an entertainment. This NYA has helped me and also my sister's family whose sole support was through my brother-in-law who earns an average of about $20.00 a month.

(The supervisor reports that since writing this letter, this young woman, one of a family of eight, has obtained private employment.)

I wish to thank you through the NYA for assisting me over a few rough spots by giving me employment on an NYA program. I graduated from high school in 1936, a typical American girl, eager and confident of my prowess to work and do my work well. I had received typing awards and shorthand certificates to further my confidence. . . . I visited the employment agencies regularly and got that so impersonal smile and "nothing for you today." A year . . . what a time to pass through when you're young and are willing and eager to work and no one wanting those services. It was when our family difficulties were at its lowest ebb that I received NYA aid. . . . To be able to have my hands and mind occupied; to get out of that mental rut; to know that I earned my carfare and lunch money and to be able to hand my check over to my mother . . . there's no describing that feeling.

(The following letter is from a Negro girl in Florida.)

When I obtained work on the NYA my mind was greatly troubled, thinking that we were going to be put out of the house which we rented due to the fact that we had no way of paying the rent. By the help of the NYA I am enabled to pay the rent.

My grandmother and I were in great distress before I obtained work. I am learning a trade which will be a benefit to me in time to come.

Before I obtained work on the NYA I was almost blind in one eye and due to financial conditions I was not able to buy proper glasses. Before going to work I was badly in need of dresses and by the help of the NYA I can buy them. I also am learning to make dresses for myself. Before going to work I could not sew. I know if I continue to work I will be a good seamstress.

(This letter was written by an NYA girl in the Kentucky mountains and was printed in the *Licking Valley Courier*.)

Pomp, Ky., Jan. 27, 1938.

Dear Mr. Whitt:

You asked me what the NYA has meant to me. It has meant everything to me and my brother. My mother died eight years ago and my father died in August 1936 and left six of us children at home. I am the oldest and my youngest sister is twelve. Neither my brother or I had ever had a job and the NYA is the only jobs we have ever had. He earns $13.00 a month and I earn $10.00 a month. This money has enabled us to provide for our other two brothers and two sisters. We rent a home from Ben Cox. We use our money to buy clothing and groceries for us all. Alice is 12 and goes to school. Tommy is 13 and goes to school. Maudie is 16 and stays at home and does the housework. Matthew is 18 and stays at home and works. Jessie is 21 and works in the NYA shops at West Liberty. I work in the sewing project and get $10.00 a month. I enjoy the work and like our new supervisor, Mrs. Price. She is good to us and is not contrary with us. I have learned a lot about sewing and can make anything I want to. It has been a lot of help to me as I can buy goods and make clothing for the other children much cheaper than we can buy them made.

Yours very truly,

Edna Riggsby.

CHAPTER VIII

A New Democracy in Education

EQUAL OPPORTUNITY AND DEMOCRACY ARE INSEPARABLE ASPIRA-
tions. No aspect of equal opportunity has been sought more
energetically by the American people than equal opportunity
for education. We have long been committed to the prin-
ciple that every child should, at public expense, be provided
with, and compelled to receive, an elementary education. Our
high schools and tax-supported colleges and universities are
the fruit of the conviction that every youth should have also
the chance for such further education as his abilities justify.

The American dream of equal educational opportunity has
never fully materialized—not even in the elementary schools.
The gap between aspiration and fact has been the widest at
the college level. Even at the State institutions, laboratory fees,
books, and incidentals are more costly than in the high schools,
and most students must meet the additional expense of board
and lodging away from home. A bridge of scholarships and
loan funds has carried a few promising but poor young people
across the gap. A wider bridge has been built by the energetic
and ambitious youths who have worked their way through
college. Entirely or partly self-supporting students have been
respected members of undergraduate communities. They have
not been unknown even at the high-tuition private colleges
catering chiefly to the children of families in the upper-income
brackets.

For a decade before the great depression the difficulty of

working one's way through college had been increasing somewhat. Between 1920 and 1930 college attendance more than
doubled. Many colleges are situated in small communities
where the number of part-time jobs did not increase in proportion to the number of students seeking them. Nor, on the
average, was there a decrease in the cost of a college education
to the individual student.[1]

With the advent of the depression, the number of students
partly or entirely dependent on their own earning capacities
sharply increased, and the number of jobs open to them
sharply decreased. Most institutions made all the concessions
that their own often dwindling resources permitted to promising students with little or no money. Some of the State universities were able to provide living quarters in limited quantity at extremely low cost. Some university cafeterias sold
balanced dinners to needy students at ten or twelve cents. Yet
this scale of living was beyond the means of many youth. At
one State university, the authorities found that one young
man had been trying to feed himself on fifty cents a week
and that another was sleeping during a cold winter in an old
automobile parked on the edge of the town. Yet these ambitious young people hung on grimly. Many of them would
have been no better off anywhere else. At the colleges they
could suffer undernourishment in attractive surroundings; and
in the classrooms and college libraries they could at least find
warmth. Thousands of other capable young people remained

---

[1] Between 1921–22 and 1931–32 income from student fees at privately
controlled institutions increased 115 per cent., while income for current expenses from productive or endowment funds increased only 86 per cent. In
the publicly controlled institutions, income from student fees increased 104
per cent., while income for current expenses from public sources increased only
63 per cent. Office of Education: *Statistics of Higher Education.* Bulletin 1933,
No. 2, pp. 2–3. Government Printing Office, Washington. Because of the
increase in enrollment, these figures do not indicate an average increase in
fees per student.

in idleness at home because they could not scrape together even enough money for incidental fees at the least expensive colleges.

In spite of all that was done, the enrollment in colleges and universities dropped about 10 per cent. between 1932 and 1934, and would have dropped further if the Federal Government had not begun to supply aid to needy students in February 1934. If this drop had meant a weeding out of the least fit, perhaps it could have been considered as not undesirable. But it was not. It meant only the loss of some of those who lacked financial means and could not find the jobs with which to pay for their own education.

With the creation of the Civilian Conservation Corps various educators began to suggest that a small amount of money be made available to help young people to go to college. Until the unused capacity of the colleges was filled, it obviously was less expensive to keep youths in college than to put them in CCC camps. Indeed, there was no cheaper way to keep a large number of people of college age off the labor market and usefully occupied. And for those capable of benefiting from a higher education, this way probably held the greatest promise of gain for society as a whole.

These considerations led President Roosevelt to approve the use of enough Federal relief money to help approximately 75,000 young people to attend college during the second half of the college year 1933–34. With a slight expansion this aid was continued by FERA during the next college year and since then has been provided through NYA.

The principal terms of the college aid program have remained unchanged since the program was instituted in February 1934. In return for work, the Federal Government pays to a needy student a maximum of $20 a month during the college year. The average of payments within any institution may not exceed $15 a month. Every bona fide non-profit-making and tax-exempt institution which requires a high school diploma or the equivalent as the minimum for entrance is eligible to participate. Each is given as a quota a percentage of its enrollment of regular students.

Unlike the work program for out-of-school youth, NYA college student aid has never been restricted to youth from relief families. The colleges and universities themselves select the students to be aided. The Federal Government requires that these students possess the ability to do good scholastic work, that they be regular students carrying at least three-fourths of the normal academic schedule, and that they be unable to enter or remain in college without Federal assistance. The institutions themselves also arrange and supervise the work which these youths do to earn their Federal wage checks. The pay is at the hourly rates for comparable work in the college or community. The chief Federal requirements are that this work be useful and that it be work not formerly done by regular employees or which could be done out of regular budgets.

Under NYA the college aid program has been expanded to include graduate students under the age of 25. The graduate students are permitted to earn a maximum of $40 a month each. For two years, graduate aid was segregated, and the graduate students assisted in any one institution were allowed to earn up to an average of $30 a month. During 1937–38, graduate aid was lumped with college aid. While an individual graduate student may still earn up to $40 a month, the funds allotted to any institution are sufficient to permit average earnings for college and graduate students combined of only $15 a month. A small special fund has been created for Negro graduate students.[2]

---

[2] $70,000 for 1937–38.

Approximately 98 per cent. of the eligible institutions, including junior colleges and normal schools, have participated in the student aid program. Most of the handful of exceptions are privately controlled colleges with limited enrollments and high tuition. A few institutions in this class accepted Federal aid for a year or two but have now dropped it. Others continue to take advantage of it, but in many cases not to the full extent of their quotas.

Of the 1656 institutions approved for participation in the college aid program in 1937–38, 618 were publicly controlled, 303 were privately controlled non-sectarian, and 692 were sectarian, institutions. Forty-three were unclassifiable. Of the youth aided, well over half were in the public institutions, one-fourth were in sectarian institutions, and one-fifth were in non-sectarian colleges. Classified differently, the list of participating institutions consisted of 263 teachers colleges or normal schools, 439 junior colleges, 911 universities, colleges, or technical schools, and 43 unclassifiable institutions.

During 1937–38, the quota of funds for each institution was based on 8 per cent. of its enrollment of resident undergraduate and graduate students under 25 years of age on October 1, 1936. Some institutions preferred to spread the assistance among more students by reducing the average individual monthly earning below $15. The original quota base fixed by FERA was 10 per cent. of the enrollment. During 1934–35, this was increased to 12 per cent. of the students enrolled in October 1934. The program reached its peak in the spring of 1937. Since then it has been contracted because of reduced funds.

The following table shows the scope of the program during each of the last four college years[3]:

---

[3] The figures for number of students aided and their average monthly earnings are for April of each college year except 1937–38, in which January 1938 is the month used. The figures for 1934–35 are for college aid under FERA.

College Aid	1934–35	1935–36	1936–37	1937–38
Institutions	1,466	1,594	1,669	1,635
Students aided	104,675	122,498	140,699	95,475
Average monthly earnings		$12.72	$12.65	$10.99
Graduate Aid				
Institutions		214	188	148
Students aided		6,707	5,416	2,501
Average monthly earnings		$19.29	$23.33	$17.84
Total number of students aided	104,675	129,205	146,115	97,976

For a limited number of students, NYA aid pays all, or substantially all, expenses during the college year. Before Federal aid was established, the University of Iowa had provided dormitory space in a field house, where 100 students were sheltered for $1.00 a week each. Subsequently this university assisted in the organization of 10 co-operative houses for a total of 300 young men and women. During 1935–36, these co-operative houses charged $15 a month for board and room, and at the end of the year were able to refund approximately one month's board to each participating student. Several State institutions have assisted in making similar provision for a few students with little money. At the University of Idaho two years ago, more than 200 students paid for all their living expenses, fees, and necessary incidentals with $18 a month each.

NYA students who live at home while going to college, as many do in the cities, often are able to pay most or all of their fees and incidental expenses from NYA earnings. For the great majority, however, NYA earnings will pay only from 50 per cent. to as little as 10 per cent. of their expenses. At the tax-supported institutions the NYA assistance usually meets from 25 to 60 per cent. of the total expenses of students who do not live at home. At the privately controlled colleges the percentage is lower.

In some cases, NYA aid is used to supplement scholarships. At the privately controlled institutions most scholarships are only rebates, in part or in whole, of tuition fees. Where scholarships exist at tax-supported institutions, they are usually only of small sums. In the whole country, the number of scholarships that pay all the essential expenses of a college student is negligible. Without assistance from NYA or other sources, many students would be unable to avail themselves of scholarships.

In many cases, NYA aid is combined with money from home, or another job, or a scholarship, or all three. A brilliant Negro student at the University of Illinois won a small scholarship. He also found a job which gave him his meals. His father, a railroad laborer earning $90 a month, sent him $6 a month. Yet, without aid from still another source, he would not have had enough to pay his expenses. The difference was made up by an NYA job as a laboratory assistant in the Department of Natural History.[4] A student at Vanderbilt University was able to pay for his education by the combination of a scholarship, summer work, $300 in loans from the student loan fund, and an NYA job. These illustrations could be multiplied many times. In most institutions, NYA assistance is under the direction of the same officials who handle other student aid funds, including the parceling out of part-time jobs. In many cases the fitting and joining and penny-by-penny calculation which college personnel officials put into the allocation of aid to needy students would excite the admiration of an efficiency engineer.

Almost one-third of the students receiving NYA college aid are from families with annual incomes of $999 or less. Three-fourths are from families having annual incomes of

---

[4] This student has had a grade average of 4.8, 5.0 being the highest grade attainable.

$1999 or less. About 16 per cent. are from families whose incomes are $2000 or more, and for 8.2 per cent. the size of the family income is unknown. More than 55 per cent. are from families containing five or more persons, and more than 34 per cent. are from families of six or more. Three out of five are boys. Negroes and other racial minorities make up 5.8 per cent.[5]

By grade in college, NYA students are distributed as follows[6]:

				Post-	
Freshman	*Sophomore*	*Junior*	*Senior*	*Graduate*	*Unknown*
29.0	28.8	20.4	17.0	2.9	1.9

It is not literally true that every student who is receiving NYA aid could not enter or remain in college without NYA aid. In a great majority of cases, these students would be unable to obtain a college education without work or other assistance of some kind. Most students who must earn part or all of their expenses prefer NYA work to other work because the hours of work are usually adjusted to their college schedules, and because the NYA jobs are more interesting or more valuable educationally or, in some instances, easier. If their applications for NYA aid are disapproved, they may fall back on other part-time jobs. By the same token, the introduction of NYA work projects has freed many part-time jobs in the college or the community for other students. There are no jobs going begging around colleges. In a small but unknown percentage of cases, NYA aid may be given to students whose parents could afford to pay a larger share of their expenses. In some instances, faculty members have pulled wires

---

[5] From a survey of all recipients of student aid made in December 1937. For tables showing distribution by size of family, family income, and occupation of head of family, see Appendix IX.

[6] In December 1937.

to obtain particular students for NYA research and departmental projects, possibly at the expense of needier students. Unless they live at home or receive substantial scholarships, NYA-aided students at private colleges in many cases probably could afford to attend State universities without NYA aid. In some State universities there was criticism of the granting of NYA aid to students belonging to fraternities or sororities. Today in most institutions students accepting the financial obligations which sororities and fraternities demand are automatically excluded from consideration for NYA aid.

At Ohio State University, 1252 students on the NYA program were asked if they knew of any students receiving NYA assistance who did not really need it. Answering anonymously, 927, or 74.0 per cent., said that they knew of no such students. One hundred and fifty-five, or 12.4 per cent., checked the word "doubtful." Eighty-three, or 6.6 per cent., gave no answer, and 7.0 per cent. answered in the affirmative. Of these same students, almost two-thirds said that they themselves could not return to college the following year without NYA assistance, and almost one-third said their return would be doubtful. Only 54, or 4.3 per cent., said that they could return or failed to answer the question.[7]

There is no reason to doubt that, on the whole, NYA college and graduate aid has been going to students who need it. It may be questioned, however, whether NYA aid should be granted to high-tuition institutions except to supplement substantial scholarships, or to help students who, because they live at home, can attend these institutions at less expense than they can go elsewhere, or in the rare cases in which it may help a graduate student of unusual endowments to work with particular equipment or teachers.

[7] W. H. Cowley: *A Study of NYA Projects at Ohio State University*. P. 19. Mimeograph, National Youth Administration, 1937.

COLLEGE AID WORK PROJECTS

Devising suitable work projects for NYA students has been a challenge to the ingenuity of college authorities. At the outset many of the work projects undoubtedly were routine in character or were frivolous "boondoggling" or were hardly more than camouflage. Even yet at some institutions many of the work projects probably are not of high quality and are taken lightly by students.

Repeated inspections by NYA officials and the descriptions of student work projects submitted to Washington indicate, however, that, as a rule, NYA-aided students perform useful work for the money they receive.

A sampling of more than 7000 college aid recipients in 338 colleges in April 1937 showed the following distribution of youth according to type of work activity:

	Per cent.
Research, surveys, statistics, etc.	21.4
Community service	20.5
Ground and building maintenance	16.3
Departmental service	9.0
Library service	8.3
Clerical assistants	7.4
Laboratory assistants	4.0
Home economics	2.8
Construction	1.9
Recreation and education	1.5
Reproduction (photography, printing, etc.)	1.3
Art and dramatics	1.2
Tutorial services	1.1
Janitorial services	0.9
Miscellaneous	2.4

The research, survey, and statistical projects cover a range

as wide as the frontiers of human knowledge. Examples selected at random include: experiments in the development
of new ceramic glazes; soil research; the preparation of local
and State historical studies; transcription of legal debates in
foreign countries; the editing and indexing of old manu-
scripts; the study of building illumination; research in cellular
metabolism; the preparation of topographical atlases and of
charts and other devices for instructional use; research into an
immense variety of economic and sociological subjects. At the
University of Minnesota, an NYA study of fish scales probably
will lead to radical changes in the methods of fish-feeding and
-stocking.

Departmental service includes the preparation of supplementary teaching material, the compilation of guides and
bibliographies, the arrangement of exhibits, the construction
of models and technical equipment, the scoring of tests, and
the grading of examination papers.

Library and clerical projects include book repair, catalogu-
ing, the extension of the hours during which the libraries are
open; stenography, typing, filing, and duplicating.

Community service includes the direction of play activities
on public playgrounds; assisting in public libraries, public
nursery schools, city health departments, and other government agencies; and work with quasi-public agencies of many
kinds.

Grounds and building maintenance and construction include landscaping and terracing; the remodeling of buildings;
the building of swimming pools, sidewalks, and retaining
walls; and the repair of furniture and windows. At the University of Nebraska 12 NYA students built an observatory on
a revolving base.

The supervision of all student work projects is either provided or arranged for by the educational institutions themselves. Most campus projects are under the direct supervision

of faculty members or maintenance officials. The Federal Government contributes nothing to either supervision or the cost of materials.

A certain percentage of these projects represents work that should be paid for out of regular college budgets—but which is not, owing to inadequate appropriations by State legislatures or reduced income from endowment funds. A great majority appear to meet the NYA requirement that in so far as possible the work projects should have educational value to the students. Many amount to small research fellowships and departmental assistantships.

In response to anonymous questionnaires in the Ohio State University survey, 88.9 per cent. of the NYA students expressed the opinion that NYA work was educationally valuable to them. More than 52 per cent. reported that their academic work had been helped by their NYA activities. Nearly 63 per cent. said that their NYA work was related to the courses they were taking. And more than 60 per cent. said that their NYA work seemed to them to be as valuable as the taking of a university course.

Of these same students, 89.8 per cent. felt the work they were doing was valuable enough to justify the expenditure of Government money. And 89 per cent. thought that the standards of work required of them were as high as private employers would expect. The individuals who conducted this survey concluded that 177 of the 530 projects investigated had very high social utility, 200 high social utility, 118 medium social utility, 31 low social utility, and 4 very low social utility. They concluded that 203 of the projects were very well supervised, 227 were well supervised, 71 were supervised in a mediocre fashion, 27 were poorly supervised, and 2 were very poorly supervised.[8]

Many educators feel that self-supporting students often are

---

[8] Ibid., pp. 113–6.

so handicapped by the drain on their energy and time that they cannot obtain full value from their college work. For at least two reasons most of the NYA work projects are less open to criticism on this score than are the usual types of part-time work done by students: first, because they have educational value and, second, because the hours and conditions of work usually are arranged with regard for the health and efficiency of the student.

College faculties generally consider the NYA student work projects of value to them, frequently of immense value. NYA students relieve some faculty members of part of their routine duties and frequently are of positive aid also in enabling faculty members to undertake research projects and special studies.[9]

The NYA college aid program has had some unforeseen incidental results. Several college administrators have reported that devising and supervising NYA projects has jostled some faculty members out of ruts, reinvigorated their imaginations, revived their ambition to do research and special studies, and brought them into closer and more harmonious relations with their students. Some institutions report that the NYA program has led generally to a better understanding between faculty members and their students.[10]

Although there is little definite information on the point, many college officials think that the employability of NYA

---

[9] In a questionnaire sent out in February 1938 by Charles W. Taussig, Chairman of the NYA National Advisory Committee, this question was asked: "To what extent has the work performed by NYA students been helpful to the faculty?" All 52 institutions that responded indicated that the work had been of help to faculty members. Many said "decidedly" or "extremely" or "enormously" or "invaluable."

[10] Of 52 institutions that responded to a question on this point in Mr. Taussig's questionnaire, 37 expressed the opinion that the NYA program had improved the relations between the faculty and the student body generally. Others said that it had improved the relations of the faculty to the particular students on NYA. Of the few who answered in the negative, nearly all indicated that they thought the relations of their faculty to their students had been all that could be desired prior to the NYA program. In general, the more decidedly positive answers came from the larger institutions.

students has been improved by their work experience on NYA projects.[11] Many employers, of course, are attracted to youth who have shown their energy or ambition by working their way through college. Perhaps especially for youth preparing to enter various professions, their NYA work often has definite occupational value. In general, these part-time jobs may serve to narrow the gap between school and work, which many progressive educators feel is far too wide.

Caliber of NYA Students

Information as to the scholastic standing of NYA students was collected in 1935–36 from 270 colleges in 31 States.

One hundred and sixty-eight reported that, on the average, NYA students made higher grades than non-NYA students.

Seventy-one reported that there was no essential difference, on the average, in the grades of NYA and non-NYA students.

Thirty-one reported that, on the average, NYA students made lower grades than non-NYA students.

Thus, in less than 12 per cent. of these institutions had the addition of NYA students lowered the scholastic average of the undergraduate body. As these reports were in average figures, it may be presumed that even in these institutions there were some NYA students of greater ability than many of the non-NYA students.

That NYA has helped many young people of superior ability to obtain college educations is strikingly indicated by more detailed data from several institutions. At the University of Illinois high scholastic standing is recognized by honor rolls

---

[11] Opinions on this point given in answer to Mr. Taussig's questionnaire were too general and varied to be classified. A substantial majority were to the effect that the NYA work experience either did or should increase employability. Many responses were marked "no data" unaccompanied by an expression of opinion.

for each class and by the special "Bronze Tablet" of seniors being graduated with high honors. The following table shows the percentages of NYA students who qualified for these honors, compared with the percentages of other students:

| | 1935–36 | | 1936–37 | |
	Honor Roll	Bronze Tablet	Honor Roll	Bronze Tablet
NYA Students	13.8	0.98	14.9	0.78
Other Students	9.0	0.49	8.8	0.23

During 1935–36, the average grade of NYA students was 3.58, while that of all other students was 3.32 (5.0 being the highest grade attainable).[12]

At Ohio State University, NYA youth were found to be "intellectually a superior group." In 1936–37, 40 per cent. of them were in the top 10 per cent. of the undergraduate body in intelligence rating. The average intelligence percentile of the entire group was more than 76. All but 10.5 per cent. of these NYA youth were making grades above the average of students who graduate from Ohio State University.[13]

Ten of the 18 seniors elected to Phi Beta Kappa at Miami University, Oxford, Ohio, in the spring of 1938 were or had been NYA students. Two of them already had been awarded scholarships in graduate institutions. The scholarship average of all NYA students in this institution (approximately 300) was 2.83. The fraternity that won a scholarship cup had an average of 2.55, and the sorority that won a similar honor had an average of 2.58.

At the State College of Washington, during the first semester of 1937–38, 17.2 per cent. of NYA students made the all-college honor roll, which contained 12 per cent. of all students enrolled in the college.

---

[12] Letter from H. B. Johnston, Secretary, University Student Relief Committee, University of Illinois.
[13] W. H. Cowley, etc., *supra*.

Of the NYA students attending the University of Minnesota during 1935–36, 35 per cent. had come from the top 10 per cent. of their high school graduating classes and 92 per cent. had come from the upper half.[14]

A study of the freshman-year work of a large section of the class that entered the University of Minnesota in the fall of 1935 brought out significant data concerning the comparative scholastic achievements of various groups. The following table shows the percentages of NYA students, other self-supporting students, dormitory students, and sorority and fraternity pledges who achieved honors and a C-average or better[15]:

	NYA	Other Workers	Dormitory	Sorority and Fraternity
Honors	15.69	13.1	11.5	5.2
C-Average	61.3	38.0	50.0	42.2

In addition to their NYA work, the NYA students carried a larger number of hours of classroom work, on the average, than did any of the other groups.

NYA has brought a college education within the reach not only of many superior students but of some whose abilities may properly be called exceptional. In February 1938 institutions forming a cross-section of all those participating were asked: "Are there any instances . . . where NYA has enabled a student of exceptional ability in some line to attend your institution?" Of the 52 institutions replying, 43 replied in the affirmative. Of the nine that gave negative or qualified answers, six are privately controlled institutions where the NYA aid can meet only a small part of the cost of attendance. Of these six, however, five reported that while NYA aid is too small to

---

[14] Alvin C. Eurich and James E. Wert: *Applicants for Federal Aid at Minnesota Colleges.* P. 36. University of Minnesota, 1937.
[15] J. B. Johnston, Dean of College of Science, Literature and the Arts, University of Minnesota. Faculty Letter, March 1, 1937. Mimeographed.

enable students to enter, it is being used in many instances to supplement the scholarships or personal resources of students of high ability.

Fifty of these institutions sent in information concerning individual students who were receiving or had received NYA college aid. Here are a few examples of NYA-aided students of superior or exceptional ability[16]:

James R——, 23 years of age, had neither parents nor other close relatives to help him. Ambitious to become a criminologist, he is now enrolled in the College of Law of the University of Illinois and works on an NYA project in the Sociology Department. "It is known that he spent about the first two weeks of the semester (and before school started) sleeping in the park, in an empty house, and in one of the school buildings, with nothing to keep him warm except a dog which is his constant companion. We were finally able to locate a room job for this boy and with the aid of the NYA he has been able to pay his fees, buy his books, and pay incidental expenses. There is no doubt that he would not have been able even to start the semester if he had not had some assurance that he would receive the job which he held last year and upon which

---

[16] The questions asked in this part of Mr. Taussig's questionnaire were: "Are there any instances . . . where NYA has enabled a student of exceptional ability in some line to attend your institution? If you know of any such individual students, would you please give one or two brief case histories? In order to obtain a cross-section picture of the average NYA student, would you please submit three or four average NYA Student Aid case histories?"

Some responses interpreted "exceptional" more strictly than others. As a result, many of the "average" cases seemed to indicate greater ability than some of the cases marked "exceptional." The examples given here are drawn from both lists, primarily with a view to giving representation to various kinds of institutions in various parts of the country. Excepting four or five extraordinary cases, we could have chosen from 50 to 100 others just as interesting and just as indicative of superior ability from examples sent in by these 50 institutions, representing only about 3 per cent. of all participating in the college aid program. Quotation marks indicate matter taken verbatim from the responses of college officials. Where full names are printed, they are genuine. Otherwise fictional first names are used to indicate sex.

he is doing excellent work." His scholastic record for his university career is "about a 5.00 average" (5.00 being the highest grade attainable).

Kay Wilson was the winner of the national poultry judging contest at the Chicago Livestock Exposition, 1937, winner of the 4-H Club State oratorical contest, runner-up in the American Legion State oratorical contest, and an excellent high school student. His parents, farmers in the drought section, were unable to give him any financial help. He worked in the harvest field during the summer months, without a shirt—so intent on saving his earnings in order to go to college that he would not spend the money for one. An NYA work-scholarship for the maximum of $20 a month enabled him to attend Oklahoma Agricultural and Mechanical College, where he has become an "outstanding leader." More than 25 other boys and girls who had proved their merit as prize-winners in agricultural competitions of the 4-H Clubs and Future Farmers of America have been enabled to attend this college by NYA student aid. Among them is the State president of the Future Farmers of America, who had been forced to withdraw from the college by family financial reverses.

Betty B—— was enabled to enter East Central Junior College, Decatur, Mississippi, by NYA aid. She worked as an accompanist for physical education and dancing classes and majored in music. At the end of two years she was awarded a scholarship to a State college. "They report to us that she is the best student of music ever to attend school there." After one year in a CCC camp, Warren J——, from a very low income family, entered this same junior college with NYA aid. He finished with honors and was immediately granted a scholarship at Millsaps College. Ellen B——, valedictorian of her high school class, came from an extremely poor family. NYA aid enabled her to complete two years at this college. She finished with the highest honors. A local civic club provided her with a scholarship to the State College for Women, where she is also finishing her education with the aid of an NYA job. "As a result she will be able to teach and help educate her very intelligent sister who is with us this year earning her entire expenses through the NYA."

Benito S—— came to the United States in 1929, acquiring American citizenship by virtue of the fact that his father, who was already here, was a citizen. While working as a shoemaker in Trenton he gained a high school education in a night school. He worked his way through Rutgers through NYA, work in a local shoe repair shop, waiting on tables, and other odd jobs. He completed his college course in three instead of the usual four years and was prominent in many undergraduate activities. His objective is a university professorship in Romance languages. "Truly a man of rare promise." Henry H—— is going through Rutgers with the aid of a State scholarship, an NYA job in the ceramics department, and money saved from his previous employment as a color matcher in a large chemical concern. "His experiments with a new ceramic green are likely to add much to the knowledge of ceramic colors."

Joseph P——, a Polish-American boy from Duluth, whose father earned about $80 a month, showed exceptional ability in mathematics in high school and junior college. Federal aid enabled him to continue his studies at the University of Minnesota. On his own initiative he had read in the field of mathematics far beyond the level of the ordinary college graduate majoring in mathematics. He was assigned as an NYA research assistant to a professor of mathematics. His work was described as "astonishing." On graduation, he was awarded a fellowship at Princeton.

Leigh Gerdin was entirely dependent on his own earning capacity to obtain a college education. (His mother was a widow with a small income and two younger children in school.) At the age of 17, he entered the University of North Dakota. For four years he paid all his expenses by working for board and room and for NYA. Carrying a scholastic load heavier than average, he made A grades (except for eight semester hours of B) throughout his college course. In addition, he practiced on the piano two hours a day and composed several numbers which have been used by orchestras and choirs. In the spring of 1938 he was elected to a Rhodes Scholarship in competition with youth from six States.

After completing four years as a radio operator in the United States Navy, Homer B—— wanted a more thorough technical education. Promised NYA aid, he entered the Georgia School of Technology. He was soon transferred from NYA to the regular pay-roll of the institution as a part-time instructor. At Georgia "Tech," a barber's son, whose NYA job is enabling him to obtain technical training, is at the head of his class scholastically.

Andrew R——, one of ten children, came to Vanderbilt University five years ago on a football scholarship. His grades were so high that he was awarded an academic scholarship for the next three years. Lacking other resources, he had to earn additional money. For three years he was helped by FERA and NYA college aid. This young man was so remarkable that he gave up his college football career to concentrate on a course "more nearly suited to his ideals for the future." He was elected president of the senior class and "was in every way one of the school's most able and admirable students." On graduation, he was immediately employed by a bank in one of the larger Southern cities.

Twin brothers, both Phi Beta Kappa students, have been attending Duke University for three years. The university has given them considerable scholarship, loan, and employment aid. But as they are almost entirely on their own, they need also their NYA jobs, which are in the college library. "In all probability, should they desire to take training and equip themselves to be professional librarians, their services would be in demand here."

Hiroto ——, an American-born Japanese, was valedictorian of his high school class in a town in the Pacific Northwest. He was so well thought of by his schoolmates that he was elected president of the student body and editor of the high school paper. The eldest of nine children, he was also the chief breadwinner of the family. With NYA assistance he is attending the State College of Washington, where he is making an excellent record.

Mabel J——'s father was on WPA. With NYA aid she was able to enter Butler University, in Indianapolis, her home city. She completed the requirements for the two-year teacher's certificate and, after a short trial, was assigned as a regular teacher in the city schools. As a result of her earnings, the family is now off relief. "A talented young woman, gifted as a teacher, who would never have had her worth brought to light had it not been for NYA."

Mary H—— was chosen for a $400 scholarship at Connecticut College. As her father could give her little help, she had to earn money to take advantage of the scholarship. She worked as a waitress in the college dining hall, made $200 last year as a correspondent for a metropolitan newspaper, and was employed on an NYA project, while carrying full-time academic work. Scholastically she stands at the head of her class.

Amy S——, valedictorian of her high school class of 175 students, is the daughter of a rug-cleaner who is irregularly employed. With the aid of scholarships and NYA she is attending Cornell University. At the end of her junior year she ranked eighth in her class. In recommending her for a position one professor stated that he doubted whether any girl better in bacteriology than she could be found in the United States. John W——, one of eight children in the family of a small farmer in the South, completed an agricultural course at his State college with an A average. NYA assistance enabled him to go to Cornell for graduate study. Within four months the quality of his work had so impressed the Agronomy Department that he was appointed to an assistantship in soil technology and taken off the NYA rolls. Another student, son of an artesian well driller with four children, was transferred from the NYA rolls to a teaching position six months after he had begun graduate work at Cornell. A third was promoted from NYA to an assistantship while still a senior.

Calvin B——'s outstanding high school record won for him two scholarship awards, totaling $350 a year, from the University of Vermont. As this university has a $300 annual tuition fee and his family could give him little help, he could not have accepted the scholarships if he had not been able to obtain NYA college aid for nearly the maximum amount. He lives with a semi-co-operative group where he gets his board for $3.15 a week and room rent for 50 cents a week, and is credited with $2.00 a week for janitor work. For three years he has made a high scholastic record in the Engineering College. At the University of Vermont are several other students who have won scholarships but could not have accepted them without the opportunity to earn the rest of their expenses.

For many years before he entered college, Harold B—— had been intensely interested in botany. His collection of fungus specimens included one which, so far as is known, had never been found before in the United States. Lacking funds to attend college, he did post-graduate work in high school, exhausting all the material and books that were accessible. NYA aid enabled him to enter the Kansas State College of Agriculture and Applied Science, where he was assigned as a laboratory assistant in the department of botany. Lloyd R—— went through Kansas State College with Federal aid, making an exceptional record both academically and in campus activities. On graduation he was given a fellowship in the Department of Agronomy of the University of Wisconsin.

Nathan I—— was assigned to an NYA out-of-school work project in Boston, in January 1936. Vocational tests showed that he had "very keen intelligence, extremely high mechanical ability, high finger dexterity and a fair ability to handle small tools." One day he brought in some blue prints of his own mechanical inventions. The supervisor arranged for his assignment to a trial job in the physics laboratory of Northeastern University. He showed such ability that the University granted him a scholarship in its Engineering School, where he is regarded as a man of "great promise."

At the University of Maine, Vergil S——, a senior who worked for NYA for four years, was the highest ranking man in the mechanical engineering group in 1937–38. Walter M——, a junior in the College of Agriculture, on the NYA program for three years, has done work on insect life which "has attracted the attention of several outstanding authorities."

Mary F—— entered Lawrence College, Appleton, Wisconsin, in 1933 and made a brilliant record. Because of her father's illness she had to leave college to contribute to the family's support. After his death, she was able to return with the assistance of an NYA job, and "is finishing this year with one of the most outstanding records we have ever had." George F——, son of a post office janitor with a large family, has worked his way through Lawrence College by summer work, NYA aid, and odd jobs. "A fine academic record" and "an unusually fine character."

At Tuskegee Institute every student who lives on the campus is required to work for at least one-half of his tuition. Only superior students are allowed to do enough work to pay for more than the cost of tuition. NYA jobs are used to supplement those regularly available. Helen D—— is the fourth of six children of a common laborer with a yearly income of approximately $450. When she finished high school, she was dependent on herself for further education. She developed a talent in making ceramics. Impressed by samples of her work, Tuskegee accepted her. She and another Negro girl on NYA have been experimenting with native clays and quartzes in the Department of Ceramics. On graduation they hope to operate a pottery department in some school or to start a ceramic business for themselves. At Tuskegee, the Agricultural Research and Experiment Station, headed by the celebrated Negro scientist, Dr. George W. Carver, is operated entirely on NYA funds for student labor.

To balance these examples of students of superior promise, we shall give thumbnail sketches of NYA students whom college officials consider "average" in ability:

Washington University, St. Louis: (A) Parents dead. No legal guardian. She pays grandmother $4.00 a week for board, room, and laundry. While working learned stenography at business school. Saved enough to finish education, with NYA aid. (B) Father a street car motorman. Finished in upper third of his high school class. NYA aid for four years. Work with St. Louis office of Red Cross has interested him in social work.

University of Wyoming: (A) Orphan. Ward of State until 21. (B) Son of carpenter earning about $700 last year. Intelligence percentile rank of 85. Studying to be engineer.

Southern Methodist University: (A) Son of widow who is not self-supporting. "Creditable work" in Engineering School. (B) Daughter of widow. Studying to be a music teacher. (C) Father has five dependents and $1000 annual salary. Boy worked for 18 months in café to save money to enter college. Making good record.

Goucher College, Baltimore, Maryland: (A) and (B) Daughters of minister with poor congregation. Family savings lost during depression. College gives scholarships and loans, which girls supplement by summer work, caring for children, and NYA jobs. Average students, active in undergraduate and church affairs. (C) Given board and lodging by friend. No aid from home. Helped by scholarships and loans. Summer work, secretarial work for member of faculty, and NYA job provide money for rest of expenses. Academic work above average. An expert stenographer. Should be self-supporting when she graduates.

Montana School of Mines, Butte: (A) Parents failed on two-acre ranch about eight miles from Butte and are now on WPA. His $10 a month from NYA gives him daily transportation to and from college. (B) Father dead. Poor surroundings. On his own. On NYA for two years. Good football player. (C) Eastern boy. On income of about $2000, parents trying to keep him in mining school and another son in Princeton. His ardent plea for assistance was rewarded with $10 a month NYA job when he made one of the two "straight A" records in the first semester of 1937–38.

Massachusetts Institute of Technology: (A) From Middle West. One of family of eight with total income of $1620. No help from home. Because good student, receives entire tuition from scholarships or loan. Has job providing meals. NYA aid meets nearly all of remaining necessary expenses. (B) First year student, age 23, had saved $600 from previous earnings to meet $500 tuition fee and part of incidentals. Lives at home. NYA job makes up balance.

Fairmont State Teachers College, West Virginia: (A) From very large underprivileged family in mountainous interior county. He arrived with one outfit of clothing. "Will leave the institution in time with much better adjustments to life and its problems." (B) Italian-American boy from mining town. Football captain.

University of Kentucky: (A) Father an epileptic. Good record in the university. Graduated last June. Employed by a large oil company. (B) Reared on the streets. Citizens of town helped to send him here. For three years, NYA has been his main support. Scholarship record not high, but his improvement has been pronounced. (C) Fine boy but poor. Aided two years by NYA. Last September entered Annapolis. (D) Son of man on direct relief. At end of first week had operation for appendicitis. With this handicap he has passed all his subjects with fair standing. (E) One of eight children. Family income low. Graduating from Law School this June. (F) Family impoverished by depression. Boy very ambitious and worthy. "One of our best NYA workers, making a fine record in every way."

The superior quality of NYA students in so many institutions is due in the first place to the opportunity for selection which college and university officials have. Every year from two to three times as many youth have applied for NYA college aid as could be appointed. In some States the ratio of applicants to appointees has been almost four to one, and at a few individual institutions it has been even greater. The average of ability is pulled up still higher by the use of NYA aid by many institutions to supplement scholarships. Some of the participating institutions attract a smaller number of promising youth. Some are extremely specialized; some are controlled by minor religious denominations; some are generally of low standard; some are high-tuition colleges with severely restricted enrollments. Other institutions are able to assist a larger number of promising students out of their own funds or through jobs in the communities in which they are situated. At a few colleges the selection of students for NYA aid, as well as the organization of the work program, probably is in the hands of slipshod or narrow-visioned officials. These various special factors probably account for the fact that in a minority of institutions NYA students, on the average, make a poorer academic record than the general run of students. In addition, individual officials and teachers in a few of the participating colleges are reported to regard NYA college aid as a kind of alms. Although intended only for students who otherwise would be unable to attend college, NYA college aid is not charity, but a work program, and as such it apparently is regarded by most higher educational institutions in the country. Because of the high caliber of so many NYA students, these work-scholarships have come to be regarded widely as an honor.

The underlying reason that most institutions are able to choose superior youths, on the average, for NYA aid is, of course, the fact that the distribution of brains in the country bears no relation to the distribution of income. That the American plutocracy has failed to develop into anything resembling an aristocracy of intelligence and culture is too well known to require argument. It is doubtful whether the upper- and middle-class groups, as a whole, have succeeded much better in that direction, although their average is raised perhaps by the inclusion of the professional classes.[17]

---

[17] Interesting data on this point come from a study of first-year scholarship at the University of Minnesota from 1931 to 1935. The students were classified in eleven groups according to the occupations of their fathers. At the top in scholarship stood the sons and daughters of clergymen and teachers and of other professional men. They were followed by the children of business men, laborers, clerical workers, and artisans. In the first six groups, therefore, there were only two classes that are in the higher economic levels: professional and business. Following these six came the children of the financial, salesmen, and farmer groupings. The tenth and next-to-bottom group consisted of the children of street car conductors, janitors, policemen, and domestic servants. These first ten groups were closely graduated, and some of them shifted up or down the scale according to the different methods used of rating scholastic achieve-

As a depression measure, NYA aid to college and graduate students probably would have been considered justified if it had kept off the labor market and usefully occupied at such small cost to the Federal Government youth capable of meeting minimum academic requirements. To a degree that was probably anticipated by no one, it has made a higher education possible for many youth of decidedly superior abilities, whose future contributions to the nation may be of incalculable value. It has made college training possible also for tens of thousands of youth, who, while they may lack unusual intellectual capacities, are of a character to become solid and useful citizens, able, as one educator expressed it, "to pull their full load in the world's work."

In the words of one distinguished educator, the NYA college aid program "has furnished experimental evidence far beyond that previously available that there are many young people having a high order of college ability who are unable to go to college for want of money."[18]

"It has done not only a great material good, but it has actually contributed to the intellectual and spiritual values of the nation," Robert E. Rienow, Dean of Men at the University of Iowa, has written of the NYA college aid program. "When the time comes that a boy or girl of great promise must feel that he is denied the opportunities of a college training because of his economic circumstances, our educational system has failed—and when that fails, democracy is destroyed."[19]

---

ment. Separated from these ten by a large gap on every measurement used was the eleventh group. It consisted of the children of owners and executives of factories. Dean J. B. Johnston, supra.

[18] Dean J. B. Johnston, supra.

[19] The Iowa Student Aid Program of the National Youth Administration. Mimeographed. Des Moines. May 1937.

School Aid

In the fall of 1935, NYA instituted a Nation-wide program of aid to needy school students 16 years of age or older. The main features of school aid were copied from the already-tested college aid, but the maximum monthly payment to any individual student was fixed at $6.00. It is supposed that the student lives at home. Federal money is intended to provide only for books, clothes, carfare, and other essential expenses of remaining in school.

Since the turn of the century, attendance at secondary schools has increased almost ninefold. During the early years of the depression certain special influences tended to accelerate the rate of growth of high school enrollments. The supply of jobs was decreasing. Stay-in-school drives were initiated. In 1933, NRA codes prohibiting the employment of youths under 16 at least temporarily barred many avenues of employment to younger workers. Between 1930 and 1932, high school enrollments for the country as a whole increased 17 per cent. Between 1932 and 1934 they increased another '10 per cent. Almost 6,000,000 boys and girls, approximately 62 per cent. of the population of high school age, are now attending public and private high schools. In 1937, the number of high school graduates in a single year passed the one-million mark for the first time. Yet there remain hundreds of thousands of students of high school age who are neither working nor in school. Many of these dropped out of school only because they lacked a few dollars a year for shoes, clothes, books, street carfare, and necessary incidental expenses. Supplying these few dollars obviously was the least expensive, and possibly the most useful, way of taking some of these young people off the labor market. At first an attempt was made to restrict this aid to youth from families on relief. But it quickly became apparent that many youth in families just above the relief level were just as badly in need of a little help in remaining in high school. Aid has been restricted, however, to young people who have passed their sixteenth birthdays.

The program is open to all non-profit-making and tax-exempt bona fide educational institutions that do not require a high school diploma or its equivalent for entrance. As in the colleges, the educational institutions themselves receive, and approve or reject, the applications for student aid and supervise or arrange the work projects.

During the first year, school aid funds were allocated on the basis of 7 per cent. of the youth relief population of each State. Since then the formula has been varied and flexible. For 1937–38, school aid was based on 10 per cent. of the total 1936 enrollment, with supplementary amounts for areas or localities in greatest need. As on the college aid program, many institutions spread these funds among more students by holding individual monthly payments below the maximums set by NYA. In some high schools in the South, the average individual monthly earning has been held to $2.00 or less.

In number of youth enrolled, school aid has been the largest division of the entire NYA program. Also it has been the cheapest division.

The following table gives the statistical high lights of the school aid program during the last three school years[20]:

	1935–36	1936–37	1937–38
No. of institutions	18,023	22,801	23,792
No. of students aided	275,544	297,871	218,871
Average wage	$5.45	$4.89	$4.40

Two-thirds of the students aided are in the junior and senior years of high school. A few are post-graduates. At the

[20] The 1935–36 and 1936–37 figures are for April, the peak month of each of these years. For 1937–38, February 1938 is the month used.

other extreme a few are youth of 16 or over who are still in grade school. For December 1937, the distribution of NYA-aided students by grades was:

7th or lower	8th	9th	10th	11th	12th	Post-Graduate
3,370	6,334	21,648	42,421	71,771	75,524	1,659

A child who has entered the first grade at the age of six and who has advanced one full grade every year should be in the eleventh grade at the age of 16. Two-thirds of the greatly retarded pupils shown in the eighth grade or lower in this table are in the Southern States. This area accounts also for a disproportionately large percentage of the ninth and tenth grade pupils receiving student aid.

Of these NYA-aided school students, almost three-fourths were from families having an annual income of $999 a year or less, and almost 40 per cent. were from families having an annual income of $499 or less. More than half were from families of six or more members. More than half were from families that had been on relief at some time during the years 1933–37.[21]

On the average, NYA school aid reaches a lower economic group than is reached by NYA college and graduate aid. This is readily understandable. Millions of families who cannot afford to send their children to college can afford the relatively small expense of keeping them in public high schools. Usually the cost of high school education is beyond the means only of those who are chronically in the lowest-income groups, or who have modest incomes but exceptionally large families, or who have been struck by such disasters as floods, droughts, and economic depressions.

At the outset many educators and many NYA officials

---

[21] Based on survey of all youth receiving student aid in December 1937. For tables showing distribution of these youth by size of family, size of family income, and occupation of head of family, see Appendix IX.

doubted the wisdom of making school aid a work program. The payments to be made were so small that only a few hours' work a month could be demanded of any individual student. There was considerable skepticism as to the willingness or ability of many high schools to develop suitable work projects. Many responsible persons felt that it would be better for the morale of the students themselves to make outright cash grants rather than to risk giving them false ideas of proper work standards through a poor program. At a few schools, NYA aid was temporarily given in the form of outright cash payments. Undoubtedly many high schools were slow in devising suitable work programs, and some may not have done so yet. But NYA State directors and their assistants have given much time to inspecting school aid work programs and to co-operating with high school administrators and teachers in improving them. As on the college aid program, the aim is to devise work that is educationally valuable to the youth who perform it in addition to being useful to the school or community. In the country as a whole the average hourly wage paid on school aid work projects is 24 cents (1936–37). Within wide range of hourly wages and monthly payments, 20 hours' work a month or five hours a week may be considered the norm for the amount of work expected from an NYA-aided student.

Many NYA high school students, thousands in the country as a whole, are assisting teachers in sorting and grading papers, and in coaching backward pupils. Some are giving clerical assistance in school offices. Some have been made into school librarians. Squeezed between restricted budgets and still-increasing enrollments, many high school teachers and administrators have found this sort of assistance of immense value.

Thousands of NYA high school students are engaged in beautifying school grounds and developing school playgrounds and athletic fields. Some are making furniture and classroom equipment. Some are doing minor repairs to buildings. Many girls are assisting in school cafeterias. A few students are assisting in research and statistical work, although this type of activity is, of course, much less extensive than at the college level. Some are assigned as helpers to local public agencies. Many are doing such simple menial tasks as sweeping out schoolrooms and halls every day—for many smaller high schools have little or no money for janitor service.

Work projects picked at random from reports on the NYA high school program in Kansas, Missouri, Indiana, and Michigan include these:

One school bought an old railroad box-car; NYA students moved it to the athletic field and fixed it up as a field house, with dressing rooms and showers; they also made and installed storm windows on an old grade-school building. Music racks built for the entire high school orchestra. Basement built under the agriculture shop. Composition board installed on ceiling of the auditorium to improve the acoustics. School doctor assisted by the keeping of clinical records for all students. School busses cleaned, oiled, washed, and checked every Saturday. School grounds graded and planted with trees and shrubbery. School paper published. Library books repaired and rebound. School towels and domestic science linen laundered. Bookcases and bicycle racks built. NYA students in advanced class assisted slow freshmen. School lunchrooms organized for the first time, many students bringing vegetables, butter, milk, and eggs from their farm homes in exchange for warm lunch prepared and served by NYA girls. School stage rebuilt, scenery repainted, and new drapes and curtains hung. Thousands engaged in checking attendance, grading papers, filing papers, mimeographing, and otherwise relieving teachers of harassing details, with the result, one school principal said, that many teachers were able to work out new sets of notes for the first time in fifteen years. Skating rinks, tennis courts, baseball diamonds, and outdoor basketball courts built (by the score). Demonstration materials prepared for home economics laboratories and various science classes. School desks refinished. Play equipment made for public nursery schools. Flower beds planted and tended on school grounds.

These illustrations can do little more than suggest the scope of the work done by NYA-aided high school students.

In Tennessee, principals in smaller high schools favor the extension of janitor services and clerical assistance as work for their NYA students. Principals in the larger high schools give a high rating to instructional work. Campus beautification work ranks high in schools of all sizes, and repairs to buildings and equipment rank only a little lower. The principals of 304 high schools were asked whether as taxpayers and citizens they felt that the NYA student aid plan was justified. Answers of "yes," usually emphatically expressed, came from 292. Three answered "no." The other nine gave various qualified answers from "to a limited extent" to "I doubt it."[22]

Although it is reasonable to suppose that the work projects for NYA-aided high school students are not uniformly of a high standard, such evidence as is available indicates that as a rule these students are faithfully performing useful work. For many students these few hours of work each week are the first job. In those States where more or less comprehensive surveys have been made, many high school principals have spoken or written with evident pride of the sense of responsibility shown by most of their NYA-aided pupils. Some of these young people are receiving experience of vocational value. In some cases the records for ability and diligence they have made on these small part-times have helped them in finding private employment.

The benefits of the high school work program are not limited to the NYA students. They spread out in concentric circles. In most high schools by far the major part of the work done

---

[22] Gordon H. Turner: *Part Time Jobs for NYA Students in Tennessee High Schools.* Pp. 5–6. NYA Mimeograph, Nashville, Tenn., 1936.

results in benefits to all students. Some of it adds to the enduring physical assets of the schools. Some of it is of direct value to other groups in the community. In some cases, the NYA student manages to save enough from his small earnings to buy some food or clothing for other members of his family. Often, we were told by high school principals, NYA aid to one youth keeps another child in school—because the NYA student buys a pair of shoes for a younger brother or sister. Some high school principals have reported that work done by NYA students has set a stimulating example to other students, with the result that some of the latter ask for the privilege of assisting teachers or of helping without pay on other projects.

Some report instances in which NYA students have set about improving their home surroundings after learning how to plant and care for shrubs, trees, and flowers on campus-improvement projects.

In 1936 and early 1937, when the country was enjoying a moderate degree of economic improvement and the Federal Government was spending more generously on other forms of relief, NYA funds for aid to high school students were sufficient to take care of 75 per cent. of the applicants. Owing to economic recession and the curtailment of NYA funds for high school aid, only about 55 per cent. of those applying in the school year 1937–38 could be chosen. And the average amount of aid per individual diminished somewhat, because many schools spread the money extremely thin in the effort to help as many worthy but needy students as possible.

Such information as is available indicates that, in the country as a whole, NYA-aided high school students measure up to the average of all high school students in their scholastic work. Of 397 high schools which were taken as a sample in 1936–37, 169 rated the NYA students higher than other students in classroom work, 139 rated them lower, and 89 reported that there was no substantial difference. Most of these NYA-aided high school students have unusually underprivileged backgrounds. Many have come from extremely poor common schools. Some are returning to school for a second trial after dropping out, perhaps as much from lack of interest as from poverty. Considering all these factors, the scholastic showing indicated by this small sample is surprisingly high. Included in the averages undoubtedly are many youth of superior promise.

NYA school aid has enabled many tens of thousands of youth to take advantage of the schools built and maintained at considerable expense by local taxpayers. As with college aid, it has not only kept youth off the labor market but has helped to prepare them to become more useful citizens. A general education, or a combination of that with vocational training, in the secondary schools is coming to be regarded as the common right of every normal youth and as a basic national requirement. Already in some States more than 80 per cent. of all youth of high school age are enrolled in high school—in Utah more than 95 per cent. But in such States as Arkansas, Alabama, South Carolina, and Mississippi, barely one-third of youth of high school age are in high school. In many other States there are areas and occupational groups with such low incomes that even in "normal" times education at the secondary level would be beyond the reach of many youth. Indeed, many areas cannot afford to sustain even good common schools. NYA aid to high school students cannot, in itself, correct these inequalities. Yet for many economically handicapped young people, NYA aid has held open, and perhaps opened a degree wider, the door to equal educational opportunity.

CHAPTER IX

Challenge to Education

NYA WAS CREATED TO HELP SOME OF THE YOUTHFUL CASUAL-
ties of an economic depression. It has found that many of the
youth with whom it deals are also educational casualties.

The 500,000 young men and women, 18 to 25 years old, who
have been on the NYA out-of-school program in the last two
and a half years have on the average attained only eighth grade
education. Among all these youth, few have had any kind of
occupational training in school or in work. Most of them have
been so much crude labor poured onto an employment market already surfeited with crude labor. They are not prepared
for the making of a living in modern industrial society. Even if
it were running more nearly at capacity, our productive econ-
omy would have no place for so vast a number of unskilled
workers as are found now in the ranks of the unemployed. With
such business recovery as we had in 1935 and 1936, the demand
for trained workers in many lines could not be filled by the
millions of people who wanted jobs.

These unemployed out-of-school youth are no better prepared for simple subsistence on the land. Many are completely
ignorant of the home production skills with which past generations maintained more adequate standards of living with small
cash outlay. Some are strangers to such simple tools as the
hammer, the saw, and the chisel. Even among farm youth,
many know nothing about raising vegetables, fruits, poultry,
and livestock for home consumption. Far too many of the girls
have no more than a fragmentary knowledge of diet, the prepa-

ration and preservation of foods, sewing, child care, home hygiene, and other essentials of sound family living.

The more one sees of the NYA program for out-of-school youth and remembers that the youngest on this program are 18 years old, the more insistent becomes the question: "Where is the celebrated American school system? How does it happen that a large segment of the youth population of the country has failed to receive any adequate foundation for satisfactory adult living?" There is no single answer. Two of the answers, both revealing aspects of the inequality of educational opportunity, are essentially economic. First, some areas and communities lack schools which are passably good by any standard of measurement. Second, many children and youth do not have the economic means to take advantage of such school facilities as are available.

As we have traveled over the country, looking at NYA work projects, talking with NYA youth, with NYA supervisors and administrators, and with educators, we have been compelled to conclude that there are additional reasons why so many young people are so poorly educated. Again and again we were forced to ask ourselves these two questions: "Why do so many of these youth, who show such an avid interest in their NYA work, and even in spare-time courses of study, have such a distaste for the orthodox schools? And how much would these young people have benefited if they had continued to attend these regular schools?"

THE UNEQUAL DISTRIBUTION OF EDUCATION

The quality of schooling that a child receives depends largely on where he lives. Schools vary within States as well as from State to State. More than three-quarters of the money spent for education in the United States comes from the taxation of property. As a rule, rural areas have the smallest funds for schools and the highest ratio of children to adults. On the whole, rural areas are inferior to the cities in school buildings, equipment, and teachers. Often the rural school year is shorter.

In Arkansas, for example, most rural schools are open only six months a year and $30 to $40 a month is the average rural school teacher's salary. Low salaries for teachers are by no means confined to the South. We saw rural schools in Kansas, where, we were informed, the teachers received $40 a month. In three States the State-wide average annual compensation for teachers and principals was less than $600 in 1935–36; and in two the average length of the school year was less than 140 days, against a national average of 173 days.[1]

New York State's school expenditures for the year 1935–36 averaged $134.13 for each pupil in actual attendance and $95.08 for each child 5 to 17 years old. In the same year Arkansas spent $24.55 per actual pupil and $15.82 per child 5 to 17. Yet, in relation to its financial ability, Arkansas was spending more money per child than New York. Mississippi, the poorest of the 48 States, spent $20.13 per child of school age in 1935–36. Yet Mississippi was making more than twice the effort that New York was; if Mississippi had spent no more than New York in relation to its financial ability it would have spent less than $10 per child. In proportion to financial ability, every Southern State in 1935–36 was spending more per child on education than were such affluent States as Delaware, Nevada, New York, California, New Jersey, Massachusetts, Connecticut, Oregon, and Rhode Island.

In 1930 the farm population of the country as a whole received 9 per cent. of the national income but was responsible for the care and education of 31 per cent. of the nation's chil-

---

[1] These and other figures in this section on Unequal Distribution of Education are taken from Report of the Advisory Committee on Education, Government Printing Office, 1938.

dren. In the Southeastern region, the farmers had only 2 per cent. of the national income but they were responsible for the care and education of 4,250,000 children 5 to 17 years old, inclusive. At the other extreme, the non-farm population of the Northeast had 42 per cent. of the national income, but only 8,500,000 children to care for and educate.

This undemocratic inequality of educational opportunity can be corrected only with the assistance of the Federal Government. It is far beyond any means and purposes of NYA.

Inequality of educational opportunity is accentuated by the fact that many of the lowest-income families cannot afford to take advantage of existing school facilities.

Again and again in many States we heard the word "shoes" used as the equation for going to school.

"The children can get to school until it's snowtime. They can't go then unless they have shoes."

"If she gets some shoes, she'll be going regular this winter."

Underwear can be made from sugar sacks. Clothes can be patched and remade. Shoes seem the insurmountable obstacle to school attendance in many impoverished families.

"I bought a pair of shoes with my first NYA money," was the story we heard many times from girls or boys on the high school aid program.

The lowest-income groups of families have the largest numbers of children. When a whole family has a yearly cash income of $200 to $400, there simply is no money for transportation, books, or school supplies for high school. Furthermore, at the very first opportunity, the older children in the family must look for work to supplement the family income.

The NYA school aid program enables a considerable number of youth to remain in the regular schools by giving them the opportunity to earn small amounts of money to cover necessary incidental expenses. This type of aid is available only to youth 16 years of age or older. In some cases, these very modest earnings also keep younger brothers and sisters in the family in school. The NYA Resident Project throws another bridge across the chasm of educational inequality.

WHY ARE MANY BOYS AND GIRLS AVERSE TO SCHOOL?

Economic handicaps are not the only reason why so many of the young people on the NYA program have not gone on through high school.

Why do so many children and young people in school have distrust, even hate, for the place where they spend so many hours of their lives? Why do youth who have left school behind them, usually at far too early an age, look back with unpleasant memories on their lives within school walls? Why is it that in many cases NYA has found it difficult to get youth interested in a workshop, for example, in a school building, and comparatively easy to interest them if the workshop is situated anywhere else in town? Why is it that so many youth will come for related training courses much more readily to a youth center, a town hall, any place, than to a school?

"Would you go back to school if you could?" we asked a number of out-of-school NYA youth.

"Not regular school," was a frequent reply.

We wanted to know why.

"It's like prison."

"They treat you like babies."

"I got to make myself a living. I want to be an auto mechanic. What's French got to do with that?"

"I don't know. It's just so dead."

These youth sketched for us a picture of school as an isolated experience in their lives. Their studies in school seemed to them to have little relation to the realities facing them.

They frequently looked on teachers as warders. Schools

seem to have failed to "sell themselves" to their consumers, the pupils. Yet most of these same youth welcome learning when working on a building, in a carpentry shop, in a home-making unit. Numbers of them study willingly spelling, arithmetic, practical physics, nutrition, hygiene, and other subjects in NYA related training programs. Most of them evince no resentment against the discipline of the NYA foremen and supervisors. Why can NYA get this co-operation where the schools have failed?

THE WHITE-COLLAR COMPLEX

"Can you get this boy a job as a bricklayer?" a school teacher asked a Junior Placement office. "I think he's feebleminded."

This is an exaggeration, perhaps, of a general feeling that manual labor is degrading and that the boy or girl who works in an office is of a far superior caste. "The dignity of honest labor" has become a faint refrain (usually reserved for Labor Day orations).

We heard of one high school where 300 students were enrolled in typing and stenographic classes. In the county in which they were living only 42 stenographers were employed in all fields. If these youth migrate to larger population centers, they find intense competition, often with other young people more highly trained for this type of work.

In a study made in Cleveland, 90.3 per cent. of the pupils in the high schools were found to be enrolled in courses supposedly leading to white-collar and professional jobs; in that city 9.3 per cent. of the population is employed in this category of work.

In 1936, the Minnesota NYA gathered some pertinent information concerning 3170 out-of-school, unemployed young people, 16 to 24 years of age, from relief families. They averaged a ninth grade education.[2] Fifty-five came from families having monthly incomes of less than $25 each. Six hundred and sixty-five came from families with incomes of $25 to $50 a month; 1047 from families with incomes of $50 to $75 a month. Almost one-third had never held any kind of job. The majority of those who had worked had been employed in manual labor, errands, or domestic service.

"What do you want to be doing ten years from now?" the youth in this group were asked. Many thought of themselves as aviators, civil, electrical, and Diesel engineers, accountants, office workers, contractors, owners of businesses, actresses, artists, authors, journalists, doctors, nurses, teachers, radio television experts, athletic directors, social scientists, etc. Very likely some of these youth have the ability to prepare for these types of jobs. Considering their limited fundamental education, their ages, their family incomes, and their own small earning power, most of these young people, however, are only indulging in wishful thinking instead of facing the actualities of employment possibilities.

NYA supervisors and Junior Placement officials reported to us that this type of romancing is pathetically prevalent. Youth 20 years old with no more than grade school education not only talk of such work as Diesel engineering, but deprive themselves of basic necessities to take correspondence courses in highly technical professions.

In America there unquestionably exists a high sense of snobbery toward manual labor, even when it is skilled work. For generations a big share of the manual labor outside of the South was done by immigrants, some of whom were artisans. The children of the later immigrants, like the descendants of the earlier immigrants, aspire to employment with more prestige than manual labor. Parents seem to derive a vicarious

---

[2] Since the survey was made the average education of youth on the Minnesota NYA out-of-school work program has dropped one year.

satisfaction in their sons' and daughters' having careers in offices rather than in factories, in construction, or in other trades. Schools also must share the responsibility for fostering the conviction that work done with the hands is inferior to desk jobs.

There is another reason why white-collar work may be especially attractive to youth and to their parents. White-collar jobs, as a rule, offer greater regularity of employment than work in factories, mills, construction, and other trades. Office workers experience comparatively fewer seasonal lay-offs and shut-downs. Their income is steadier. Regular vacations with pay, shorter working days, and other more inviting working conditions accrue to them. Labor and industry must insure greater security of income, shorter hours, and generally better working conditions before they can expect youth to choose work with the hands in preference to white-collar jobs.

The less work experience a youth has had, we were told many times, the more illusions he entertains about the desirability and the feasibility of a white-collar or a professional job. NYA is probably helping many youth to correct their occupational fixations by giving them work experience and vocational information and guidance that they could obtain in no other way in this period of depression.

NYA AND THE EDUCATIONAL SYSTEM

Because NYA touches large groups of young people who might be termed educational fatalities, it challenges the educational system to improve and enlarge itself.

We asked several high school principals and teachers if they felt that the NYA program for out-of-school youth had any significance educationally.

"We in schools have lost the faith of young people," one

principal said. "They do not look to us to guide them or to
help them in the ways of the modern world. And they're right,
because we ourselves don't know this world. We've prided ourselves in keeping aloof from it. NYA has captured the confidence of youth because it has given them more honest ways of
learning."

A college president who was in intimate touch with a Resident Project on his campus felt that the interest and progress
of the NYA youth (most of whom had completed no more
than the eighth grade), both in their work and in their related
studies, opened new doors for education.

"These young people are learning much that they will use
every day of their lives," he said, in speaking of the NYA resident students. "They make us face the fact that we have concentrated in preparing young people to meet the abnormalities
of living rather than the normalities of work, of family life, of
responsible citizenship. We must take inventory of the educational system, forget our own defenses, and set the educational house in better order."

Leaders of educational thought recognize that the traditional high school linguistic-mathematical curriculum, originally devised as a foundation for a small number of youth who
would enter the learned professions, fails to satisfy the needs of
the vast numbers of young people in high schools today. The
NYA experience with large numbers of out-of-school youth
deserves, we believe, a thorough examination by the educators
who are now concerning themselves with the problem of revision of high school methods and curricula.

Educators and taxpayers may also find it worth their time to
investigate the development of the NYA youth center, where
the young people and sometimes all the members of the community find opportunities for learning, recreation, and work
under one roof. Undoubtedly there are schools that integrate
the whole community life—where during the day children come

for eager hours of learning, where young people want to gather for dancing, plays, music, discussion groups, athletics, where parents and children find satisfying family recreation, where the important local and national questions of the day are threshed out in public forums, where teachers are leaders and where buildings and equipment continue their useful services after the formal school day is over. They are too few and far between.

Of necessity the NYA out-of-school program has been experimental. The positive encouragement to experiment given by the administrative officers in this decentralized and flexible organization has led to the breaking of many new trails. In its rough and ready pioneering the NYA out-of-school program has had the counsel of many educators—on the administrative staff, on advisory committees, and among co-operating local agencies. Much of the work that NYA is doing for these young people properly belongs within the province of the regular schools. NYA has evinced no ambition to usurp the rightful prerogatives of the educational system. But it has been forced to make an effort, wide in its significance and deep in its effects, to salvage many educational outcasts and wrecks of the past decade—young people unequipped to meet problems of living far more complicated than youth of other generations have confronted.

CHAPTER X

The Balance Sheet for NYA

THE NYA PROGRAM IS IN A FLUID, CHANGING STATE. IT IS AN emergency measure, designed to provide some of the less privileged youth with at least a measure of participation in the economic, social, and educational life of an era which frequently seems to have no place for many of them. In this informal survey of NYA, it is necessary to include some of the new aspects, problems, and evaluations that have emerged as the program has developed.

NYA YOUTH AND HEALTH

NYA has no national health program. In every State, health education is carried on to some degree, according to the community resources that NYA can command, since its own limited funds prevent expansion in this important field. Red Cross nurses, county and State public health officials, personnel from public hospitals, and in a number of instances social-minded physicians and dentists assist in spreading knowledge of healthy living to boys and girls from relief families. All these preventive measures, inadequate as they are, have significance in the general health picture.

But what of the 18-to-24-year-old boys and girls who need medical and dental care? It is extremely difficult to figure in any way how youth who earn on an average $15.44 a month and whose families are on relief can afford the services of private doctors, dentists, and hospitals. Clinical facilities are non-existent in most rural areas and in many towns. Few cities make investments in the health of their citizens adequate to meet more than the most desperate demands.

Students receiving NYA college aid use whatever medical services the colleges provide for their student bodies. NYA youth in Resident Projects receive physical examinations, and, when these projects are established at educational institutions, arrangements are usually made for the youth to receive the institution's regular medical services.

In some cases, NYA has provided medical examinations for its out-of-school youth. Every boy and girl on the Rhode Island program receives a physical examination, and is assigned to work according to his physical as well as his potential occupational abilities. Youth in need of medical care are referred to hospitals and clinics. Ohio has a well-developed health program. In other States, we have found several instances in which medical examinations are now an accepted routine in NYA, but this practice is by no means general. Furthermore, without available clinical follow-up for those who need it, medical examinations are futile.

Some indications of the health of NYA out-of-school youth are startling. In one Middle-Western industrial city, 1800 boys and girls were given thorough physical examinations. Forty-three per cent. of them were found to be unemployable (by private industry) because of their physical condition. It was estimated that with corrective medical treatment this large portion of youth who were occupationally handicapped because of physical defects could be reduced to 8 or 10 per cent.

In giving a skin tuberculin test to 506 Negro youth in Chicago, the Tuberculosis Institute found that 87.5 per cent. reacted positively, indicating past tubercular histories or present infections. Of the 370 of this group who were X-rayed, only 207 showed healthy chests. In Atlanta, Georgia, 371 Negro girls were given the Kahn test for syphilis; 138, or 37 per cent., showed positive reactions. This was an exceptionally high percentage in comparison with other groups of NYA youth who have received Wassermann or Kahn tests. In rural communities in Georgia, the percentage of positive reactions was very low. In a Minnesota report, one per cent. showed positive reaction. In general, in these scattered reports, cities have shown a greater incidence of venereal disease among relief youth than have rural areas. In many States NYA is co-operating with the United States Public Health Service in its broad program for the control and eradication of venereal diseases.

All investigations into the physical conditions of relief youth indicate a very serious situation. Those youth now suffering from ill health become less and less able to care for themselves when no medical treatment is available for them. If this country is not to carry the burden of large groups of adults unemployable because of ill health, wider medical and hospital facilities must be brought within the reach of underprivileged youth.

ENGINEERS' REPORT ON NYA WORK PROGRAM

Whether raw youth under the limited expert supervision that NYA funds permit could do satisfactory construction work was an open question in the minds of NYA administrators. In the late summer of 1937, a confidential engineers' evaluation of the construction and shop program was made by the WPA engineering organization under the direction of Colonel F. C. Harrington, of the United States Army, Assistant WPA Administrator. This survey covered 108 projects in 27 States—sufficient in the opinion of the engineers to give a fair cross-section of the program.

The summary of the survey, prepared by Mr. Perry A.

Fellows, Chief Assistant Engineer of WPA, was intended exclusively for administrative guidance and has not been published. It contained a number of frank criticisms and minor recommendations, which have been followed by NYA officials in improving the work program. However, the general conclusion of the report was that "the National Youth Administration construction program as a whole is very good." The expressions *excellent, very good, good,* and *mediocre* were the principal adjectives used in evaluating various aspects of the program.

In brief summary, the ratings given to various aspects of the construction and shop work as a whole were these:

Public value of work done and facilities created: *Excellent.*

Educational value of work to youth employed: *Good,* with great variations from project to project.

Location of projects, with view to their operation and their later use: *Excellent.*

Design factors: *Good, very good,* and *excellent.*

Employment value of work: *Very good.*

Operating methods, safety, etc.: *Very good*—in some sections *excellent.*

Supervision: *Very good* and *excellent.*

The report cited examples of rather large projects—one consisting of the construction of a dormitory for 72 boys, a mess hall, a poultry house, dairy facilities, and other facilities— where the class of construction work done was "excellent" and where the foreman deserved praise for training the boys to lay out details of work and "insisting on a high quality of workmanship."

As a testimonial to the ability of inexperienced young men under limited supervision to do high-grade construction and shop work this engineers' report is arresting. It was influential in the decision of NYA to expand this phase of its work program.

Like others who have inspected the NYA work program in the field, these engineers were impressed with the effect of the work on the social attitudes of the youth employed. One engineer-inspector reported:

"When the project first started there was considerable 'soldiering' on the job. A few fights occurred between boys and some drunkenness was evident. This particular city had a reputation of juvenile delinquency. Since the project has been in operation it was found that the spirit of the youths has been aroused to a pride in a participation in a public enterprise. The boys on the project have formed a social unit and for the past five months there have been no complaints from the local peace officers, who have attributed the lack of delinquency to this project."

NYA AND ORGANIZED LABOR

Organized labor is represented on the National and State advisory committees and many of the local advisory committees of NYA. On the whole, the NYA out-of-school work program appears to enjoy the approval of organized labor. In a few States NYA has refrained from going into the construction field in deference to the objections of certain trade union bodies. In some, organized labor has tacitly approved NYA work in the fields of the various trades. In a number of States and localities, organized labor has warmly endorsed the NYA out-of-school program and is actively co-operating with it.

Where union men are available it is the general practice to employ them as foremen on NYA construction and workshop projects. This, in itself, has added in a small way to employment within the ranks of organized labor.

For at least two reasons the NYA work program is not generally regarded as a threat by organized workers in those fields in which NYA affords vocational experience. The first is that the NYA program is turning out very few skilled workers. Probably the only exceptions to the rule are the wood-carvers and cabinet-makers developed among the Spanish-American youth of New Mexico and in a few other of the best woodworking shops, such as some of those in the Kentucky mountains. Ordinarily the NYA construction and shop program affords a youth no more than a chance to discover his aptitudes and to obtain a little experience as a beginner.

Secondly, the NYA program has adhered to the rule that these out-of-school youth shall not engage in productive work which might be done in any other way. From fairly extensive observation, we are convinced that the instances in which it might be displacing regular adult workers are so rare as to be negligible. There is no displacement of regular labor when NYA youth, under skilled supervision, build a new school in a poverty-ridden county that could not otherwise have one. There is none when they build a co-operative dormitory where they themselves, and youth to come in later years, can pool their tiny resources to obtain an education. There is none when they convert a piece of waste ground into a playground, or when they make play equipment for the use of underprivileged children, or when they make chairs and desks for rural schools that cannot afford to buy them.

On the NYA out-of-school program, youth creates for youth. A large portion of the benefits of NYA work goes directly to the children and youth of the laboring groups of the population.

Many instances could be cited in which the endorsement by organized labor groups of the NYA out-of-school program has been accompanied by intimate co-operation.

In Schenectady, New York, NYA youth are starting to remodel the entire plant of the abandoned county home. Both A. F. of L. and CIO organizations in that city have agreed to furnish volunteer technical supervision from the following trade unions: Local 146, Brotherhood of Carpenters and Joiners; Local 16, Masons (covering masonry, bricklaying, tile terrazzo); Local 105, Plumbers and Steamfitters; Local 166, Electrical Workers; Local 62, Decorators, Painters, and Paperhangers; Local 12, Structural and Ornamental Iron Workers.

The following is from a resolution passed in June 1937 by the Building Trades Council of Santa Clara County, California:

Whereas the National Youth Administration is an agency of the Federal Government and a part of the Works Progress Administration whose purpose is the training and assistance of young American citizens so that they may become upright, self-supporting, and self-reliant citizens, and

Whereas the Building Trades Council of Santa Clara County, State of California . . . is vitally interested in promotion of the welfare of youth and of the cause of good citizenship, and

Whereas we believe it to be right and proper that young men being assisted by the National Youth Administration should have an opportunity to learn the honorable skilled trades at which we work . . .

Be it resolved that young men now being assisted or that may hereafter be assisted by the National Youth Administration in this county and who may be recommended by said Administration be and they are hereby given permission to be employed as apprentices in the several crafts represented in this building trades council.

In setting up a Resident Project at San Marcos, Texas, where NYA youth are getting vocational experience in the woodwork and metal trades, Mr. Travis J. Lewis, Co-ordinator for the Fort Worth public schools and labor's representative on the Texas Planning Board, worked out a system by which in each locality two members of unions would sit on a committee with two representatives of industry and one educator to select youth for the project and to advise on the general conduct of the project. In a report Mr. Lewis stated: "Thoughtful labor union members have been concerned by the number of occupational misfits now being accepted for apprenticeship."

In Atlanta, Georgia, the garment makers' union wrote in their contract with textile mills a clause which states that only NYA workers from a project in power machine operation are to be accepted as apprentices. In Macon, Georgia, the building trades unions advise with NYA supervisors as to the type of work project most desirable from the points of view both of youth and of the possibility of absorption in the various trades. For example, the painters' union figures that eight more youth can be absorbed during the year into the apprenticeship class. In its project planning NYA co-ordinates the number of youth it employs in this field with the openings which the union has indicated are likely to occur. The preliminary try-out on NYA gives the youth a chance to show his aptitude and the union a chance to judge it.

Organized labor has an important stake in the youth of the country; from them in a short time must come the strength, the patterns, and the leadership for labor. It seems inconceivable that a large group of youth, unemployable because of lack of training and general occupational disintegration, can contribute to the progress of organized labor. The derelict on the wharf, the sleeper on the park bench, the transient on the road—the youth to whom education and work experience have been alien—cannot add to labor's strength.

ADMINISTRATIVE PERSONNEL

The central staff of NYA consists of 25 administrative officials. Mr. Aubrey Williams, Deputy Administrator of WPA, receives no compensation for his special duties as Executive Director of NYA. Actively in charge under Mr. Williams is

Mr. Richard R. Brown, Deputy NYA Administrator. Under Mr. Brown are five regional directors, who spend most of their time in the field, six directors of administrative divisions, and twelve assistants. Counting all field workers and clerical, stenographic, and custodial employees, the entire national office force consisted of 67 persons in May 1938, and has never exceeded that number by more than four or five.

The 48 States, New York City, and the District of Columbia each have a Youth Director. Their salaries range from $3000 to $6000, a great majority being less than $4800. Attached to the State offices are 110 administrative assistants and district supervisors. Their salaries range from $1000 to $3600. Including all clerical, stenographic, and miscellaneous employees in the national office and all State offices, there were approximately 915 persons on the NYA administrative pay-roll in April 1938.

In addition, there are some county supervisors and approximately 6000 supervisors of individual work projects. They receive from $60 to $120 a month, the average being less than $70. As in the WPA, these job supervisors, or foremen, are not classified as administrative employees. Their wages are charged to the costs of the individual projects, and they account for nearly all the non-relief workers on the rolls of the NYA work program.

The administrative and supervisory personnel in NYA is too limited. Project and county supervisors, particularly, receive quite inadequate compensation for the varied duties demanded of them. In the earlier NYA days, many of these came from the ranks of teachers. As the program developed, and the work projects became more diverse, men and women of broader practical experience were needed. We noted a tendency to employ young engineers as district and county supervisors.

As we traveled from county to county and from State to State, we were impressed with the efficiency, the deep interest, and the long hours that NYA administrators and supervisors devote to their work.

"It gets you," one young man who was a county supervisor in West Virginia told us. "There's something I can't just define about it, but when you see boys and girls who never have had a chance before, learning to do something, actually making something that other people will use, changing their own habits of living, developing toward each other a sense of responsibility, you decide maybe there's something more to a job than a pay-check."

How Much Does It Cost?

More than 475,000 youth were working on NYA programs in March 1938. Of these approximately 154,000 were out-of-school youth and approximately 325,000 were high school, college, and graduate students. Since the out-of-school program has got well under way, and excepting the summer months when student aid is not given, the number of youth working on all NYA programs has ranged between the peak of 630,000, reached in April 1937, and the low point of 360,000, reached in October 1937.

For the twelve months ending June 30, 1938, the total cost of the NYA programs to the Federal Government was approximately $58,000,000. The annual cost to the Federal Government of each NYA youth was approximately[1]:

> For high school students: $40
> For college students: $105
> For out-of-school youth: $242

These figures include costs of administration, supervision, materials, and all other overhead items in both national and

[1] For full statistics on costs of various NYA programs, including youth enrolled, average hourly and monthly earnings, etc., see Appendix.

State NYA offices paid for by the Federal Government, nearly all of which are chargeable to the out-of-school program. The Federal cost of administering the student aid programs is probably only a small fraction of one per cent. of the total outlay. The total administrative overhead for the entire NYA amounts to about $2,500,000 annually, or less than 5 per cent. of the total Federal expenditure of NYA. For the fiscal year 1937–38, it was approximately 4.6 per cent. In 1936–37, when more youth were employed, it was only 3.78 per cent. To these figures should be added a small but incalculable allowance for the free services which NYA receives from WPA. WPA handles NYA pay-rolls and requisitions and compensation claims arising from accidents, and provides NYA with a certain amount of free statistical service—an arrangement that is economical for the Federal Government.

Under the NYA program, the annual Federal cost of keeping a youth in high school is about one-thirtieth that of keeping him in a CCC camp. College student aid costs less than one-tenth as much per youth annually as the CCC. The out-of-school work program costs only slightly more than one-fifth as much as the CCC per youth. The Resident Centers, which are the NYA enterprises most nearly comparable to the CCC, are being operated for approximately one-fourth of the cost of the CCC per youth. The cost of the Resident Centers per youth will rise as this division of the NYA program is enlarged, since there is a limit to the subsidies in the form of materials, supervision, and instruction which they can obtain from existing educational institutions. The full cost of the CCC is borne by the Federal Government. The CCC provides full-time employment whereas the NYA provides only part-time employment. As most CCC youths send home from $20 to $25 of the $30 or more monthly that they are paid in cash, in addition to the food, lodging, clothing, and incidentals with which they are provided, part of the higher CCC cost is a contribution to the support of the general relief burden. Part of the NYA expenditure also is offset by reduced relief payments through other channels. But as NYA has had annually only about one-tenth as much as the CCC for out-of-school youth, the NYA contribution to the general relief burden necessarily has been the smaller of the two.

Through November 30, 1937, only $1,506,581 of Federal funds had been spent by NYA for materials, supplies, equipment, rentals, and services for work projects. Local sponsors had put up $3,697,241, or 71 per cent. of the cost of these items in the out-of-school program. At all times since the out-of-school program got under way, more than 95 per cent. of all persons employed on it—including county and project supervisors—have been persons certified as in need of relief.

There is no way of computing the money value of the counsel and active attention given to the out-of-school program and related educational work by thousands of local agencies and individual citizens. Also unascertainable is the value of the materials and supervision provided by high schools and colleges for student work projects.

The low cost per youth of the NYA program as a whole is due largely to the maximum use of existing State and local facilities. The Federal money is chiefly a thinly spread subsidy which puts to work the surplus capacity of these facilities. Beyond that, NYA serves largely as an agency of stimulation and organization.

The monetary worth of the thousands of public improvements and the many thousands of articles of furniture, clothing, hospital supplies, and other products made by NYA youth cannot be computed. Nor can any dollar value be fixed for the expansion of public services made possible by NYA youth. In total these increased services and inanimate assets probably amount to a good many millions of dollars. However valuable they are, they are unimportant in comparison with the incalculable return to the nation in the conservation and improvement of its human assets.

The Future of NYA

If NYA were to cease to function, thousands of college students of superior ability would be forced to leave college. Many thousands of high school girls and boys also would drop out. With employment opportunities at a low ebb, many thousands of youth on the out-of-school program would be "on the bum," with no work to do, small chance to learn how to work, no earnings for personal and family needs, no feeling that they are part of the national life. The annual investment that NYA is making in the less privileged youth of the United States is less than the cost of one battleship.

With the needs of youth as wide as they are, and with the future of the country as dependent as it patently is on the character and capability of youth, it would be reckless to neglect the minimum needs of this populous group of economically disabled young people. An important benefit of NYA is the integration of large numbers of youth into the general community life. Youth working on a public school, a playground, a park, or sewing for public institutions, acquire a sense and specific knowledge of the interdependence of human beings within their own communities, of social organization, and of the responsibilities of citizenship. Public and private organizations and individuals who contribute money, time, and advice to NYA activities are brought in closer touch with the difficulties and aspirations of youth.

NYA touches only part of the youth who are in the most desperate circumstances. In May 1938, there were many thousands of boys and girls already certified for NYA who could not be assigned because funds were not available. Apart from the youth who were being helped to remain in colleges and schools by NYA wage checks, there were probably between 5,000,000 and 6,000,000 youth, 18 to 24 years of age, who in May 1938 were out of school and seeking work but unable to find it.

In addition there were several hundred thousand youth in a group which NYA does not reach: those 17 years of age or younger who are out of school and unemployed. NYA might well consider bringing some of these younger youth to Resident Projects where they can earn subsistence while receiving education and practical training. On the other hand, the unmarried youth of 23 or older, who form a small percentage of the enrollees on NYA out-of-school projects, might be cared for on some other public program. They are usually less plastic occupationally and educationally than the younger people, and consequently do not receive correspondingly valuable returns from NYA.

Within NYA's present restricted scope, there is room for improvement and enlargement. Much of this is dependent upon the availability of additional funds. In some ways, NYA's lack of money may have been an asset in its first phases, as it demanded ingenuity in planning and exploration of all resources for co-operation within communities. But insufficient money for materials for work projects has been and still is a serious handicap. Frequently communities with the least abilities to contribute have the largest reservoirs of relief youth and the greatest opportunities for improvement of public property. More flexibility in the use of funds for materials seems desirable. The results of the new NYA Resident Projects indicate that expansion in this field of closely related work and training can benefit increased numbers of youth. There are limits, however, to the willingness and ability of existing educational institutions to take on these new and experimental units. If NYA is to set them up as independent work and educational centers, more funds will be needed if the rest of the NYA work program is not to suffer.

The turn-over of youth on the NYA out-of-school program has been high. Although the average number of out-of-school youth employed by NYA at any one time has been around 150,000, more than 500,000 different youth have been on the program in its first two and one-half years. Approximately one-third of the youth who left the program between March 1937 and February 1938 did so to take private employment. Some of these jobs were seasonal. Other separations from the NYA rolls were attributable to general curtailment of the program, loss of family relief status, attainment of the 25-year upper age limit prescribed for NYA, employment on other public programs, and the loss of eligibility through marriage. Married youth are classified as primary wage earners. With the decline of private employment opportunities which began in the fall of 1937, separations from the NYA program have been fewer, while the number of youth seeking admission to the NYA work program has increased.

We questioned State Youth Directors and supervisors closely concerning the possibility of a dearth of desirable projects for NYA out-of-school work. Except in a few communities, we found no indication that there is likely to be any shortage of sound projects in the near future. Because of NYA's characteristic decentralization into small working units, many minor but useful public work projects may be undertaken, such as the repair of a one-room school house, the development of a neighborhood playground, and the building of smaller structures than it would be feasible for WPA to handle. There is apparently an almost inexhaustible demand throughout the country for the improvement and creation of youth facilities.

After a careful scrutiny and analysis of the needs of youth, the President's Advisory Committee on Education recommended in February 1938 that NYA and CCC activities be placed under one agency, which might be designated the National Youth Service Administration and which should be placed in a department including public health, education, and welfare, if such a department should be established. Specifically this comprehensive report states:

The student aid program now being carried on by the National Youth Administration should be continued. It should not be made permanent until after further experience but might well be placed upon a basis of specific and continuing statutory authorization for a period ending in 1945. . . . Aid for college students and for other students 18 years of age and older, except those physically disabled, should be authorized only on a work basis. Aid should be continued for needy high school pupils 16 and 17 years of age. The administrative agency should be given freedom to experiment with high school aid both on a work and on a non-work basis until a sound general policy can be determined. . . . The work projects program of the existing National Youth Administration should be continued along much the same lines as at present, with additional effort to increase the educational value of the projects and to stimulate the educational interests of the youth concerned. Some form of educational activity should be provided in connection with all work projects.

A consolidation of the present CCC and NYA programs under one administration might prove to be a desirable development. Each organization has a wealth of experience to contribute to a more comprehensive appreciation of the problems of present-day youth. Each has developed varying techniques which could be objectively analyzed with possible immediate benefit. We have noted a number of youth who after serving in the CCC have come home to face unimproved working opportunities and have been assigned to NYA. A careful study of these youth who have experienced both programs might be of help in determining the most efficient, economical, and productive methods of assisting depression youth.

NYA has not solved and cannot solve the basic problems of the groups of youth it has touched. These problems are interwoven with and inseparable from the general social and economic enigmas of this era. NYA does demonstrate that, given the chance, these youth show a willingness, often an eagerness, to work, to learn, and to assume their responsibilities in this civilization.

APPENDIX I

NATIONAL YOUTH ADMINISTRATION

The National Youth Administration is organized within the framework of the Works Progress Administration and is under the direction of Mr. Harry L. Hopkins, Administrator of the Works Progress Administration. The administrative staff of the Washington office of the National Youth Administration is as follows:

Mr. Aubrey Williams, Executive Director
Mr. Richard R. Brown, Deputy Executive Director
Dr. Mary H. S. Hayes, Director, Division of Guidance and Placement
Mr. David R. Williams, Director, Division of Work Projects
Mrs. Mary McLeod Bethune, Director, Division of Negro Affairs
Miss Thelma C. McKelvey, Director, Division of Reports and Records
Mr. Sam Gilstrap, Director, Division of Finance
Mr. W. Thacher Winslow, Director, Division of Public Relations
Mr. Leon J. Kowal, Field Director, Northeast Region
Mr. Orin W. Kaye, Field Director, Mid-Atlantic Region
Mr. Garth Akridge, Field Director, South Central Region
Mr. O. H. Lull, Field Director, Western Region
Mr. C. B. Lund, Field Director, Midwestern Region

NATIONAL ADVISORY COMMITTEE
Appointed by Executive Order 7123, Dated August 1, 1935

Mr. Charles W. Taussig, President of the American Molasses Company, New York City; *Chairman*

Mr. Adolf Augustus Berle, Jr., New York City (now Assistant Secretary of State)

Mrs. Mary McLeod Bethune, President, Bethune-Cookman College, Daytona Beach, Florida

Miss Selma Borchardt, Vice-President, American Federation of Teachers, Washington, D. C.

Mr. Frank L. Boyden, Headmaster, Deerfield Academy, Deerfield, Massachusetts

Dr. Howard S. Braucher, Secretary, National Recreation Association, New York City

Mr. Louis Brownlow, Director, Public Administration Clearing House, Chicago, Illinois

Mr. Glenn Cunningham, Peabody, Kansas

Mr. Henry Dennison, Dennison Manufacturing Company, Framingham, Massachusetts

220 *A New Deal for Youth*

Miss Amelia Earhart, New York City (deceased)
Mr. Kenneth Farrier, Pembroke, Virginia
Mr. William Green, President, American Federation of Labor, Washington, D. C.
Mr. George Harrison, Grand President, Brotherhood of Railway and Steamship Clerks, Cincinnati, Ohio
Mr. Sidney Hillman, President, Amalgamated Clothing Workers, New York City
Reverend George W. Johnson, Director, Department of Education, National Catholic Welfare Association, Washington, D. C.
Dr. Mordecai Johnson, President, Howard University, Washington, D. C.
Dr. Charles H. Judd, Chairman, Department of Education, University of Chicago, Chicago, Illinois
Dr. E. H. Lindley, Chancellor, University of Kansas, Lawrence, Kansas
Mr. Bernarr Macfadden, Macfadden Publishing Company, New York City
Mr. Hiram Percy Maxim, Hartford, Connecticut (deceased)
Bishop Francis J. McConnell, Methodist Episcopal Church, New York City
Mr. Thomas J. McInerney, Grange League Federation, Ithaca, New York
Reverend Edward Roberts Moore, Catholic Charities of the Archdiocese of New York, New York City
Dr. Elizabeth Morrissy, Professor of Economics, College of Notre Dame of Maryland, Baltimore, Maryland
Mr. Thomas Neblett, National Labor Relations Board, New Orleans, Louisiana
Mrs. Julia O'Connor Parker, Boston, Massachusetts
Dr. Clarence Poe, Editor, *Progressive Farmer*, Raleigh, North Carolina
Dr. David deSola Pool, Spanish and Portuguese Synagogue, New York City
Miss Agnes Samuelson, Superintendent of Public Instruction, Des Moines, Iowa
Miss Mae K. Sargent, Catholic Welfare Bureau, Los Angeles, California
Mr. M. W. Thatcher, Representative of Farmers Union and the Farmers National Grain Corporation, St. Paul, Minnesota
Miss Florence Thorne, American Federation of Labor, Washington, D. C.
Dr. David E. Weglein, Superintendent of Public Instruction, Baltimore, Maryland
Mr. Owen D. Young, Chairman of the Board, General Electric Company, New York City
Dr. George F. Zook, President, American Council on Education, Washington, D. C.

EXECUTIVE COMMITTEE

Appointed by Executive Order 7096, Dated July 9, 1935

Miss Josephine Roche, Assistant Secretary of the Treasury, Department of the Treasury, Washington, D. C. (resigned from position with the

Department of the Treasury, November 1937, but continues to serve as Chairman of the Executive Committee); *Chairman*

Dr. Arthur J. Altmeyer, Member of Social Security Board, Washington, D. C.

Dr. John Studebaker, Commissioner of Education, Office of Education, Washington, D. C.

Mr. M. L. Wilson, Under-Secretary of Agriculture, Department of Agriculture, Washington, D. C.

The following were members of the original Executive Committee, but are no longer connected with the Government. The positions indicated are those held at the time of the Executive Order.

Mr. Lee Pressman, General Counsel, Federal Emergency Relief Administration, Washington, D. C.

Mr. Chester H. McCall, Special Assistant to the Secretary of Commerce, Department of Commerce, Washington, D. C.

NATIONAL YOUTH ADMINISTRATION

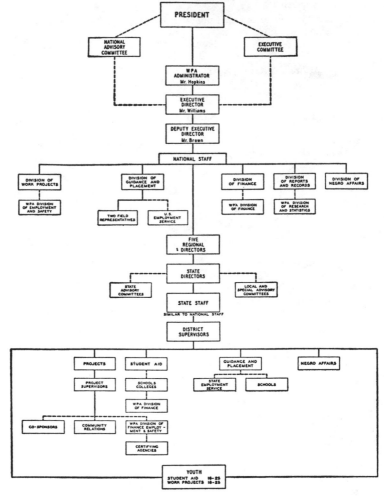

WPA 2562

EXAMPLES OF CO-SPONSORING AGENCIES

A sampling of 130 representative NYA work projects for out-of-school youth disclosed the following 73 co-sponsoring agencies:

A. NATIONAL

Bureau of Entomology and Plant Quarantine, U. S. Dept. of Agriculture

Bureau of Home Economics, U. S. Dept. of Agriculture

B. STATE

Universities and Colleges
Librarian
Library Board
University Hospital
College Extension Service
Department of Education
Department of Labor
Department of Public Welfare
Department of Conservation

Attorney General
Agricultural Extension Service
Agricultural Experiment Station
Forestry Service
Soil Conservation Service
Game, Forestation, and Parks Commission
Forestry Commission
Planning Board

C. COUNTY

School Board
Superintendent of Education
Training School
Consolidated School
Children's Home
Librarian
Board of Commissioners
Advisory Board or Committee

Judge
Court
Garden Club
Farm Agent
Home Demonstration Club
Health Department
Road Department
Mechanic

D. CITY OR TOWNSHIP

School Nurse
Schools
Opportunity School
Board of Education
Parent-Teacher Association
Adult Education Department
Youth Committee
Council of Social Agencies

Relief Agencies
Emergency Bureau
Planning Commission
Board of Supervisors
City Commission
Officers and Departments
Council
Mayor

City or Town
Park Board
Recreation Department (or Commission)
Park

Public Library
Township Road Supervisor
Game Farm
Chamber of Commerce

E. OTHER ORGANIZATIONS

Colleges and Universities (Not State)
Church Asylum
Home for Crippled Children
Medical Research Laboratory
Women's Club
Junior Women's Club
Rotary Club

Lions Club
Kiwanis Club
American Legion
County and Civic Organizations
Anaconda Mining Company
YMCA and YWCA

TYPES OF WORK ACTIVITY

A sampling of 150 NYA work projects for out-of-school youth showed that the youth employed on them were engaged in these 169 types of work:

Agricultural experimentation
Agricultural testing
Airport floodlight installed
Art work (maps and illustrations)
Athletic courts constructed
Automobile mechanics
Awnings made and installed
Baby cribs made and screened
Beautification of grounds, parks, parkways, etc.
Bleachers built
Book renovation and repair
Bricklaying
Bridges (small, log, stone, metal)
Bridle path constructed
Broom making
Buildings (adobe) constructed
Buildings (brick) constructed
Buildings (concrete) constructed
Buildings (frame) constructed
Buildings (log) constructed
Buildings repaired, remodeled, and renovated
Cabinet work
Canning of vegetables, fruits
Carpentry
Cement forms made for construction work
Cement spindles for bridge-railing cast
Child care in "Homes"
City street-lighting system overhauled
Cleaned and grubbed ravine in park
Cleaned bricks for re-use
Cleaned grounds around completed construction projects (sewers)
Cleaned lagoon banks
Cleaned poultry houses
Cleaned sewers and drains
Cleaned skating pond
Cleared land
Clerical work—
    recording, stenographic, indexing, filing, machine calculation, addressograph, etc.
Clipping service in library
Concrete and mortar mixed and laid
Cooking (home, etc.)
Cooking for lunchrooms, etc.
Dams (small) constructed
Delivered information on insects, weeds, etc., to farmers
Dishwashing
Dismantled buildings
Dismantled building partitions
Domestic service (general)
Drafting
Driveways construction
Dug treatment pool
Dutch oven construction in park
Employment Office work
Excavation for artifacts
Extension of home hygiene, household management, and domestic science
Farm short course directory prepared
Feeding game
Fences and walls constructed
Fireplaces constructed (in parks)
Fish and game conservation
Forest conservation program
Furniture made
Furniture repaired

Gardening

Golf course rehabilitation (put in sandtraps and hazards, resurfaced tees)

Graded land

Graded roads

Granite columns constructed

Guide service (at historical sites)

Handicraft work

Hauled (and removed) old road bed

Hauled top-soil

Helped prepare and serve hot lunches for needy school children

Hospital and dispensary services

Improvement of playgrounds

Installation of plumbing and electric fixtures

Instruction in taxidermy and craft work

Iron work (ornamental) assistants

Janitorial

Kindergarten supervision

Landscaping

Laundering

Leveled top-soil

Library indexing

Library study hour assistance

Magazine renovating

Manufactured playground equipment

Manufactured toys

Map making

Mapped farms

Maps copied

Masonry

Musical instruments constructed

Nursery education work

Nursery work (plant)

Nursing (general)

Painting

Painting (curbs, signs, etc.)

Painting (murals)

Papering and varnishing

Parking areas constructed

Pavement construction

Pipes laid

Planted grass

Planted seedlings and trees

Planted shrubbery

Plastering

Play areas prepared

Playground equipment installed

Playground equipment made

Playground park area constructed

Posts set

Pottery

Poultry raising

Poultry reports kept

Prepared flower beds for winter

Pruned trees and shrubs

Pump house constructed

Quarried stone

Recorded information on basic township maps

Recreational equipment (nets, etc.) made

Recreational facilities improved

Recreational supervision or leadership

Rehabilitation or remodeling of parks

Repaired buildings

Repaired school busses and trucks

Research work

Reservoir constructed

Retaining walls built

Rip-rapping along river banks constructed, etc.

Roads and roadways constructed

Roofing

Sawed fallen timber

Sewer mains relaid

Sewers and drains constructed

Sewing
    clothing
    costumes
    curtains
    dolls and animals
    fancy work
    home furnishings
    hospital supplies
    quilting
    renovated old clothes
    rugs

Sheet-metal work

Shelters and feed stations for birds and animals constructed

Shelters for golf course

Shelters for skating rink

Sidewalks and trails
Skating rink construction
Soil conservation
Statistical study of data
Statistical surveys made
Statistics compiled and checked
Stenographic work
Street and highway markers built and installed
Studies in classes co-ordinated with work project
Surveyed land (farms)
Tables and benches (wood and concrete) constructed
Tanks (reaction) constructed
Temporary classrooms constructed
Temporary dormitories constructed
Terracing

Tile setting
Track construction
Traveling library service
Treatment of diseased trees
Tree surgery
Tuberculosis cottages
Typing and copying
Visual-aid material made (posters, scrap books, etc.)
Walks constructed
Watertower constructed
Weaving
Windows and doors installed
Wiring for electricity
Woodcraft
Woodcraft shop supervised in home for boys

TYPES OF WORK
PERFORMED ON A SINGLE PROJECT

Illustrative of the variety of work experience afforded by the renovation of a building is the following list of 93 different jobs done by NYA out-of-school youth in reconditioning the Pawtucket, Rhode Island, Boys' Club:

LIBRARY

Floor washed and varnished
Tables and benches cleaned and varnished
Door knob and door check repaired

GAMES ROOM

Windows cleaned
Bicycle rack erected
Overhead pipes dusted
Vocational award certificates placed on walls
Walls cleaned, stained, and varnished
Tables and benches repaired and varnished
Floor washed, repaired, and floor dressing applied

UPPER LOCKER ROOM

Benches varnished
New wringer installed
Comb machine repaired
5 hair driers overhauled
Painted table, towel bin, and doors
Entire floor grouted
Placed all keys and lockers in working order .

SWIMMING POOL

Windows repaired
Tile walls cleaned
Light shades cleaned
Diving board fulcrum repaired
Loose shower pipes strengthened
Bell in pool office repaired
New flushometer placed in pool toilet
Return line on radiator repaired
Cleaned and grouted entire floor and pool proper

Painted ceiling, girders, windows, doors, radiators, pipes, exhaust fans, and pool office

Replaced 6 measuring showers with manual control equipment; screen placed over fan at rear of pool

Made 2 new diving boards

Pool license and swim notices placed on wall

Cleaned mixing valve

GYMNASIUM

Lights repaired
Cleaned under stage
Gym mats repaired
Tile walls stippled
Holes in walls plastered
Windows washed and painted
Entire ceiling painted
Quadrant on windows repaired
Exit light repaired
Movie screen painted
All bleachers repaired and painted
All auditorium chairs repaired
End basketball backboards painted
Side backboards repaired and varnished
Floor washed and varnished (3 coats)
Basketball and badminton lines repainted
Walls and stairways leading to gym varnished
Walls, stage, and stage doors varnished
Doors under stage repaired
Apparatus room cleaned
Repaired molding around and oiled Thermolier
Washed and varnished floor in Physical Director's office
Radiator, walls, and ceiling painted in Physical Director's office

BADMINTON ROOM

Entire floor grouted
Walls and ceiling of showers painted
Walls, ceiling, and radiator of room painted
Molding for clothes hooks placed on wall

ART CLASS

Windows washed
Cleaned all paint jars
Work benches varnished
Doors and locks on storage cabinets repaired
Walls and stairway to room painted
Floor washed, varnished, and waxed
Stools, chairs, easels, bench, and potter's wheel painted

LOWER LOCKER ROOM

New lockers set in place
3 benches and 7 catwalks made
Applied dressing to floor
Cleaned windows
New key cabinet made
Weighing scales repaired
Stock room cleaned
Under sidewalk cleaned
Lights and shades cleaned
Ceiling at stairway replaced
Storage space made under stairway
Repaired and painted stairway to pool
New slide for window of towel room made
Painted walls of toilet and towel room
Varnished and painted benches and bases

BOILER ROOM AND WORKSHOP

Cleaned both filters
Tool cabinet cleaned
Recirculating pump cleaned
Top of oil tank cleaned
Pipe fitting rack sorted
Hot water valve repaired
Installed new circulating pump and changed piping for same

SHOPS

Repaired jig-saw in woodwork shop
New bookshelf made for print shop
Work benches in electric shop refinished
Woodwork shop cleaned and painted
Electric shop cleaned and painted

RESIDENT PROJECTS IN OPERATION, MARCH 31, 1938, BY STATES

At the end of March 1938, 95 Resident Projects were in operation in 29 States with 4460 youths receiving work experience and related instruction. These Resident Projects are being set up rapidly and there is every reason to believe that, by the end of June, 175 Resident Projects will be in operation employing 7000 or 8000 NYA youths.

REPORT OF NATIONAL YOUTH ADMINISTRATION

State	City	County	Total	White Male	White Female
United States			4,460	2,323	1,020
Alabama			*142*	*48*	—
	Huntsville	Madison	38	—	—
	Gadsden	Etowah	48	48	—
	Calhoun	Lowndes	11	—	—
	Montgomery	Montgomery	45	—	—
Arkansas			*438*	*356*	*30*
	Stella	Izard	106	106	—
	Beebe	White	14	14	—
	Solgohachia	Conway	95	95	—
	Camp Couchdale	Hot Spring	48	48	—
	Pine Bluff	Jefferson	54	—	—
	Magnolia	Columbia	22	22	—
	Conway	Faulkner	68	38	30
	Russellville	Pope	31	31	—
California	Riverside	Riverside	26	21	5
Florida			*103*	*103*	
	Winter Haven	Polk	18	18	—
	Youngstown	Bay	85	85	—
Georgia			*517*	*168*	*169*
	Fort Valley	Peach	81	—	—
	Walker Park	Walton	105	61	44
	Tifton	Tift	79	54	25
	Milledgeville	Baldwin	56	—	56
	McIntosh	Liberty	29	—	—
	Clarkesville	Habersham	49	35	14
	Carrollton	Carroll	48	18	30
	Savannah	Chatham	70	—	—
Idaho			*203*	*101*	*102*
	Pocatello	Bannock	84	57	27
	Moscow	Latah	43	43	—
	Coeur d'Alene	Kootenai	15	—	15
	Weiser	Washington	50	—	50
	Boise	Ada	11	1	10
Iowa	Tabor	Fremont	20	14	6

RESIDENT PROJECTS IN OPERATION AS OF MARCH 31, 1938

Youths Employed		Major Work Activity
Negro and Other		
Male	Female	
620	497	
43	*51*	
38	—	Construction of boys' dormitory
—	—	Construction and wiring of buildings, drainage, auto repair
5	6	Manufacture of school desks, sewing, and handicraft
—	45	College equipment
54		
—	—	Construction of county court house
—	—	Construction of administration building
—	—	Repairing of Government-owned autos and woodworking for schools and public buildings
—	—	Development of camp, workshop, and construction of buildings
54	—	General farming, landscaping, workshop, and kitchen work
—	—	General farming, workshop, and power plant operation
—	—	Carpentry, workshop, farming, gardening, sewing, and care of co-operative home
—	—	Auto mechanics, farming, carpentry, workshop, power plant operation
—	—	Building-plant rehabilitation
—	—	Concrete block construction of two-story vocational shop building
—	—	Demolition of CCC camp buildings
114	*66*	
56	25	Construction of Negro recreational camp
—	—	School construction
—	—	Georgia coastal plains experimental station
—	—	Assistance in school functions and public welfare institutions of city
21	8	Construction of 4-H club house and swimming pool
—	—	Finish second floor of school building and operation of farm
—	—	Construction and improvement of school property, operation of school farm, assistance in school functions
37	33	Construction work on school property, operation of school farm
—	—	Construction of co-operative dormitory and airplane hangar, renovation of CCC clothing salvage
—	—	Agricultural training, construct stock judging pavilion, Boy Scout cabins, and chicken house
—	—	Home economics, renovation of CCC salvage and sewing for State institutions
—	—	Renovation of CCC salvage, making clothes for State institutions
—	—	General library and clerical work
—	—	Rehabilitation of college, remodeling of buildings, sewing

REPORT OF NATIONAL YOUTH ADMINISTRATION

State	City	County	Total	White Male	White Female
Kansas			*134*	*46*	*45*
	Kingman	Kingman	15	—	15
	Topeka	Shawnee	43	—	—
	Hays	Ellis	76	46	30
Louisiana			*433*	*176*	*173*
	Scotlandville	E. Baton Rouge	34	—	—
	Lafayette	Lafayette	89	89	—
	Alexandria	Rapides	49	—	49
	Pineville	Rapides	22	22	—
	Shreveport	Caddo	46	—	46
	Ruston	Lincoln	24	24	—
	Grambling	Lincoln	33	—	—
	Mansfield	De Soto	17	—	—
	Natchitoches	Natchitoches	119	41	78
Michigan	Chelsea	Washtenaw	61	61	—
Minnesota	Crookston	Polk	18	—	6
Mississippi			*210*	*63*	*15*
	Piney Woods	Rankin	55	—	—
	Alcorn	Claiborne	48	—	—
	Clarksdale	Coahoma	29	—	—
	Poplarville	Pearl River	38	23	15
	Ellisville	Jones	40	40	—
Nebraska	Kearney	Buffalo	32	32	—
New Hampshire	Durham	Strafford	36	36	—
New Mexico	Camp Capitan	Lincoln	110	—	110
North Carolina			*91*	*41*	*4*
	Elizabeth City	Pasquotank	18	—	—
	Fayetteville	Cumberland	28	—	—
	Raleigh	Wake	41	41	—
	Crossmore	Avery	4	—	4
North Dakota			*55*	*27*	*28*
	Bottineau	Bottineau	27	27	—
	Dickinson	Stark	28	—	28
Ohio	New Philadelphia	Tuscarawas	144	123	—
Oklahoma			*514*	*301*	*150*
	Briston	Creek	57	57	—
	Cordell	Washita	47	47	—
	Goodwell	Texas	59	37	22

RESIDENT PROJECTS IN OPERATION AS OF MARCH 31, 1938

Youths Employed

Negro and Other

Male	Female	Major Work Activity
11	*32*	
—	—	Sewing and knitting
11	32	Mattress making for State welfare department
—	—	Building construction and clerical survey
50	*34*	
19	15	Agricultural training
—	—	Agricultural training
—	—	Homemaking
—	—	Auto mechanics
—	—	Hospital assistance
—	—	Agricultural training
14	19	Agricultural training
17	—	Construction
—	—	Agricultural training
—	—	Assistance in construction, carpentry, landscaping, plumbing, and labor
—	12	Chart making and sewing
99	*33*	
22	33	Cooking, sewing, canning, minor construction and furniture repair
48	—	Dormitory and school building repairs, soil conservation and general farming, shop work, and subsistence gardening
29	—	Minor construction and repair of school, plant, farming, shop, and home gardening
—	—	Building vocational shop, subsistence gardening, homemaking
—	—	Construction of vocational building, subsistence gardening, shop work
—	—	Construct school equipment, alter school auditorium, construct ticket office at athletic field
—	—	Repair, modernize, and improve educational plant
—	—	Manufacturing of State flags for public schools and furnishings for New Mexico crippled children's hospital
33	*13*	
18	—	Construction and improvements
15	13	Sewing, repairs, lunchroom service in grade schools
—	—	Construction, mechanics, and clerical work
—	—	Assisting in school lunchrooms and offices
—	—	Construction of two-story wooden dormitory
—	—	Clerical and stenographic work for college and county officials
21	—	Conservation and development of park and recreational areas
27	*36*	
—	—	Woodwork shop, build furniture for Resident Projects
—	—	Woodwork shop, build furniture for Resident Projects
—	—	Farm, mechanics' shops, canning process, and sewing

REPORT OF NATIONAL YOUTH ADMINISTRATION

State	City	County	Total	White Male	White Female
	Langston	Logan	63	—	—
	Lawton	Comanche	89	39	50
	Stillwater	Payne	101	45	56
	Wetumka	Hughes	50	50	—
	Wilburton	Latimer	48	26	22
Pennsylvania	Lancaster	Lancaster	16	16	—
South Carolina			*355*	*58*	*112*
	McCormick	McCormick	32	32	—
	Trenton	Edgefield	42	—	—
	Columbia	Rickland	235	—	112
	McColl	Marlboro	26	26	—
	Jenkinsville	Fairfield	20	—	—
South Dakota	Pukwana	Brule	60	—	60
Tennessee	Whiteville	Hardeman	46	—	—
Texas			*209*	*116*	—
	San Marcos	Hays	54	54	—
	Prairie View	Waller	45	—	—
	Prairie View	Waller	48	—	—
	Lubbock	Lubbock	51	51	—
	Luling	Caldwell	11	11	—
Utah	Cedar	Iron	30	25	5
Virginia			*56*	*20*	
	Christiansburg	Montgomery	36	—	—
	Lee Hall	Warwick	20	20	—
Washington	Pullman	Whitman	49	49	—
West Virginia			*50*	*22*	
	Institute	Kanawha	28	—	—
	Keyser	Mineral	22	22	—
Wisconsin			*302*	*302*	
	Antigo	Langlade	20	20	—
	Chippewa Falls	Chippewa	21	21	—
	Green Bay	Brown	31	31	—
	Madison	Dane	66	66	—
	Marinette	Marinette	27	27	—
	Menomonie	Dunn	21	21	—
	Platteville	Grant	21	21	—
	Racine	Racine	30	30	—
	Superior	Douglas	36	36	—
	Wausau	Marathon	29	29	—

Youths Employed

Negro and Other

Male	Female	Major Work Activity
27	36	Minor construction and sewing
—	—	Woodwork shops, farm irrigation, canning, and sewing
—	—	Landscaping on campus, cooking, and sewing
—	—	Build furniture for Resident Projects
—	—	Major and minor construction, cooking and sewing
—	—	Furniture construction
62	123	
—	—	Agricultural work on public land
42	—	Agricultural work on public land
—	123	Woodwork, craftwork, and sewing
—	—	Agricultural work on public land
20	—	Agricultural work on public land
—	—	Sewing and handicraft
16	30	Construction work and crafts
45	48	
—	—	Reconstruction and remodeling of building into NYA co-operative dormitory
45	—	Home economics practice house
—	48	Home economics in dormitory
—	—	Construction of NYA co-operative dormitory
—	—	Operation of 1200-acre experimental farm
—	—	Construction of dormitories
17	19	
17	19	Soil and food conservation, general farm work, home economics
—	—	Demolition and prefabrication of buildings, repairing school busses and playground equipment
—	—	Construction of dormitories
28		
28	—	Build rock gardens, hot beds, cold frames, plant trees and shrubbery, beautify college campus
—	—	Soil erosion and improve general farming, build fences
—	—	School and farm building, woodwork project, tourist information center
—	—	School furniture construction
—	—	Park and sanctuary improvement, proposed dormitory construction
—	—	Agricultural research and experiment, and auditorium equipment construction
—	—	Park and building improvement, proposed dormitory construction
—	—	Establishment and repair of recreational facilities
—	—	Farm experiment and demolition of CCC building for dormitory use
—	—	Construction of furniture and airplane hangar for school
—	—	School dormitory, farm building, experimental hostels, and furniture construction
—	—	Establishing and improving of recreational facilities and grounds

JUNIOR PLACEMENT OFFICES STARTED IN CO-OPERATION WITH STATE EMPLOYMENT SERVICES

OFFICES STARTED PREVIOUS TO JULY 1936

California (Los Angeles, San Francisco)............................ June 1936
Connecticut (Bridgeport, Hartford, New Haven).................... March 1936
Illinois (Chicago, Danville, Decatur, East St. Louis, Joliet, Peoria, Rockford, Springfield)... March 1936
Indiana (Indianapolis).. March 1936
Iowa (Cedar Rapids, Council Bluffs, Davenport, Dubuque, Des Moines, Fort Dodge, Sioux City, Waterloo)............................... March 1936
Massachusetts (Boston, Springfield, Worcester)..................... March 1936
New Hampshire (Concord, Manchester, Nashua)..................... March 1936
New York City (Bronx, Brooklyn)................................. March 1936
North Carolina (Asheville, Charlotte, Durham, Raleigh, Winston-Salem) March 1936
Texas (Dallas, Fort Worth, Houston, San Antonio).................. March 1936
Virginia (Richmond).. June 1936

OFFICES STARTED FROM JULY 1, 1936, TO JUNE 30, 1937

Alabama (Birmingham, Bessemer)................................. Dec. 1936
Arkansas (Little Rock, Fort Smith)................................ Nov. 1936
District of Columbia.. Oct. 1936
Florida (Jacksonville, Tampa, Miami)............................. Sept. 1936
Kansas (Topeka)... March 1937
Kentucky (Louisville).. Nov. 1936
Louisiana (New Orleans).. Oct. 1936
Michigan (Detroit)... Nov. 1936
Minnesota (Minneapolis, St. Paul, Duluth, Rochester)............... Feb. 1937
Nebraska (Omaha, Lincoln)....................................... Nov. 1936
Nevada (Las Vegas, Reno)... Jan. 1937
New Mexico (Albuquerque, Santa Fe)............................. Jan. 1937
Oklahoma (Oklahoma City, Tulsa)................................ Dec. 1936
Rhode Island (Providence).. Oct. 1936
West Virginia (Charleston, Wheeling)............................. June 1937
Wisconsin (Milwaukee)... March 1937

OFFICES STARTED FROM JULY 1, 1937, TO JANUARY 31, 1938

Colorado (Denver)... Nov. 1937
Georgia (Atlanta).. Dec. 1937
Idaho (Boise, Pocatello, Lewiston)............................... Jan. 1938
Missouri (Kansas City, St. Louis)................................. Aug. 1937
Tennessee (Chattanooga, Knoxville, Memphis)..................... July 1937
Vermont (Rutland)... Jan. 1938

INDUSTRIAL AND OCCUPATIONAL STUDIES
PREPARED BY NYA IN DIFFERENT STATES

INDUSTRIAL STUDIES

Air Conditioning....... Illinois†
"   "   .... Kentucky
"   "   .... Wisconsin
Air Transportation..... Illinois†
Automotive.......... Illinois†
Aviation Manufacturing Illinois†
Baking Industry........ Kentucky†
Candy Making......... Illinois
Canning (Vegetables)... Indiana*
Citrus Fruit.......... Florida*
Cotton Growing....... Texas*
Dairying.............. Wisconsin*
Electrical Appliance
   Manufacturing....... Illinois†
Farming.............. Illinois†
Fruit Packing......... California*
Furniture Making...... Illinois
Garment Industry...... Illinois
Glass................ Ohio*

Hosiery and Knit Goods
   Industries.......... Wisconsin*
Hotel Occupations..... Illinois†
Insurance............. Illinois†
Laundry Occupations... Illinois
Law................. Massachusetts*
Lumber.............. Washington*
Meat Packing......... Illinois|
Metal Manufacturing
   (Heavy)............. Wisconsin*
Milk Distribution...... Illinois†
Millinery............. Illinois
Oil Industry.......... Texas*
Pottery.............. Ohio*
Radio Industry........ Illinois†
Restaurant........... Illinois†
Rubber Industry....... Ohio
Tanning.............. Illinois†
Tobacco Industry....... Kentucky†

INDUSTRIAL AND OCCUPATIONAL STUDIES—Continued

OCCUPATIONAL STUDIES

Auto Mechanics........ Wisconsin	Maid Service......... Wisconsin
Aviation............. Wisconsin	Mining and Metallurgi-
Barber............... Ohio*	cal Engineering...... Wisconsin
Barber and Beautician.. Kentucky*	Music............... Illinois†
Beauty Culture........ Illinois†	Nursing............. Illinois†
" " .... Georgia	" .... Kansas*
" " .... Ohio	" .... Wisconsin
" " .... Wisconsin	Photography......... Wisconsin
Clerical............. Illinois†	Plant Pathology....... Georgia
" .... Ohio	Policeman............ Ohio*
" .... Kentucky	Power Sewing........ Georgia
Office Machine Opera-	Professional Salesman... Kentucky†
tor................. Ohio	Radio Broadcasting..... Illinois†
Secretarial Occupations.. Wisconsin	Radio Service......... Kentucky†
Diesel Engineering..... Illinois†	Recreational Worker.... Ohio*
" " .... Ohio*	Sales Person.......... Kansas*
Domestic Occupations.. Illinois†	" " .... Kentucky
" " .. Kentucky†	Soil Science........... Georgia
Dress Designing........ Illinois†	Store Occupations...... Illinois†
Forestry.............. Wisconsin	Structural Iron........ Illinois†
Gasoline Station....... Ohio	Teaching............. West Virginia
Laboratory Technician.. Wisconsin	" .... Wisconsin
Landscaping.......... Wisconsin	Undertaker........... Ohio*
Machinist............ Illinois†	Waitress.............. Kentucky*

* In preparation.
† Brief also was prepared with study.

MEDIAN WEEKLY WAGE OF YOUTH PLACED BY JUNIOR PLACEMENT OFFICES

This list shows the median weekly wage as of October 1937 earned by youth receiving employment through NYA Junior Placement Offices in 57 different cities:

MEDIAN WAGE

$ 8.03	Charlotte, N.C. (Negro)	$12.22	Charlotte, N.C.
8.29	Little Rock, Ark.	12.26	St. Paul, Minn.
8.75	Durham, N.C. (Negro)	12.27	Duluth, Minn.
9.49	Chicago, Ill. (Negro)	12.31	Des Moines, Iowa
9.74	Louisville, Ky.	12.47	Dubuque, Iowa
9.88	Birmingham, Ala.	12.50	Chicago, Ill.
10.00	Topeka, Kan.	12.73	Sioux City, Iowa
10.18	Springfield, Mass.	12.73	Nashua, N.H.
10.34	Decatur, Ill.	12.75	Manchester, N.H.
10.43	Joliet, Ill.	12.78	Rochester, Minn.
10.50	Las Vegas, N.M.	12.85	Charleston, W.Va.
10.71	New Orleans, La.	12.97	Detroit, Mich.
10.96	Kansas City, Mo.	13.02	Minneapolis, Minn.
11.07	Rochester, N.Y.	13.07	Davenport, Iowa
11.12	Rockford, Ill.	13.36	Council Bluffs, Iowa
11.22	Omaha, Neb.	13.37	District of Columbia
11.25	Tulsa, Okla.	13.38	Lincoln, Neb.
11.30	Fort Smith, Ark.	13.50	Hartford, Conn.
11.33	East St. Louis, Ill.	13.52	Indianapolis, Ind.
11.35	Concord, N.H.	13.65	Durham, N.C.
11.77	St. Louis, Mo.	13.86	Knoxville, Tenn.
11.82	Fort Dodge, Iowa	14.02	Worcester, Mass.
11.82	Denver, Colo.	14.79	Los Angeles, Calif.
11.82	Albuquerque, N.M.	14.86	Waterloo, Iowa
12.01	District of Columbia (Negro)	15.57	New Haven, Conn.
12.13	Danville, Ill.	15.64	San Francisco, Calif.
12.16	Peoria, Ill.	17.19	Bridgeport, Conn.
12.17	Wheeling, W.Va.	18.29	Reno, Nev.
12.22	Queens, N.Y.		

APPROVED STUDENT AID APPLICANTS

A special study was made of all applications approved for NYA Student Aid for the school year 1937–38 as of December 1937. The study includes 227,007 approved School Aid applicants and 107,214 College Aid applicants and presents the first information concerning the yearly family income, size of family, and occupation of the family head of students receiving school and college aid.

TABLE I

PER CENT. DISTRIBUTION OF APPROVED APPLICANTS FOR NATIONAL YOUTH ADMINISTRATION STUDENT AID BY YEARLY FAMILY INCOME

United States

Yearly Family Income	Total	Approved Applicants for NYA School Aid	Approved Applicants for NYA College Aid
Total..........................	100.0	100.0	100.0
None...........................	1.7	2.0	1.0
$ 0– 99...................	1.9	2.7	0.3
100– 199...................	4.7	6.3	1.1
200– 299...................	6.3	8.5	1.7
300– 399...................	7.8	10.2	2.6
400– 499...................	7.1	9.1	2.8
500– 599...................	7.9	9.6	4.3
600– 699...................	7.7	9.1	4.6
700– 799...................	6.7	7.8	4.5
800– 899...................	5.2	5.4	4.9
900– 999...................	4.9	4.8	5.1
1,000–1,249...................	12.5	9.0	19.9
1,250–1,499...................	3.2	2.0	5.9
1,500–1,749...................	4.8	1.9	10.9
1,750–1,999...................	2.4	0.7	6.2
2,000–2,499...................	3.3	0.5	9.3
2,500–2,999...................	1.2	0.1	3.4
3,000–3,999...................	0.8	0.1	2.5
4,000–4,999...................	0.2	(A)	0.5
5,000 and over..............	0.1	(A)	0.3
Unknown.....................	9.6	10.2	8.2

(A) Less than .05 per cent.

TABLE 2

PER CENT. DISTRIBUTION OF APPROVED APPLICANTS FOR
NATIONAL YOUTH ADMINISTRATION STUDENT AID BY SIZE OF FAMILY

United States

Size of Family	Total	Approved Applicants for NYA School Aid	Approved Applicants for NYA College Aid
Total	100.0	100.0	100.0
1	0.5	0.4	0.6
2	4.0	3.9	4.3
3	12.4	11.0	15.2
4	18.5	16.2	23.4
5	18.4	17.2	20.8
6	14.5	14.9	13.8
7	10.8	11.9	8.6
8	7.7	8.8	5.2
9	5.1	6.1	3.1
10 and over	7.2	8.8	3.9
Unknown	0.9	0.8	1.1

TABLE 3

DISTRIBUTION OF APPROVED APPLICANTS FOR
NATIONAL YOUTH ADMINISTRATION STUDENT AID
BY OCCUPATION OF FAMILY HEADS

United States

| Occupation | Family Heads of Approved Applicants for NYA Student Aid | | | | | |
| | Total | | For School Aid | | For College Aid | |
	Number	Per Cent.	Number	Per Cent.	Number	Per Cent.
Total...................	334,221	100.0	227,007	100.0	107,214	100.0
Professional and Technical.................	12,770	3.8	2,891	1.3	9,879	9.2
Proprietors, Managers, and Officials (A)......	14,690	4.4	3,577	1.6	11,113	10.4
Office Workers..........	11,292	3.4	3,785	1.7	7,507	7.0
Salesmen and Kindred Workers.............	12,350	3.7	4,159	1.8	8,191	7.6
Skilled Workers........	32,036	9.6	18,398	8.1	13,638	12.7
Semi-Skilled Workers....	33,047	9.9	23,269	10.3	9,778	9.1
Unskilled Workers (B)..	31,259	9.3	26,389	11.6	4,870	4.5
Domestic and Personal Service Workers......	22,016	6.6	16,275	7.2	5,741	5.4
Farm Operators and Laborers..............	73,168	21.9	53,251	23.4	19,917	18.6
Unemployed...........	56,577	16.9	43,631	19.2	12,946	12.1
Employed on WPA......	31,671	9.5	28,957	12.8	2,714	2.5
Occupation Unknown...	3,345	1.0	2,425	1.0	920	0.9

(A) Excludes farm operators.
(B) Excludes farm laborers.

INSTITUTIONS PARTICIPATING IN THE STUDENT AID PROGRAM

TABLE 4

NUMBER OF INSTITUTIONS PARTICIPATING IN THE
NATIONAL YOUTH ADMINISTRATION STUDENT AID PROGRAM
BY TYPES OF INSTITUTIONS

Monthly—September 1935 through March 1938

Month	Total	Schools	Colleges	Graduate Schools
1935				
September..............	4,159	3,923	232	4
October..............	10,689	9,039	1,485	165
November..............	14,955	13,235	1,529	191
December..............	17,236	15,455	1,586	195
1936				
January................	18,403	16,654	1,553	196
February..............	19,613	17,800	1,599	214
March................	20,076	18,271	1,585	220
April................	19,831	18,023	1,594	214
May................	18,474	16,658	1,604	212
June ,,,,,,,,,,,,,,,,	6,932	5,821	952	159
July................	39	39	—	—
August................	163	163	—	—
September...	4,875	4,717	152	6
October...............	19,906	18,128	1,598	180
November..............	23,247	21,393	1,660	194
December..............	23,794	21,977	1,628	189
1937				
January................	24,458	22,601	1,666	191
February..............	24,743	22,880	1,670	193
March................	24,930	23,068	1,671	191
April................	24,658	22,801	1,669	188
May................	22,672	20,816	1,668	188
June................	10,555	9,293	1,114	148
July................	—	—	—	—
August................	12	12		

TABLE 4—CONTINUED

Month	Total	Schools	Colleges	Graduate Schools
September...............	4,439	4,329	107	3
October.................	19,497	17,851	1,529	117
November...............	22,558	20,860	1,573	125
December...............	24,293	22,521	1,625	147
1938				
January.................	25,367	23,584	1,635	148
February................	25,568	23,792	1,627	149
March..................	25,566	23,907	1,636	152

TABLE 5

NUMBER OF STUDENTS ASSISTED UNDER THE
NATIONAL YOUTH ADMINISTRATION STUDENT AID PROGRAM
BY TYPES OF INSTITUTIONS

Monthly—September 1935 through March 1938

Month	Total	Schools	Colleges	Graduate Schools
1935				
September...............	34,924	26,163	8,700	61
October.................	183,594	75,033	104,969	3,592
November...............	234,450	118,273	111,500	4,677
December...............	282,829	159,158	118,453	5,218
1936				
January.................	306,490	189,031	112,654	4,805
February................	351,302	227,629	118,623	5,050
March..................	380,099	256,706	117,287	6,106
April...................	404,749	275,544	122,498	6,707
May....................	398,362	266,304	125,758	6,300
June....................	214,603	127,121	80,932	6,550
July....................	239	239	—	—
August.................	1,707	1,707	—	—
September...............	62,969	52,155	10,730	84
October.................	341,583	207,954	128,771	4,858
November...............	400,253	257,475	137,250	5,528
December...............	412,210	270,464	136,572	5,174
1937				
January.................	418,721	276,584	136,733	5,404
February................	428,818	283,738	139,541	5,539
March..................	442,100	294,456	142,127	5,517
April...................	443,986	297,871	140,699	5,416
May....................	425,694	280,427	139,841	5,426
June....................	249,826	153,168	92,382	4,276
July	—	—	—	—
August.................	36	36	—	—
September...............	36,581	31,758	4,688	135
October.................	244,648	155,793	86,831	2,024
November...............	284,535	189,180	93,037	2,318
December...............	303,253	204,762	95,967	2,524
1938				
January.................	309,306	211,330	95,475	2,501
February................	318,401	218,871	96,996	2,534
March..................	327,484	226,166	98,705	2,613

EMPLOYMENT ON WORK PROJECTS

TABLE 6

EMPLOYMENT ON NATIONAL YOUTH ADMINISTRATION WORK PROJECTS,
BY SEX AND BY RELIEF STATUS

Monthly—January 1936 through March 1938

Month	Total	Male	Female	Persons Certified As in Need of Relief	
				Number	Per Cent.
1936					
January	16,751	10,179	6,572	15,760	94.0
February	78,755	47,676	31,079	75,130	95.4
March	163,491	97,872	65,619	157,240	96.2
April	181,279	105,743	75,536	174,015	95.9
May	177,846	99,935	77,911	170,436	95.8
June	184,256	100,989	83,267	176,291	95.6
July	164,792	88,600	76,192	156,699	95.0
August	161,571	85,385	76,186	154,131	95.4
September	166,664	87,773	78,891	159,048	95.4
October	165,730	85,385	80,345	158,411	95.6
November	171,940	87,416	84,524	164,412	95.6
December	177,303	90,872	86,431	169,750	95.7
1937					
January	183,648	94,748	88,900	176,042	95.8
February	187,737	96,931	90,806	179,695	95.7
March	189,790	97,659	92,131	182,130	95.9
April	189,866	96,305	93,561	182,507	96.1
May	182,149	89,041	93,108	175,063	96.1
June	170,498	81,853	88,645	163,694	96.0
July	148,554	70,203	78,351	142,328	95.8
August	131,731	62,087	69,644	126,185	95.7
September	126,191	59,054	67,137	120,867	95.7
October	122,407	56,819	65,588	117,342	95.8
November	126,526	58,858	67,668	121,558	96.0
December	135,981	65,862	70,119	130,465	95.9
1938					
January	145,934	73,294	72,640	140,025	96.0
February	152,089	78,234	73,854	146,075	96.1
March	154,851	81,119	73,732	148,906	96.1

TABLE 7

TOTAL EMPLOYMENT ON NATIONAL YOUTH ADMINISTRATION
WORK PROJECTS BY TYPE OF WORK, RELIEF STATUS, AND SEX

Continental United States

Month Ending March 31, 1938*

(Subject to Revision)

Type of Project	Total		Number of Persons Employed					
			Certified			Non-Certified		
	Number	Per Cent	Total	Male	Female	Total	Male	Female
GRAND TOTAL	154,750	100.00	148,821	77,877	70,944	5,929	3,195	2,734
Highways, Roads, and Streets—Total	6,242	4.03	6,098	5,977	121	144	116	28
Roadside improvement	3,022		2,951	2,940	11	71	61	10
Other highway, road, and street projects	3,220		3,147	3,037	110	73	55	18
Public Building Projects—Total	19,884	12.85	19,301	18,823	478	583	532	51
Construction of new buildings	7,242		6,957	6,880	77	285	277	8
Remodeling and repair of public buildings	4,632		4,506	4,338	168	126	113	13
Improvement of grounds	8,010		7,838	7,605	233	172	142	30
Recreational Facilities (Excl. Bldgs.)	19,850	12.83	19,312	18,864	448	538	466	72
Conservation	2,170	1.40	2,128	2,044	84	42	34	8
Goods Projects—Total	27,800	17.96	26,904	9,993	16,911	896	411	485
Sewing	14,566		14,140	182	13,958	426	41	385
Workshops	13,234		12,764	9,811	2,953	470	370	100
Education Projects—Total	8,070	5.22	7,717	2,747	4,970	353	203	150
Nursery schools	3,831		3,742	145	3,597	89	11	78
Resident projects	4,239		3,975	2,602	1,373	264	192	72
Recreational Leadership Projects	10,195	6.59	9,604	4,800	4,804	591	312	279
Clerical Projects—Total	30,323	19.59	28,831	6,409	22,422	1,492	513	979
For Government agencies	23,742		22,587	4,977	17,610	1,155	408	747
For other than Government agencies	6,581		6,244	1,432	4,812	337	105	232
Professional and Technical Projects—Total	9,063	5.86	8,733	2,361	6,372	330	113	217
Agricultural demonstration	2,145		2,095	1,239	856	50	32	18
Library service and book repair	6,107		5,857	867	4,990	250	67	183
Museum work	811		781	255	526	30	14	16
Survey and Research Projects	356	.23	344	141	203	12	3	9
Art, Music, Drama, and Writing	1,006	.65	851	389	462	155	114	41
Home Economics Projects—Total	7,685	4.97	7,535	134	7,401	150	12	138
School lunches	2,051		2,030	55	1,975	21	2	19
Homemaking	5,634		5,505	79	5,426	129	10	119
Youth Center Activities (not elsewhere classified)	1,781	1.15	1,669	849	820	112	52	60
Projects not elsewhere classified	10,323	6.67	9,794	4,346	5,448	531	314	217

* Total of 154,750 represents revisions and is 101 less than total figure for employment on Work Projects, Table 6.

TOTAL EMPLOYMENT (RELIEF AND NON-RELIEF) ON NATIONAL YOUTH

Continental

Month Ending

(Subject to

NUMBER OF

State	Grand Total	Highways, Roads, and Streets Projects			Public Building Projects			
		Total	Roadside Improvements	Other	Total	Construction of New Buildings	Remodeling and Repair of Public Buildings	Improvement of Grounds around Buildings
United States	154,750	6,242	3,022	3,220	19,884	7,242	4,632	8,010
Alabama	3,084	234	15	219	794	219	126	449
Arizona	452	—	—	—	221	29	6	186
Arkansas	4,024	140	80	60	1,517	1,292	175	50
California	5,342	7	—	7	581	—	112	469
Colorado	2,004	101	—	101	369	132	37	200
Connecticut	1,558	39	12	27	44	—	15	29
Delaware	161	30	30	—	7	—	—	7
District of Columbia	336	—	—	—	44	—	—	44
Florida	2,902	5	5	—	508	279	23	206
Georgia	2,517	14	—	14	603	518	29	56
Idaho	850	18	—	18	141	1	76	64
Illinois	9,456	893	245	648	633	—	106	527
Indiana	2,225	65	52	13	166	26	36	104
Iowa	1,390	103	—	103	221	131	7	83
Kansas	4,594	199	—	199	745	241	23	481
Kentucky	6,374	279	—	279	983	84	610	289
Louisiana	2,384	9	9	—	568	314	254	—
Maine	751	—	—	—	—	—	—	—
Maryland	625	14	—	14	68	35	33	—
Massachusetts	3,632	—	—	—	34	10	24	—
Michigan	4,806	84	—	84	718	75	423	220
Minnesota	3,458	415	366	49	279	239	40	—
Mississippi	2,555	28	—	28	865	828	27	10
Missouri	4,147	601	311	290	321	8	56	257
Montana	1,350	53	17	36	132	14	84	34
Nebraska	1,855	306	7	299	306	166	95	45
Nevada	121	—	—	—	—	—	—	—
New Hampshire	560	12	—	12	31	—	31	—
New Jersey	3,507	77	—	77	261	—	100	161
New Mexico	1,104	47	15	32	112	68	—	44
New York City	8,843	—	—	—	—	—	—	—
New York (excl. N.Y.C.)	7,125	264	247	17	523	16	254	253
North Carolina	2,518	15	—	15	385	9	376	—
North Dakota	2,394	33	—	33	164	30	54	80
Ohio	6,468	298	190	108	193	138	—	55
Oklahoma	7,307	—	—	—	1,141	1,141	—	—
Oregon	619	—	—	—	53	25	—	28
Pennsylvania	11,768	404	404	—	829	56	395	378
Rhode Island	529	—	—	—	—	—	—	—
South Carolina	2,592	—	—	—	181	181	—	—
South Dakota	3,886	39	39	—	344	—	66	278
Tennessee	3,085	133	—	133	1,047	272	418	357
Texas	7,319	958	943	15	591	122	55	414
Utah	936	12	—	12	372	208	24	140
Vermont	310	9	—	9	52	—	52	—
Virginia	3,054	85	—	85	629	58	182	389
Washington	1,649	14	—	14	305	19	19	267
West Virginia	2,632	171	35	136	1,434	257	181	996
Wisconsin	3,268	—	—	—	347	1	—	346
Wyoming	324	34	—	34	22	—	8	14

8

ADMINISTRATION WORK PROJECTS BY TYPE OF PROJECT AND BY STATE
United States
March 31, 1938
Revision)

PERSONS EMPLOYED

Recreational Facilities (Excluding Buildings)	Conservation Projects	Goods Projects			Education Projects		
		Total	Sewing	Workshops	Total	Nursery Schools	Resident Projects
19,850	*2,170*	*27,800*	*14,566*	*13,234*	*8,070*	*3,831*	*4,239*
99	—	395	238	157	312	180	132
—	—	66	66	—	—	—	—
171	—	465	47	418	581	75	506
308	358	980	399	581	281	262	19
81	—	353	177	176	114	114	—
241	14	280	21	259	—	—	—
—	—	4	4	—	31	31	—
—	—	60	—	60	15	15	—
78	—	357	231	126	174	151	23
12	—	403	205	198	596	31	565
20	—	100	21	79	216	19	207
437	100	1,803	940	863	241	241	—
610	—	417	287	140	59	59	—
191	23	227	12	215	32	15	17
1,411	—	861	771	90	145	64	81
65	—	4,296	2,885	1,411	73	73	—
36	—	784	583	201	401	118	284
150	5	376	118	248	14	14	—
71	27	74	21	53	100	100	—
883	116	719	420	299	237	227	10
497	269	487	226	261	122	122	—
402	11	650	367	283	42	20	22
17	85	682	368	314	176	—	176
483	4	785	529	256	95	95	—
138	20	322	91	231	106	106	—
169	—	547	355	192	—	—	—
—	—	36	—	36	5	5	—
97	56	85	—	85	23	23	—
1,079	—	567	—	567	49	49	—
35	3	409	111	298	141	29	112
1,736	—	—		—	638	638	—
861	19	1,107	352	755	143	143	—
—	—	644	96	548	168	67	101
330	84	789	514	275	87	32	55
2,092	233	375	224	151	147	—	147
2,278	75	52	—	52	553	—	553
151	3	113	31	82	25	25	—
1,269	316	1,371	541	830	350	333	17
—	23	286	128	158	—	—	—
—	—	1,214	—	1,214	339	—	339
1,262	—	307	97	210	113	—	113
234	46	913	660	253	97	67	30
1,129	—	1,613	1,484	129	302	106	196
160	—	41	41	—	61	30	31
—	—	32	—	32	28	28	—
—	114	360	290	70	100	42	58
126	—	217	114	103	50	—	50
221	14	166	122	44	135	71	64
220	143	561	363	198	331	—	331
—	—	39	6	33	11	11	—

TABLE 8

TOTAL EMPLOYMENT (RELIEF AND NON-RELIEF) ON NATIONAL YOUTH

Continental

Month Ending

(Subject to

NUMBER OF

State	Recreational Leadership Projects	Clerical Projects			Professional and	
		Total	For Government Agencies	For Other Than Government Agencies	Total	Agricultural Demonstration
United States	10,195	30,323	23,742	6,581	9,063	2,145
Alabama	174	434	416	18	313	105
Arizona	11	76	76	—	25	—
Arkansas	—	915	904	11	208	—
California	280	1,259	525	734	433	52
Colorado	79	419	356	63	365	86
Connecticut	240	496	398	98	27	6
Delaware	9	24	8	16	7	—
District of Columbia	87	73	36	37	15	—
Florida	205	871	773	98	418	181
Georgia	—	348	348	—	67	45
Idaho	63	171	170	1	89	—
Illinois	788	1,699	1,092	607	744	107
Indiana	212	359	359	—	163	—
Iowa	69	305	215	90	117	23
Kansas	108	678	678	—	326	166
Kentucky	77	395	395	—	70	—
Louisiana	1	253	253	—	182	38
Maine	40	108	108	—	33	—
Maryland	12	83	79	4	15	5
Massachusetts	541	798	554	244	168	—
Michigan	421	1,483	1,106	377	155	—
Minnesota	333	751	541	210	279	88
Mississippi	—	423	423	—	231	—
Missouri	334	519	314	205	315	40
Montana	41	377	377	—	96	—
Nebraska	121	109	85	24	250	26
Nevada	46	22	6	16	12	—
New Hampshire	4	90	82	8	32	—
New Jersey	322	1,090	513	577	—	—
New Mexico	113	131	131	—	61	25
New York City	1,606	2,468	945	1,523	—	—
New York (excl. N.Y.C.)	765	1,700	1,362	338	919	221
North Carolina	24	416	416	—	128	62
North Dakota	89	363	345	18	107	9
Ohio	619	1,669	1,669	—	118	—
Oklahoma	38	857	857	—	285	285
Oregon	33	83	70	13	48	8
Pennsylvania	1,047	2,593	2,152	441	758	—
Rhode Island	138	81	81	—	—	—
South Carolina	—	393	393	—	80	80
South Dakota	294	615	615	—	—	—
Tennessee	50	194	194	—	115	8
Texas	104	1,363	1,363	—	463	410
Utah	72	32	32	—	133	—
Vermont	63	60	60	—	17	3
Virginia	143	627	531	96	261	43
Washington	51	496	437	59	157	19
West Virginia	105	193	121	72	66	—
Wisconsin	161	1,233	650	583	152	2
Wyoming	40	117	117	—	40	2

(Concluded)

ADMINISTRATION WORK PROJECTS BY TYPE OF PROJECT AND BY STATE

United States

March 31, 1938

Revision)

PERSONS EMPLOYED

Technical Projects		Survey and Research Projects	Art, Music, Drama, and Writing	Home Economics Projects			Youth Center Activities Not Elsewhere Classified	Projects Not Elsewhere Classified
Library Service and Book Repair	Museum Work			Total	School Lunches	Home-making		
6,107	*811*	*356*	*1,006*	*7,685*	*2,051*	*5,634*	*1,781*	*10,325*
203	5	61	—	236	87	149	—	31
25	—	—	—	23	19	4	—	29
180	28	—	—	23	—	23	—	4
234	147	3	207	77	59	18	94	474
206	73	36	4	66	44	22	17	—
19	2	—	8	10	—	10	69	90
7	—	—	—	12	12	—	27	10
—	15	—	—	—	—	—	—	42
116	11	—	6	113	110	3	—	167
22	—	—	—	241	—	241	215	18
89	—	—	3	11	—	11	—	8
637	—	25	171	165	—	165	331	1,426
158	5	33	—	119	12	107	—	12
44	50	—	13	29	—	29	10	50
160	—	—	—	5	5	—	18	98
70	—	—	—	21	21	—	—	115
144	—	—	—	—	—	—	101	48
33	—	—	—	—	—	—	16	9
10	—	—	—	56	15	41	75	30
168	—	—	23	18	—	18	80	15
147	8	—	—	80	64	16	—	490
191	—	23	73	97	97	—	44	59
209	22	—	—	—	—	—	—	48
275	—	108	—	42	42	—	198	342
85	11	—	—	29	29	—	—	27
214	10	—	—	44	22	22	—	3
12	—	—	—	—	—	—	—	—
9	23	—	—	125	2	123	—	5
—	—	61	—	—	—	—	—	—
31	5	4	—	—	—	—	38	—
—	—	—	—	—	—	—	—	2,395
538	160	—	79	393	199	194	168	184
66	—	—	—	687	218	469	—	51
97	1	—	5	57	57	—	—	286
118	—	—	109	605	—	605	—	—
—	—	—	54	1,974	—	1,974	—	—
40	—	—	—	37	29	8	—	73
637	121	—	217	33	—	33	208	2,373
—	—	—	—	—	—	—	—	385
—	—	—	—	902	60	842	—	—
35	72	—	—	130	78	52	—	126
53	—	—	—	460	450	10	11	325
133	—	—	—	53	53	—	—	—
14	—	—	—	49	49	—	—	—
218	—	—	—	490	148	342	—	245
134	4	—	23	87	31	56	—	123
34	32	—	—	17	—	17	61	49
144	6	—	9	50	20	30	—	60
38	—	—	2	19	19	—	—	—

FUND ALLOCATIONS AND EMPLOYMENT
NATIONALLY AND BY STATES

The following tables give fund allocations since the beginning of the National Youth Administration Program through the present fiscal year ending June 30, 1938, nationally and by States. During the year 1935–36, the Work Projects Program operated only for a six months' period, January 1, 1936, through June 30, 1936. Consequently, the fund allocations to Work Projects for this year are smaller than for the succeeding two years.

Employment, total earnings, average hours worked, average hourly earnings, and average monthly earnings are given on the Work Projects Program and the Student Aid Program, nationally and by States, for the month of March 1938, the most recent available figures. (These statistics are subject to revisions due to the receipt of late pay-rolls which slightly change the totals.)

TABLE 9

FUND ALLOCATIONS FOR NATIONAL YOUTH ADMINISTRATION WORK PROJECTS PROGRAM AND STUDENT AID PROGRAM FOR FISCAL YEAR ENDING JUNE 30, 1938, BY STATES

| | Work Projects | Student Aid | | |
		Total	School Aid	College and Graduate Aid
TOTAL.........	$35,800,000.00	$19,091,039.00	$8,549,018.00	$10,542,021.00
Alabama...........	581,180.00	275,115.00	112,500.00	162,615.00
Arizona............	127,609.00	84,495.00	39,000.00	45,495.00
Arkansas...........	804,056.00	209,640.00	120,000.00	89,640.00
California..........	1,303,523.00	1,075,230.00	300,000.00	775,230.00
Colorado...........	406,083.00	275,130.00	135,000.00	140,130.00
Connecticut........	418,901.00	154,580.00	71,250.00	83,330.00
Delaware..........	30,325.00	17,085.00	7,500.00	9,585.00
District of Columbia	94,438.00	140,400.00	16,500.00	123,900.00
Florida............	526,299.00	226,920.00	120,000.00	106,920.00
Georgia............	619,310.00	402,000.00	183,750.00	218,250.00
Idaho..............	200,982.00	112,935.00	52,050.00	60,885.00
Illinois............	2,246,188.00	1,050,300.00	465,000.00	585,300.00
Indiana............	652,557.00	473,445.00	195,000.00	278,445.00
Iowa..............	276,428.00	372,015.00	126,000.00	246,015.00
Kansas............	812,246.00	449,332.00	210,000.00	239,332.00

TABLE 9 (*Continued*)

	Work Projects	Student Aid		
		Total	School Aid	College and Graduate Aid
Kentucky..........	$1,099,170.00	$416,655.00	$247,500.00	$169,155.00
Louisiana..........	694,204.00	291,285.00	90,000.00	201,285.00
Maine.............	150,791.00	83,700.00	33,750.00	49,950.00
Maryland..........	153,732.00	179,617.00	67,500.00	112,117.00
Massachusetts......	1,095,965.00	553,950.00	262,500.00	291,450.00
Michigan..........	1,114,654.00	678,390.00	285,000.00	393,390.00
Minnesota.........	927,042.00	493,020.00	216,000.00	277,020.00
Mississippi........	493,981.00	211,230.00	93,750.00	117,480.00
Missouri..........	963,306.00	539,130.00	252,000.00	287,130.00
Montana..........	296,905.00	149,125.00	85,000.00	64,125.00
Nebraska..........	343,625.00	253,935.00	94,500.00	159,435.00
Nevada...........	37,982.00	17,820.00	5,400.00	12,420.00
New Hampshire....	186,173.00	80,250.00	26,250.00	54,000.00
New Jersey........	1,177,137.00	398,707.00	243,750.00	154,957.00
New Mexico.......	362,144.00	82,185.00	48,750.00	33,435.00
New York City.....	2,419,969.00	1,060,320.00	375,000.00	685,320.00
New York (excl. N.Y.C.)..........	2,015,103.00	729,962.00	352,500.00	377,462.00
North Carolina.....	498,394.00	409,935.00	138,750.00	271,185.00
North Dakota......	434,026.00	211,405.00	130,000.00	81,405.00
Ohio..............	1,849,018.00	1,024,545.00	480,000.00	544,545.00
Oklahoma..........	1,100,290.00	590,535.00	342,000.00	248,535.00
Oregon...........	163,314.00	158,040.00	42,750.00	115,290.00
Pennsylvania.......	3,332,973.00	1,520,715.00	862,500.00	658,215.00
Rhode Island.......	205,553.00	84,375.00	33,750.00	50,625.00
South Carolina.....	529,949.00	266,220.00	131,250.00	134,970.00
South Dakota......	572,152.00	246,685.00	175,000.00	71,685.00
Tennessee..........	554,586.00	376,410.00	178,500.00	197,910.00
Texas..............	1,037,359.00	895,170.00	345,000.00	550,170.00
Utah..............	183,808.00	159,795.00	56,250.00	103,545.00
Vermont...........	68,149.00	51,600.00	16,500.00	35,100.00
Virginia...........	485,907.00	335,205.00	131,250.00	203,955.00
Washington........	401,403.00	320,405.00	106,500.00	213,905.00
West Virginia......	653,259.00	302,325.00	195,000.00	107,325.00
Wisconsin..........	1,018,411.00	474,963.00	195,000.00	279,963.00
Wyoming..........	79,441.00	34,920.00	14,400.00	20,520.00
Alaska.............		6,890.00	5,000.00	1,890.00
Hawaii............		38,520.00	23,130.00	15,390.00
Puerto Rico........		44,478.00	13,788.00	30,690.00

TABLE 10

NATIONAL YOUTH ADMINISTRATION

(A) GRAND TOTAL OF STATE TABLES SHOWING FUND ALLOCATIONS AND EMPLOYMENT FOR MARCH 1938

Fund Allocations

	Total	Work Projects	Student Aid
1935–1936[1]	$ 39,356,811	$15,257,101	$24,099,710
1936–1937	65,501,239	36,601,239	28,900,000
1937–1938	54,891,039	35,800,000	19,091,039
Grand Total......	$159,749,689	$87,658,340	$72,090,749

Employment on National Youth Administration Programs for March 1938[2]:

Program	Number Institutions	Number of Persons			Total Earnings	Average Hours Worked	Average Hourly Earnings	Average Monthly Earnings
		Total	Male	Female				
Work Projects								
Total all persons......		154,851	81,119	73,732	$2,739,990	49.1	$.361	$17.69
Relief.............		148,906	77,920	70,986	2,366,759	47.0	.338	15.89
Non-relief..........		5,945	3,199	2,746	373,231	101.7	.617	62.78
Student Aid								
Total all programs.....	25,559	327,484	165,466	162,018	$2,111,784	23.7	$.272	$6.45
School Aid..........	23,907	226,166	105,139	121,027	1,002,509	18.3	.243	4.43
College Aid.........	1,636	98,705	58,395	40,310	1,163,537	35.7	.330	11.79
Graduate Aid........	152	2,613	1,932	681	46,738	37.2	.481	17.89
Total Employment.......		482,335	246,585	235,750				

[1] Allocations for Work Projects were for a six-month period only, January 1, 1936 through June 30, 1936.

[2] Preliminary figures, subject to revision.

(B) State by State Summary Tables Showing Fund Allocations and Employment for March 1938[1]

ALABAMA

State Youth Director: J. E. Bryan
325 First Nat. Bank Bldg.
Montgomery

Fund Allocations

	Total	Work Projects	Student Aid
1935–1936	$ 552,288.81	$ 211,352.22	$340,936.59
1936–1937	973,718.00	601,850.00	371,868.00
1937–1938	856,295.00	581,180.00	275,115.00
Grand Total........	$2,382,301.81	$1,394,382.22	$987,919.59

Employment on National Youth Administration Programs for March 1938:

Program	Number Institutions	Number of Persons			Total Earnings	Average Hours Worked	Average Hourly Earnings	Average Monthly Earnings
		Total	Male	Female				
Work Projects								
Total all persons........		3,084	1,333	1,751	$38,274	53.8	$.231	$12.41
Relief..............		3,020	1,303	1,717	33,693	51.7	.216	11.16
Non-relief..........		64	30	34	4,581	152.7	.469	71.58
Student Aid								
Total all programs.....	728	4,875	2,292	2,583	$32,017	31.0	$.212	$ 6.57
School Aid...........	701	3,332	1,456	1,876	13,850	24.1	.173	4.15
College Aid..........	27	1,514	815	699	17,722	45.2	.259	11.71
Graduate Aid	2	29	21	8	465	97.2	.165	16.03
Total Employment........		7,959	3,625	4,334				

[1] Including also Alaska, District of Columbia, Hawaii, New York City, and Puerto Rico.

ALASKA

John W. Troy
Governor
Juneau

Fund Allocations	Total	Work Projects[1]	Student Aid
1935–1936	—		—
1936–1937	$2,031		$2,031
1937–1938	6,890		6,890
Grand Total.......	$8,921		$8,921

Employment on National Youth Administration Programs for March 1938:

Program	Number Institutions	Number of Persons			Total Earnings	Average Hours Worked	Average Hourly Earnings	Average Monthly Earnings
		Total	Male	Female				
Student Aid								
Total all programs.....	2	21	9	12	$261	24.9	$.500	$12.43
School Aid...........	1	6	2	4	36	12.0	.500	6.00
College Aid..........	1	15	7	8	225	30.0	.500	15.00
Graduate Aid.........	—	—	—	—	—	—	—	—
Total Employment.......		21	9	12				

[1] No Work Projects Program in operation in Alaska.

ARIZONA

State Youth Director: Miss Jane Rider
203 Orpheum Theatre Bldg.
Phoenix

Fund Allocations

	Total	Work Projects	Student Aid
1935–1936	$181,527.14	$ 65,610.82	$115,916.32
1936–1937	213,806.00	93,820.00	119,986.00
1937–1938	212,104.00	127,609.00	84,495.00
Grand Total.......	$607,437.14	$287,039.82	$320,397.32

Employment on National Youth Administration Programs for March 1938:

Program	Number Institutions	Number of Persons			Total Earnings	Average Hours Worked	Average Hourly Earnings	Average Monthly Earnings
		Total	Male	Female				
Work Projects								
Total all persons......		452	260	192	$6,819	47.7	$.316	$15.09
Relief.............		443	254	189	6,362	47.0	.305	14.36
Non-relief...........		9	6	3	457	82.2	.618	50.78
Student Aid								
Total all programs.....	78	1,315	680	635	$9,342	23.8	$.299	$ 7.10
School Aid...........	73	887	464	423	4,351	18.2	.269	4.91
College Aid..........	5	424	213	211	4,938	35.3	.330	11.65
Graduate Aid.........	1	4	3	1	53	37.8	.351	13.25
Total Employment........		1,767	940	827				

ARKANSAS

State Youth Director: J. W. Hull
Russellville

Fund Allocations	Total	Work Projects	Student Aid
1935–1936	$ 506,317.65	$ 220,855.89	$285,461.76
1936–1937	1,048,345.00	652,170.00	396,175.00
1937–1938	1,013,696.00	804,096.00	209,640.00
Grand Total.......	$2,568,358.65	$1,677,081.89	$891,276.76

Employment on National Youth Administration Programs for March 1938:

Program	Number Institutions	Number of Persons			Total Earnings	Average Hours Worked	Average Hourly Earnings	Average Monthly Earnings
		Total	Male	Female				
Work Projects								
Total all persons.....		4,024	2,800	1,224	$61,404	66.3	$.230	$15.26
Relief............		3,912	2,698	1,214	51,751	63.8	.207	13.23
Non-relief...........		112	102	10	9,653	154.3	.558	86.19
Student Aid								
Total all programs.....	516	4,356	1,992	2,364	$22,724	29.5	$.177	$ 5.22
School Aid..........	492	3,276	1,420	1,856	11,257	21.3	.162	3.44
College Aid..........	24	1,080	572	508	11,467	54.7	.194	10.62
Graduate Aid..........	—	—	—	—	—	—	—	—
Total Employment........		8,380	4,792	3,588				

CALIFORNIA

State Youth Director: Mrs. Anne Treadwell
49 Fourth Street
San Francisco

Fund Allocations

	Total	Work Projects	Student Aid
1935–1936	$2,100,969.91	$ 614,532.52	$1,486,437.39
1936–1937	2,653,019.00	1,164,850.00	1,488,169.00
1937–1938	2,378,753.00	1,303,523.00	1,075,230.00
Grand Total......	$7,132,741.91	$3,082,905.52	$4,049,836.39

Employment on National Youth Administration Programs for March 1938:

Program	Number Institutions	Number of Persons			Total Earnings	Average Hours Worked	Average Hourly Earnings	Average Monthly Earnings
		Total	Male	Female				
Work Projects								
Total all persons........		5,302	2,529	2,773	$109,961	41.8	$.496	$20.74
Relief.............		5,143	2,455	2,688	98,386	40.3	.475	19.13
Non-relief...........		159	74	85	11,575	89.9	.810	72.80
Student Aid								
Total all programs.....	509	14,913	7,656	7,257	$117,067	23.7	$.360	$ 8.52
School Aid..........	428	7,383	3,173	4,210	35,503	16.4	.293	4.81
College Aid.........	77	7,162	4,216	2,946	84,667	30.3	.390	11.82
Graduate Aid........	9	368	267	101	6,897	38.7	.484	18.74
Total Employment........		20,215	10,185	10,030				

COLORADO

State Youth Director: Kenneth W. Rowe
810 14th Street
Denver

Fund Allocations

	Total	Work Projects	Student Aid
1935–1936	$ 519,199.66	$186,551.11	$332,648.55
1936–1937	730,682.00	381,050.00	349,632.00
1937–1938	681,213.00	406,083.00	275,130.00
Grand Total......	$1,931,094.66	$973,684.11	$957,410.55

Employment on National Youth Administration Programs for March 1938:

Program	Number Institutions	Number of Persons			Total Earnings	Average Hours Worked	Average Hourly Earnings	Average Monthly Earnings
		Total	Male	Female				
Work Projects								
Total all persons........		2,004	896	1,108	$32,777	47.2	$.346	$16.36
Relief..............		1,932	874	1,058	28,746	45.9	.324	14.88
Non-relief..........		72	22	50	4,031	82.2	.681	55.99
Student Aid								
Total all programs.....	360	4,822	2,367	2,455	$32,818	23.5	$.289	$ 6.81
School Aid..........	343	3,620	1,613	2,007	17,836	18.1	.272	4.93
College Aid.........	17	1,185	743	442	14,770	39.9	.312	12.46
Graduate Aid........	3	17	11	6	212	30.4	.411	12.47
Total Employment........		6,826	3,263	3,563				

CONNECTICUT

State Youth Director: Thomas J. Dodd
1044 Chapel Street
New Haven

Fund Allocations

	Total	Work Projects	Student Aid
1935–1936	$ 381,579.27	$188,014.09	$193,565.18
1936–1937	544,953.00	329,100.00	215,853.00
1937–1938	573,481.00	418,901.00	154,580.00
Grand Total......	$1,500,013.27	$936,015.09	$563,998.18

Employment on National Youth Administration Programs for March 1938:

Program	Number Institutions	Number of Persons			Total Earnings	Average Hours Worked	Average Hourly Earnings	Average Monthly Earnings
		Total	Male	Female				
Work Projects								
Total all persons........		1,558	863	695	$35,254	51.9	$.436	$22.63
Relief.............		1,491	821	670	30,252	49.5	.410	20.29
Non-relief.............		67	42	25	5,002	105.1	.710	74.66
Student Aid								
Total all programs.....	127	2,259	1,121	1,138	$17,941	23.7	$.335	$ 7.94
School Aid...........	107	1,467	671	796	7,887	19.8	.271	5.38
College Aid..........	20	655	336	319	7,298	30.4	.367	11.14
Graduate Aid........	2	137	114	23	2,756	33.7	.597	12.47
Total Employment........		3,817	1,984	1,833				

DELAWARE

State Youth Director: Benjamin Abelman
6th and King Streets
Wilmington

Fund Allocations

	Total	Work Projects	Student Aid
1935–1936	$ 33,984.01	$13,417.37	$20,566.64
1936–1937	47,833.00	24,615.00	23,218.00
1937–1938	47,410.00	30,325.00	17,685.00
Grand Total	$129,227.01	$68,357.37	$60,869.64

Employment on National Youth Administration Programs for March 1938:

Program	Number Institutions	Number of Persons Total	Male	Female	Total Earnings	Average Hours Worked	Average Hourly Earnings	Average Monthly Earnings
Work Projects								
Total all persons		161	75	86	$2,677	44.5	$.374	$16.63
Relief		159	74	85	2,498	43.4	.362	15.71
Non-relief		2	1	1	179	130.0	.688	89.50
Student Aid								
Total all programs	37	284	165	119	$2,027	26.6	$.269	$ 7.14
School Aid	35	168	80	88	958	25.3	.225	5.70
College Aid	2	116	85	31	1,069	28.4	.325	9.22
Graduate Aid	—	—	—	—	—	—	—	—
Total Employment		445	240	205				

DISTRICT OF COLUMBIA

State Youth Director: Miss Francoise Black
460 C Street, N.W.
Washington

Fund Allocations

	Total	Work Projects	Student Aid
1935–1936	$160,564.12	$ 27,979.02	$132,585.10
1936–1937	273,292.00	81,066.00	192,226.00
1937–1938	234,838.00	94,438.00	140,400.00
Grand Total.......	$668,694.12	$203,483.02	$465,211.10

Employment on National Youth Administration Programs for March 1938:

Program	Number Institutions	Number of Persons			Total Earnings	Average Hours Worked	Average Hourly Earnings	Average Monthly Earnings
		Total	Male	Female				
Work Projects								
Total all persons......		336	128	208	$ 5,788	44.6	$.387	$17.23
Relief...............		324	123	201	4,812	42.1	.353	14.85
Non-relief...........		12	5	7	976	112.0	.726	81.33
Student Aid								
Total all programs.....	35	1,226	712	514	$15,359	33.3	$.376	$12.53
School Aid..........	24	356	116	240	1,820	17.4	.293	5.11
College Aid.........	11	747	522	225	10,934	39.6	.370	14.64
Graduate Aid........	5	123	74	49	2,605	41.2	.514	21.18
Total Employment........		1,562	840	722				

FLORIDA

State Youth Director: Joe A. Youngblood
611-614 Dyal Upchurch Bldg.
Jacksonville

Fund Allocations

	Total	Work Projects	Student Aid
1935-1936	$ 493,775.71	$ 212,767.47	$281,008.24
1936-1937	718,260.00	427,490.00	290,770.00
1937-1938	753,219.00	526,299.00	226,920.00
Grand Total	$1,965,254.71	$1,166,556.47	$798,698.24

Employment on National Youth Administration Programs for March 1938:

Program	Number Institutions	Number of Persons			Total Earnings	Average Hours Worked	Average Hourly Earnings	Average Monthly Earnings
		Total	Male	Female				
Work Projects								
Total all persons		2,901	1,027	1,874	$34,854	51.3	$.234	$12.01
Relief		2,793	936	1,857	31,925	51.3	.223	11.43
Non-relief		108	91	17	2,929	52.5	.517	27.12
Student Aid								
Total all programs	526	4,238	1,904	2,334	$25,699	23.3	$.261	$ 6.06
School Aid	511	3,310	1,391	1,919	13,474	18.0	.227	4.07
College Aid	15	924	511	413	12,150	42.2	.312	13.15
Graduate Aid	2	4	2	2	75	43.5	.431	18.75
Total Employment		7,139	2,931	4,208				

GEORGIA

State Youth Director: D. B. Lasseter
10 Forsyth Street Bldg.
Atlanta

Fund Allocations

	Total	Work Projects	Student Aid
1935–1936	$ 818,285.33	$ 276,854.78	$ 541,430.55
1936–1937	1,445,697.00	728,500.00	717,197.00
1937–1938	1,021,310.00	619,310.00	402,000.00
Grand Total......	$3,285,292.33	$1,624,664.78	$1,660,627.55

Employment on National Youth Administration Programs for March 1938:

Program	Number Institutions	Number of Persons			Total Earnings	Average Hours Worked	Average Hourly Earnings	Average Monthly Earnings
		Total	Male	Female				
Work Projects								
Total all persons........		2,517	1,311	1,206	$40,495	50.1	$.321	$16.09
Relief..............		2,454	1,287	1,167	35,151	47.6	.301	14.32
Non-relief............		63	24	39	5,344	147.8	.574	84.83
Student Aid								
Total all programs.....	704	8,134	3,521	4,613	$45,671	25.1	$.224	$ 5.61
School Aid...........	655	5,931	2,381	3,550	20,760	19.1	.183	3.50
College Aid..........	46	2,103	1,093	1,010	22,921	40.5	.269	10.90
Graduate Aid.........	7	100	47	53	1,990	54.3	.367	19.90
Total Employment........		10,651	4,832	5,819				

HAWAII

Oren E. Long
Honolulu

Fund Allocations	Total	Work Projects[1]	Student Aid
1935–1936	—		—
1936–1937	$50,777.05		$50,777.05
1937–1938	38,520.00		38,520.00
Grand Total......	$89,297.05		$89,297.05

Employment on National Youth Administration Programs for March 1938:

Program	Number Institutions	Number of Persons			Total Earnings	Average Hours Worked	Average Hourly Earnings	Average Monthly Earnings
		Total	Male	Female				
Student Aid								
Total all programs.....	27	724	470	254	$4,779	25.8	$.256	$ 6.60
School Aid...........	26	557	361	196	3,015	22.4	.242	5.41
College Aid..........	1	158	104	54	1,599	36.5	.277	10.12
Graduate Aid........	1	9	5	4	165	45.8	.400	18.33
Total Employment.......		724	470	254				

[1] No Work Projects Program in operation in Hawaii.

IDAHO

State Youth Director: William W. Gartin
Room 408
Capitol Securities Bldg.
Boise

Fund Allocations

	Total	Work Projects	Student Aid
1935–1936	$213,717.38	$ 62,013.18	$151,704.20
1936–1937	362,778.66	212,182.00	150,596.66
1937–1938	313,917.00	200,982.00	112,935.00
Grand Total.......	$890,413.04	$475,177.18	$415,235.86

Employment on National Youth Administration Programs for March 1938:

Program	Number Institutions	Number of Persons			Total Earnings	Average Hours Worked	Average Hourly Earnings	Average Monthly Earnings
		Total	Male	Female				
Work Projects								
Total all persons........		850	458	392	$15,696	47.7	$.387	$18.47
Relief.................		810	431	379	13,635	45.9	.367	16.83
Non-relief............		40	27	13	2,061	84.5	.610	51.53
Student Aid								
Total all programs.....	190	2,002	974	1,028	$13,748	21.9	$.314	$ 6.87
School Aid...........	180	1,390	592	798	6,456	16.6	.280	4.64
College Aid..........	10	604	374	230	7,083	33.7	.348	11.73
Graduate Aid.........	1	8	8	—	209	52.4	.499	26.13
Total Employment.......		2,852	1,432	1,420				

ILLINOIS

State Youth Director: Wm. J. Campbell
Merchandise Mart
222 West North Bank Drive
Chicago

Fund Allocations

	Total	Work Projects	Student Aid
1935–1936	$2,161,201.56	$ 657,341.06	$1,503,860.50
1936–1937	3,954,654.00	2,213,970.00	1,740,684.00
1937–1938	3,296,488.00	2,246,188.00	1,050,300.00
Grand Total......	$9,412,343.56	$5,117,499.06	$4,294,844.50

Employment on National Youth Administration Programs for March 1938:

Program	Number Institutions	Number of Persons			Total Earnings	Average Hours Worked	Average Hourly Earnings	Average Monthly Earnings
		Total	Male	Female				
Work Projects								
Total all persons........		9,456	4,996	4,460	$182,985	54.7	$.354	$19.35
Relief..............		8,690	4,681	4,009	149,586	52.4	.329	17.21
Non-relief.............		766	315	451	33,399	81.2	.537	43.60
Student Aid								
Total all programs.....	998	18,738	9,963	8,775	$123,989	22.4	$.296	$ 6.62
School Aid..........	915	13,042	6,447	6,595	56,756	17.9	.244	4.35
College Aid........	74	5,485	3,336	2,149	64,105	32.8	.356	11.69
Graduate Aid........	9	211	180	31	3,128	29.2	.508	14.82
Total Employment........		28,194	14,959	13,235				

INDIANA

State Youth Director: Robert S. Richey
745 Century Building
Indianapolis

Fund Allocations

	Total	Work Projects	Student Aid
1935–1936	$1,091,701.21	$ 471,068.45	$ 620,632.76
1936–1937	1,408,454.00	743,700.00	664,754.00
1937–1938	1,126,002.00	652,557.00	473,445.00
Grand Total........	$3,626,157.21	$1,867,325.45	$1,758,831.76

Employment on National Youth Administration Programs for March 1938:

Program	Number Institutions	Number of Persons			Total Earnings	Average Hours Worked	Average Hourly Earnings	Average Monthly Earnings
		Total	Male	Female				
Work Projects								
Total all persons........		2,225	1,221	1,004	$41,711	39.2	$.478	$18.75
Relief..............		2,183	1,198	985	37,885	37.6	.461	17.35
Non-relief.............		42	23	19	3,816	120.4	.757	91.10
Student Aid								
Total all programs....	695	8,702	4,742	3,960	$57,253	23.6	.279	$ 6.58
School Aid...........	657	5,923	2,864	3,059	25,929	18.8	.233	4.38
College Aid..........	38	2,726	1,836	890	30,449	33.8	.331	11.17
Graduate Aid.........	3	53	42	11	875	37.4	.442	16.51
Total Employment........		10,927	5,963	4,964				

IOWA

State Youth Director: R. W. Tallman
Royal Union Life Bldg.
Des Moines

Fund Allocations

	Total	Work Projects	Student Aid
1935–1936	$ 574,321.68	$ 95,663.17	$ 478,658.51
1936–1937	809,947.00	191,880.00	618,067.00
1937–1938	648,443.00	276,428.00	372,015.00
Grand Total.......	$2,032,711.68	$563,971.17	$1,468,740.51

Employment on National Youth Administration Programs for March 1938:

Program	Number Institutions	Number of Persons			Total Earnings	Average Hours Worked	Average Hourly Earnings	Average Monthly Earnings
		Total	Male	Female				
Work Projects								
Total all persons........		1,390	792	598	$21,972	41.2	$.383	$15.81
Relief................		1,359	773	586	20,188	39.6	.375	14.86
Non-relief............		31	19	12	1,784	112.0	.514	57.55
Student Aid								
Total all programs.....	800	5,743	2,986	2,757	$41,767	26.7	$.272	$ 7.27
School Aid..........	735	3,314	1,497	1,817	13,848	19.7	.223	4.18
College Aid..........	65	2,363	1,441	922	26,677	37.6	.301	11.29
Graduate Aid.........	3	66	48	18	1,242	40.4	.466	18.82
Total Employment........		7,133	3,778	3,355				

KANSAS

State Youth Director: Anne Laughlin
801 Harrison Street
Topeka

Fund Allocations

	Total	Work Projects	Student Aid
1935–1936	$ 884,934.19	$ 369,753.30	$ 515,180.89
1936–1937	1,580,387.00	836,570.00	743,817.00
1937–1938	1,261,578.00	812,246.00	449,332.00
Grand Total........	$3,726,899.19	$2,018,569.30	$1,708,329.89

Employment on National Youth Administration Programs for March 1938:

Program	Number Institutions	Number of Persons			Total Earnings	Average Hours Worked	Average Hourly Earnings	Average Monthly Earnings
		Total	Male	Female				
Work Projects								
Total all persons........		4,594	2,794	1,800	$64,044	46.4	$.301	$13.94
Relief...............		4,461	2,717	1,744	54,271	43.3	.281	12.17
Non-relief............		133	77	56	9,773	148.3	.496	73.48
Student Aid								
Total all programs.....	753	9,449	4,598	4,851	$55,562	23.6	$.249	$ 5.88
School Aid...........	688	6,819	3,183	3,636	25,660	17.4	.217	3.76
College Aid..........	45	2,602	1,394	1,208	29,456	39.7	.285	11.32
Graduate Aid.........	3	28	21	7	446	37.2	.428	15.93
Total Employment........		14,043	7,392	6,651				

KENTUCKY

State Youth Director: Robert K. Salyers
9th and Broadway
Louisville

Fund Allocations

	Total	Work Projects	Student Aid
1935–1936	$1,001,522.61	$ 474,799.26	$ 526,723.35
1936–1937	2,261,494.00	1,474,150.00	787,344.00
1937–1938	1,515,825.00	1,099,170.00	416,655.00
Grand Total.......	$4,778,841.61	$3,048,119.26	$1,730,722.35

Employment on National Youth Administration Programs for March 1938:

Program	Number Institutions	Number of Persons			Total Earnings	Average Hours Worked	Average Hourly Earnings	Average Monthly Earnings
		Total	Male	Female				
Work Projects								
Total all persons......	—	6,374	2,881	3,493	$80,707	47.0	$.269	$12.66
Relief.............	—	6,156	2,778	3,378	64,711	43.8	.240	10.51
Non-relief.........	—	218	103	115	15,996	136.7	.537	73.38
Student Aid								
Total all programs.....	725	8,578	4,005	4,573	$50,575	26.0	$.226	$ 5.90
School Aid..........	692	6,786	3,089	3,697	31,516	22.2	.209	4.64
College Aid.........	33	1,792	916	876	19,059	40.7	.262	10.64
Graduate Aid.........	—	—	—	—	—	—	—	—
Total Employment........		14,952	6,886	8,066				

State Youth Director: A. J. Sarré
910 Canal Bank Bldg.
New Orleans

LOUISIANA

Fund Allocations

	Total	Work Projects	Student Aid
1935–1936	$ 535,399.12	$ 188,745.14	$ 346,653.98
1936–1937	841,314.00	470,568.00	370,746.00
1937–1938	985,489.00	694,204.00	291,285.00
Grand Total.......	$2,362,202.12	$1,353,517.14	$1,008,684.98

Employment on National Youth Administration Programs for March 1938:

Program	Number Institutions	Number of Persons			Total Earnings	Average Hours Worked	Average Hourly Earnings	Average Monthly Earnings
		Total	Male	Female				
Work Projects								
Total all persons........		2,384	1,094	1,290	$39,964	67.3	$.249	$16.76
Relief............		2,123	872	1,251	29,168	65.6	.209	13.74
Non-relief...........		261	221	39	10,796	80.6	.513	41.36
Student Aid								
Total all programs.....	595	4,350	2,114	2,236	$33,447	29.3	$.263	$ 7.69
School Aid..........	570	2,279	987	1,292	10,189	21.4	.209	4.47
College Aid.........	25	2,067	1,115	942	23,144	37.9	.296	11.20
Graduate Aid........	1	4	2	2	114	56.8	.502	28.50
Total Employment........		6,734	3,208	3,526				

MAINE

State Youth Director: Charles G. Hewett
Congress Building
142 High Street
Portland

Fund Allocations

	Total	Student Aid	Work Projects
1935–1936	$185,270.86	$107,871.18	$ 77,399.68
1936–1937	398,090.00	127,110.00	270,980.00
1937–1938	234,491.00	83,700.00	150,791.00
Grand Total.......	$817,851.86	$318,681.18	$499,170.68

Employment on National Youth Administration Programs for March 1938:

Program	Number Institutions	Number of Persons			Total Earnings	Average Hours Worked	Average Hourly Earnings	Average Monthly Earnings
		Total	Male	Female				
Work Projects								
Total all persons......		778	523	255	$14,146	47.7	$.381	$18.18
Relief.............		753	503	250	12,190	45.5	.355	16.19
Non-relief...........		25	20	5	1,956	116.2	.673	78.24
Student Aid								
Total all programs.....	202	1,251	666	585	$ 9,746	25.6	$.304	$ 7.79
School Aid...........	186	768	390	378	3,826	17.9	.279	4.98
College Aid..........	16	483	276	207	5,920	38.0	.323	12.25
Graduate Aid.........	—	—	—	—	—	—	—	—
Total Employment.......		2,029	1,189	840				

MARYLAND

State Youth Director: Ryland N. Dempster
1245 Baltimore Trust Bldg.
Baltimore

Fund Allocations

	Total	Work Projects	Student Aid
1935–1936	$ 330,345.63	$ 95,647.74	$234,697.89
1936–1937	381,187.00	129,560.00	251,627.00
1937–1938	333,349.00	153,732.00	179,617.00
Grand Total.......	$1,044,881.63	$378,939.74	$665,941.89

Employment on National Youth Administration Programs for March 1938:

Program	Number Institutions	Number of Persons			Total Earnings	Average Hours Worked	Average Hourly Earnings	Average Monthly Earnings
		Total	Male	Female				
Work Projects								
Total all persons......		625	326	299	$10,036	51.2	$.314	$16.06
Relief...............		604	313	291	8,191	48.5	.280	13.56
Non-relief...........		21	13	8	1,845	129.8	.677	87.86
Student Aid								
Total all programs.....	174	2,553	1,355	1,198	$19,748	24.5	$.316	$ 7.74
School Aid..........	147	1,406	670	736	7,038	19.9	.251	5.01
College Aid..........	27	1,109	653	456	12,139	30.4	.360	10.95
Graduate Aid.........	3	38	32	6	571	20.0	.753	15.03
Total Employment		3,178	1,681	1,497				

MASSACHUSETTS

State Youth Director: E. L. Casey
Park Square Building
31 St. James Avenue
Boston

Fund Allocations

	Total	Work Projects	Student Aid
1935–1936	$1,177,865.26	$ 578,153.38	$ 599,711.88
1936–1937	1,937,529.00	1,206,300.00	731,229.00
1937–1938	1,649,915.00	1,095,965.00	553,950.00
Grand Total.......	$4,765,309.26	$2,880,418.38	$1,884,890.88

Employment on National Youth Administration Programs for March 1938:

Program	Number Institutions	Number of Persons			Total Earnings	Average Hours Worked	Average Hourly Earnings	Average Monthly Earnings
		Total	Male	Female				
Work Projects								
Total all persons........		3,632	1,955	1,677	$86,046	56.6	$.419	$23.69
Relief.................		3,496	1,877	1,619	76,595	54.0	.406	21.91
Non-relief.............		136	78	58	9,451	123.4	.563	69.49
Student Aid								
Total all programs.....	378	9,106	4,801	4,305	$62,402	21.0	$.327	$ 6.85
School Aid............	327	6,253	2,986	3,267	29,687	26.2	.293	4.75
College Aid...........	51	2,652	1,644	1,008	29,161	30.6	.359	11.00
Graduate Aid.........	11	201	171	30	3,554	41.9	.422	17.68
Total Employment.......		12,738	6,756	5,982				

MICHIGAN

State Youth Director: C. R. Bradshaw
127 North Cedar Street
Lansing

Fund Allocations

	Total	Work Projects	Student Aid
1935–1936	$1,511,297.70	$ 678,292.46	$ 843,005.24
1936–1937	2,274,290.00	1,190,000.00	1,084,290.00
1937–1938	1,793,044.00	1,114,654.00	678,390.00
Grand Total......	$5,588,631.70	$2,982,946.46	$2,605,685.24

Employment on National Youth Administration Programs for March 1938:

Program	Number Institutions	Number of Persons			Total Earnings	Average Hours Worked	Average Hourly Earnings	Average Monthly Earnings
		Total	Male	Female				
Work Projects								
Total all persons........		4,806	2,658	2,148	$88,913	55.7	$.332	$ 18.50
Relief..............		4,725	2,607	2,118	79,427	54.3	.310	16.81
Non-relief............		81	51	30	9,486	141.7	.826	117.11
Student Aid								
Total all programs.......	748	10,704	5,567	5,137	$79,323	24.6	$.301	$ 7.41
School Aid...........	706	7,070	3,198	3,872	33,679	19.4	.245	4.76
College Aid..........	42	3,455	2,223	1,232	42,858	34.8	.356	12.40
Graduate Aid.........	2	179	146	33	2,786	31.1	.500	15.56
Total Employment........		15,510	8,225	7,285				

MINNESOTA

State Youth Director: George A. Selke
Minnesota Building
4th and Cedar Streets
St. Paul

Fund Allocations

	Total	Work Projects	Student Aid
1935–1936	$ 979,344.64	$ 385,694.20	$ 593,650.44
1936–1937	1,584,911.00	858,270.00	726,641.00
1937–1938	1,420,062.00	927,042.00	493,020.00
Grand Total.......	$3,984,317.64	$2,171,006.20	$1,813,311.44

Employment on National Youth Administration Programs for March 1938:

Program	Number Institutions	Number of Persons			Total Earnings	Average Hours Worked	Average Hourly Earnings	Average Monthly Earnings
		Total	Male	Female				
Work Projects								
Total all persons......		3,458	1,919	1,539	$66,334	42.8	$.448	$19.18
Relief.............		3,254	1,808	1,446	55,995	41.3	.417	17.21
Non-relief..........		204	111	93	10,339	67.3	.753	50.68
Student Aid								
Total all programs.....	545	8,073	3,744	4,329	$55,101	20.7	$.330	$ 6.83
School Aid..........	510	5,295	2,046	3,249	22,711	14.1	.305	4.29
College Aid.........	35	2,766	1,687	1,079	32,179	33.4	.349	11.63
Graduate Aid........	1	12	11	1	211	37.6	.468	17.58
Total Employment......		11,531	5,663	5,868				

MISSISSIPPI

State Youth Director: J. C. Flowers
1705 Tower Building
Jackson

Fund Allocations

	Total	Work Projects	Student Aid
1935–1936	$ 445,879.47	$ 160,254.09	$285,625.38
1936–1937	718,962.00	425,770.00	293,192.00
1937–1938	705,211.00	493,981.00	211,230.00
Grand Total....	$1,870,052.47	$1,080,005.09	$790,047.38

Employment on National Youth Administration Programs for March 1938:

Program	Number Institutions	Number of Persons			Total Earnings	Average Hours Worked	Average Hourly Earnings	Average Monthly Earnings
		Total	Male	Female				
Work Projects								
Total all persons.......		2,555	1,556	999	$34,924	57.7	$.237	$13.67
Relief.............		2,452	1,477	975	27,519	55.0	.204	11.22
Non-relief............		103	79	24	7,405	121.3	.592	71.89
Student Aid								
Total all programs.....	739	4,663	2,309	2,354	$25,036	28.1	$.191	$ 5.37
School Aid..........	701	3,092	1,440	1,652	11,891	24.2	.159	3.85
College Aid..........	38	1,570	869	701	13,125	35.8	.233	8.36
Graduate Aid.........	1	1	—	1	20	80.0	.250	20.00
Total Employment.......		7,218	3,865	3,353				

MISSOURI

State Youth Director: C. Clark Buckner
210 E. Capitol Avenue
Jefferson City

Fund Allocations

	Total	Work Projects	Student Aid
1935–1936	$1,010,676.54	$ 382,512.71	$ 628,163.83
1936–1937	2,001,020.00	1,056,020.00	945,000.00
1937–1938	1,502,436.00	963,306.00	539,130.00
Grand Total.......	$4,514,132.54	$2,401,838.71	$2,112,293.83

Employment on National Youth Administration Programs for March 1938:

Program	Number Institutions	Number of Persons Total	Male	Female	Total Earnings	Average Hours Worked	Average Hourly Earnings	Average Monthly Earnings
Work Projects								
Total all persons.......		4,147	2,243	1,904	$74,181	50.2	$.356	$17.89
Relief.............		4,015	2,186	1,829	67,298	48.6	.345	16.76
Non-relief...........		132	57	75	6,883	99.2	.526	52.14
Student Aid								
Total all programs.....	894	9,932	4,745	5,187	$61,357	23.9	$.258	$ 6.18
School Aid...........	834	7,163	3,236	3,927	29,107	17.9	.226	4.06
College Aid...........	60	2,734	1,485	1,249	31,616	39.3	.294	11.56
Graduate Aid.........	4	35	24	11	634	39.9	.454	18.11
Total Employment.......		14,079	6,988	7,091				

MONTANA

State Youth Director: James B. Love
Silver Bow Club Bldg.
Butte

Fund Allocations

	Total	Work Projects	Student Aid
1935–1936	$ 268,187.07	$100,470.15	$167,716.92
1936–1937	483,356.00	234,140.00	249,216.00
1937–1938	446,030.00	296,905.00	149,125.00
Grand Total.......	$1,197,573.07	$631,515.15	$566,057.92

Employment on National Youth Administration Programs for March 1938:

Program	Number Institutions	Number of Persons			Total Earnings	Average Hours Worked	Average Hourly Earnings	Average Monthly Earnings
		Total	Male	Female				
Work Projects								
Total all persons.......		1,349	688	661	$25,200	39.7	$ .470	$18.68
Relief..............		1,321	671	650	22,838	37.8	.458	17.29
Non-relief...........		28	17	11	2,362	133.0	.634	84.36
Student Aid								
Total all programs.....	203	3,295	1,585	1,710	$20,075	19.7	$ .310	$ 6.09
School Aid...........	193	2,616	1,206	1,410	12,835	16.8	.292	4.91
College Aid..........	10	678	378	300	7,209	30.6	.348	10.63
Graduate Aid.........	1	1	1	—	31	77.0	.403	31.00
Total Employment.......		4,644	2,273	2,371				

NEBRASKA

State Youth Director: Miss Gladys J. Shamp
Union Terminal Warehouse Bldg.
900 N. 16th St.
Lincoln

Fund Allocations

	Total	Work Projects	Student Aid
1935–1936	$ 464,612.05	$163,735.90	$ 300,876.15
1936–1937	753,538.00	299,582.00	453,956.00
1937–1938	597,560.00	343,625.00	253,935.00
Grand Total......	$1,815,710.05	$866,942.90	$1,008,767.15

Employment on National Youth Administration Programs for March 1938:

Program	Number Institutions	Number of Persons			Total Earnings	Average Hours Worked	Average Hourly Earnings	Average Monthly Earnings
		Total	Male	Female				
Work Projects								
Total all persons.......		1,855	1,000	855	$28,993	43.8	$.356	$15.63
Relief..............		1,776	965	811	25,476	42.4	.338	14.34
Non-relief..........		79	35	44	3,517	76.9	.579	44.52
Student Aid								
Total all programs.....	561	4,346	2,291	2,055	$29,949	25.5	$.270	$ 6.89
School Aid..........	538	2,724	1,307	1,417	10,756	16.9	.233	3.95
College Aid.........	23	1,610	974	636	19,033	39.9	.296	11.82
Graduate Aid........	2	12	10	2	160	36.9	.361	13.33
Total Employment........		6,201	3,291	2,910				

NEVADA

State Youth Director: Miss Margaret Griffin
303 South Center Street
Reno

Fund Allocations

	Total	Work Projects	Student Aid
1935–1936	$ 21,101.07	$ 4,712.70	$16,388.37
1936–1937	28,575.00	8,190.00	20,385.00
1937–1938	55,802.00	37,982.00	17,820.00
Grand Total.......	$105,478.07	$50,884.70	$54,593.37

Employment on National Youth Administration Programs for March 1938:

Program	Number Institutions	Number of Persons			Total Earnings	Average Hours Worked	Average Hourly Earnings	Average Monthly Earnings
		Total	Male	Female				
Work Projects								
Total all persons.....		121	61	60	$1,987	39.2	$.419	$16.42
Relief...............		120	61	59	1,952	38.9	.418	16.27
Non-relief...........		1	—	1	35	70.0	.500	35.00
Student Aid								
Total all programs.....	34	251	136	115	$2,312	22.9	$.402	$ 9.21
School Aid...........	33	129	52	77	686	15.9	.335	5.32
College Aid..........	1	122	84	38	1,616	30.4	.439	13.33
Graduate Aid.........	—	—	—	—	—	—	—	—
Total Employment.......		372	197	175				

NEW HAMPSHIRE

State Youth Director: Harold C. Bingham
Silver and Lincoln Sts.
Manchester

Fund Allocations

	Total	Work Projects	Student Aid
1935–1936	$118,317.37	$ 45,390.01	$ 72,927.36
1936–1937	237,232.00	147,420.00	89,812.00
1937–1938	266,423.00	186,173.00	80,250.00
Grand Total.......	$621,972.37	$378,983.01	$242,989.36

Employment on National Youth Administration Programs for March 1938:

Program	Number Institutions	Number of Persons			Total Earnings	Average Hours Worked	Average Hourly Earnings	Average Monthly Earnings
		Total	Male	Female				
Work Projects								
Total all persons........		560	315	245	$10,936	73.8	$.265	$19.53
Relief................		534	303	231	8,878	70.7	.235	16.63
Non-relief............		26	12	14	2,058	137.4	.576	79.15
Student Aid								
Total all programs.....	98	1,127	594	533	$ 9,332	27.2	$.305	$ 8.28
School Aid..........	90	596	271	325	2,988	18.5	.271	5.01
College Aid..........	8	528	320	208	6,320	31.1	.323	11.97
Graduate Aid........	2	3	3	—	24	14.7	.545	8.00
Total Employment........		1,687	909	778				

NEW JERSEY

State Youth Director: Daniel S. Kealey
1060 Broad Street
Newark

Fund Allocations

	Total	Work Projects	Student Aid
1935–1936	$ 878,800.05	$ 455,951.20	$ 422,840.85
1936–1937	1,861,992.00	1,312,014.00	549,978.00
1937–1938	1,575,844.00	1,177,137.00	398,707.00
Grand Total.......	$4,316,636.05	$2,545,102.20	$1,371,525.85

Employment on National Youth Administration Programs for March 1938:

Program	Number Institutions	Number of Persons Total	Male	Female	Total Earnings	Average Hours Worked	Average Hourly Earnings	Average Monthly Earnings
Work Projects								
Total all persons.....	279	3,507	2,091	1,416	$76,065	44.1	$.492	$21.69
Relief...............	249	3,412	2,036	1,376	70,768	42.9	.484	20.74
Non-relief...........		95	55	40	5,297	87.0	.641	55.76
Student Aid								
Total all programs....		6,644	3,704	2,940	$45,524	22.8	$.301	$ 6.85
School Aid...........		5,143	2,686	2,457	27,757	20.3	.265	5.40
College Aid..........	30	1,495	1,012	483	17,643	31.1	.379	11.80
Graduate Aid........	3	6	6	—	124	50.7	.408	20.67
Total Employment......		10,151	5,795	4,356				

NEW MEXICO

State Youth Director: Thos. L. Popejoy
117 South Third Street
Albuquerque

Fund Allocations

	Total	Work Projects	Student Aid
1935–1936	$ 234,927.42	$132,254.72	$102,672.70
1936–1937	412,236.28	305,655.00	106,581.28
1937–1938	444,329.00	362,144.00	82,185.00
Grand Total.......	$1,091,492.70	$800,053.72	$291,438.98

Employment on National Youth Administration Programs for March 1938:

Program	Number Institutions	Number of Persons			Total Earnings	Average Hours Worked	Average Hourly Earnings	Average Monthly Earnings
		Total	Male	Female				
Work Projects								
Total all persons........		1,246	472	774	$23,310	54.1	$.346	$18.71
Relief.............		1,190	454	736	19,027	50.0	.320	15.99
Non-relief........		56	18	38	4,283	141.7	.540	76.48
Student Aid								
Total all programs.....	212	1,499	783	716	$ 9,559	24.4	$.261	$ 6.38
School Aid..........	205	1,084	566	518	5,393	20.2	.247	4.98
College Aid.........	7	414	216	198	4,146	35.5	.282	10.01
Graduate Aid........	1	1	1	—	20	66.0	.303	20.00
Total Employment........		2,745	1,2,5	1,490				

NEW YORK CITY

Youth Director: Carroll N. Gibney
265 W. 14th Street
New York City

Fund Allocations

	Total	Work Projects	Student Aid
1935–1936	$2,237,674.45	$780,403.03	$1,457,271.42
1936–1937	3,767,076.00	2,151,300.00	1,615,776.00
1937–1938	3,480,289.00	2,419,969.00	1,060,320.00
Grand Total........	$9,485,039.45	$5,351,672.03	$4,133,367.42

Employment on National Youth Administration Programs for March 1938:

Program	Number Institutions	Number of Persons			Total Earnings	Average Hours Worked	Average Hourly Earnings	Average Monthly Earnings
		Total	Male	Female				
Work Projects								
Total all persons......		8,843	4,805	4,038	$198,634	43.9	$.511	$22.46
Relief.............		8,341	4,539	3,802	174,254	41.7	.501	20.89
Non-relief.........		502	266	236	24,380	81.1	.599	48.57
Student Aid								
Total all programs.....	220	15,881	8,656	7,225	$121,808	16.7	$.460	$7.67
School Aid..........	170	10,096	4,721	5,375	42,538	10.6	.399	4.21
College Aid.........	48	5,454	3,701	1,753	73,710	27.2	.497	13.51
Graduate Aid........	10	331	234	97	5,560	29.4	.572	16.80
Total Employment........		24,724	13,461	11,263				

NEW YORK STATE

State Youth Director: Karl D. Hesley
30 Lodge Street
Albany

Fund Allocations

	Total	Work Projects	Student Aid
1935–1936	$1,623,237.15	$ 677,972.82	$ 945,264.33
1936–1937	3,173,229.00	2,160,450.00	1,012,779.00
1937–1938	2,745,065.00	2,015,103.00	729,962.00
Grand Total	$7,541,531.15	$4,853,525.82	$2,688,005.33

Employment on National Youth Administration Programs for March 1938:

Program	Number Institutions	Number of Persons			Total Earnings	Average Hours Worked	Average Hourly Earnings	Average Monthly Earnings
		Total	Male	Female				
Work Projects								
Total all persons........		7,125	3,493	3,632	$165,898	44.9	$.519	$23.28
Relief..............		6,956	3,384	3,572	146,486	42.9	.491	21.06
Non-relief.........		169	109	60	19,412	127.7	.899	114.86
Student Aid								
Total all programs.....	824	11,998	6,207	5,791	$ 86,588	22.2	$.325	$ 7.22
School Aid...........	773	8,307	3,983	4,324	41,516	17.3	.289	5.00
College Aid..........	51	3,629	2,182	1,447	44,039	33.1	.366	12.14
Graduate Aid.........	5	62	42	20	1,033	36.1	.462	16.66
Total Employment........		19,123	9,700	9,423				

NORTH CAROLINA

State Youth Director: C. E. McIntosh
204-10 Masonic Temple Bldg.
Raleigh

Fund Allocations	Total	Work Projects	Student Aid
1935–1936	$ 624,522.74	$ 115,924.79	$ 508,597.95
1936–1937	1,070,436.00	440,600.00	629,836.00
1937–1938	908,329.00	493,394.00	409,935.00
Grand Total	$2,603,287.74	$1,054,918.79	$1,548,368.95

Employment on National Youth Administration Programs for March 1938:

Program	Number Institutions	Number of Persons			Total Earnings	Average Hours Worked	Average Hourly Earnings	Average Monthly Earnings
		Total	Male	Female				
Work Projects								
Total all persons		2,518	851	1,667	$32,489	55.8	$.231	$12.90
Relief		2,423	829	1,594	26,146	52.6	.205	10.79
Non-relief		95	22	73	6,343	136.8	.488	66.77
Student Aid								
Total all programs	977	5,876	2,846	3,030	$46,255	32.8	$.240	$ 7.87
School Aid	926	3,183	1,515	1,668	15,025	25.0	.189	4.72
College Aid	51	2,676	1,320	1,356	30,905	42.0	.275	11.55
Graduate Aid	2	17	11	6	325	41.4	.462	19.12
Total Employment		8,394	3,697	4,697				

NORTH DAKOTA

State Youth Director: Robert Byrne
Box 810
Bismarck

Fund Allocations

	Total	Work Projects	Student Aid
1935–1936	$ 404,970.93	$ 184,745.39	$220,225.54
1936–1937	765,518.00	416,300.00	349,218.00
1937–1938	645,431.00	434,026.00	211,405.00
Grand Total	$1,815,919.93	$1,035,071.39	$780,848.54

Employment on National Youth Administration Programs for March 1938:

Program	Number Institutions	Number of Persons			Total Earnings	Average Hours Worked	Average Hourly Earnings	Average Monthly Earnings
		Total	Male	Female				
Work Projects								
Total all persons		2,394	1,117	1,267	$37,736	45.2	$.349	$15.76
Relief		2,370	1,114	1,256	35,198	44.2	.336	14.85
Non-relief		24	13	11	2,538	141.1	.750	105.75
Student Aid								
Total all programs	460	5,026	2,357	2,669	$32,774	24.1	$.271	$ 6.52
School Aid	448	4,107	1,803	2,304	23,744	22.1	.262	5.78
College Aid	12	919	554	365	9,030	33.0	.298	9.83
Graduate Aid	—	—	—	—	—	—	—	—
Total Employment		7,420	3,484	3,936				

OHIO

Fund Allocations

	Total	Work Projects	Student Aid
1935–1936	$2,135,007.37	$ 853,862.90	$1,281,144.47
1936–1937	3,237,453.00	1,881,700.00	1,355,753.00
1937–1938	2,873,563.00	1,849,018.00	1,024,545.00
Grand Total	$8,246,023.37	$4,584,580.90	$3,661,442.47

Employment on National Youth Administration Programs for March 1938:

Program	Number Institutions	Number of Persons			Total Earnings	Average Hours Worked	Average Hourly Earnings	Average Monthly Earnings
		Total	Male	Female				
Work Projects								
Total all persons......		6,468	3,620	2,848	$144,966	48.0	$.467	$22.41
Relief...............		6,173	3,467	2,706	144,740	45.5	.444	20.21
Non-relief..........		295	153	142	20,226	100.4	.683	68.56
Student Aid								
Total all programs.....	1,136	16,244	8,243	8,001	$120,021	25.2	$.294	$ 7.39
School Aid..........	1,069	11,387	5,242	6,145	55,800	19.9	.247	4.90
College Aid.........	67	4,746	2,922	1,824	62,037	37.6	.348	13.07
Graduate Aid........	6	111	79	32	2,184	38.8	.507	19.68
Total Employment.......		22,712	11,863	10,849				

OKLAHOMA

State Youth Director: Houston A. Wright
431 West Main Street
Oklahoma City

Fund Allocations	Total	Work Projects	Student Aid
1935–1936	$1,134,663.21	$ 427,507.49	$ 707,155.72
1936–1937	2,441,530.00	1,267,870.00	1,173,660.00
1937–1938	1,690,825.00	1,100,290.00	590,535.00
Grand Total	$5,267,018.21	$2,795,667.49	$2,471,350.72

Employment on National Youth Administration Programs for March 1938:

Program	Number Institutions	Number of Persons			Total Earnings	Average Hours Worked	Average Hourly Earnings	Average Monthly Earnings
		Total	Male	Female				
Work Projects								
Total all persons.......		7,307	4,302	3,005	$97,475	44.3	$.301	$13.34
Relief..............		7,135	4,190	2,945	82,151	41.4	.278	11.51
Non-relief..........		172	112	60	15,324	166.6	.535	89.09
Student Aid								
Total all programs.....	1,012	13,563	6,139	7,424	$67,231	22.1	$.224	$ 4.96
School Aid...........	970	11,081	4,945	6,136	39,688	17.5	.205	3.58
College Aid..........	42	2,469	1,185	1,284	27,351	42.8	.259	11.08
Graduate Aid.........	2	13	9	4	192	49.3	.300	14.77
Total Employment.......		20,870	10,441	10,429				

OREGON

State Youth Director: Ivan Munro
1123 Bedell Building
Portland

Fund Allocations

	Total	Work Projects	Student Aid
1935–1936	$282,248.32	$ 77,941.80	$204,306.52
1936–1937	314,018.00	105,900.00	208,118.00
1937–1938	321,354.00	163,314.00	158,040.00
Grand Total......	$917,620.32	$347,155.80	$570,464.52

Employment on National Youth Administration Programs for March 1938:

Program	Number Institutions	Number of Persons			Total Earnings	Average Hours Worked	Average Hourly Earnings	Average Monthly Earnings
		Total	Male	Female				
Work Projects								
Total all persons........		619	368	251	$11,020	46.5	$.383	$17.80
Relief..............		613	366	247	10,392	45.6	.372	16.95
Non-relief............		6	2	4	628	145.0	.722	104.67
Student Aid								
Total all programs.....	206	2,480	1,204	1,276	$18,393	23.9	$.310	$ 7.42
School Aid...........	183	1,316	524	792	5,217	16.0	.248	3.96
College Aid..........	23	1,162	678	484	13,148	33.0	.343	11.31
Graduate Aid.........	1	2	2	—	28	28.0	.500	14.00
Total Employment........		3,099	1,572	1,527				

PENNSYLVANIA

State Youth Director: Walter S. Cowing
219 South Front Street
Harrisburg

Fund Allocations

	Total	Work Projects	Student Aid
1935-1936	$ 3,553,763.48	$1,636,750.21	$1,917,013.27
1936-1937	5,972,679.00	3,953,620.00	2,019,059.00
1937-1938	4,853,688.00	3,333,973.00	1,520,715.00
Grand Total.......	$14,380,130.48	$8,923,343.21	$5,456,787.27

Employment on National Youth Administration Programs for March 1938:

Program	Number Institutions	Number of Persons			Total Earnings	Average Hours Worked	Average Hourly Earnings	Average Monthly Earnings
		Total	Male	Female				
Work Projects								
Total all persons........		11,768	6,362	5,406	$256,456	47.6	$.458	$21.79
Relief..............		11,144	6,049	5,095	215,377	45.5	.445	19.33
Non-relief..........		624	313	311	41,079	84.9	.775	65.83
Student Aid								
Total all programs......	1,204	26,018	14,474	11,544	$168,873	20.7	$.314	$ 6.49
School Aid...........	1,118	19,939	10,451	9,488	93,685	16.8	.280	4.70
College Aid..........	84	5,917	3,897	2,020	72,321	33.4	.366	12.22
Graduate Aid........	13	162	126	36	2,867	36.7	.482	17.70
Total Employment........		37,786	20,836	16,950				

PUERTO RICO

Mr. E. E. Glover
Washington, D. C.

Fund Allocations

	Total	Work Projects[1]	Student Aid
1935–1936	—		—
1936–1937	$33,942.00		$33,942.00
1937–1938	44,478.00		44,478.00
Grand Total.......	$78,420.00		$78,420.00

Employment on National Youth Administration Programs for March 1938:

Program	Number Institutions	Number of Persons			Total Earnings	Average Hours Worked	Average Hourly Earnings	Average Monthly Earnings
		Total	Male	Female				
Student Aid								
Total all programs[2]....	32	492	266	226	$3,993	39.5	$.205	$8.12
School Aid[2]...........	32	492	266	226	3,993	39.5	.205	8.12

[1] No Work Projects Program in operation in Puerto Rico.
[2] Employment figures for month of November 1937 are last available.

State Youth Director: Peter E. Donnelly
Steiner Building
509 Westminster Street
Providence

RHODE ISLAND

Fund Allocations

	Total	Work Projects	Student Aid
1935–1936	$192,268.96	$ 70,670.32	$121,598.64
1936–1937	291,494.00	170,880.00	120,614.00
1937–1938	289,928.00	205,553.00	84,375.00
Grand Total.......	$773,690.96	$447,103.32	$326,587.64

Employment on National Youth Administration Programs for March 1938:

Program	Number Institutions	Number of Persons			Total Earnings	Average Hours Worked	Average Hourly Earnings	Average Monthly Earnings
		Total	Male	Female				
Work Projects								
Total all persons........		529	300	229	$11,666	52.7	$.419	$22.05
Relief..............		510	286	224	10,518	51.2	.402	20.62
Non-relief..........		19	14	5	1,148	90.6	.667	60.42
Student Aid								
Total all programs.....	57	1,126	646	480	$ 9,744	24.4	$.355	$ 8.65
School Aid...........	49	652	303	349	3,777	22.1	.262	5.79
College Aid..........	8	458	331	127	5,691	27.6	.450	12.42
Graduate Aid........	2	16	12	4	276	24.8	.695	17.25
Total Employment........		1,655	946	709				

SOUTH CAROLINA

State Youth Director: Roger L. Coe
29 Arcade Building
Columbia

Fund Allocations

	Total	Work Projects	Student Aid
1935-1936	$ 584,935.96	$ 236,692.12	$ 348,243.84
1936-1937	1,097,429.00	631,540.00	465,889.00
1937-1938	796,169.00	529,949.00	266,220.00
Grand Total........	$2,478,533.96	$1,398,181.12	$1,080,352.84

Employment on National Youth Administration Programs for March 1938:

Program	Number Institutions	Number of Persons			Total Earnings	Average Hours Worked	Average Hourly Earnings	Average Monthly Earnings
		Total	Male	Female				
Work Projects								
Total all persons........		2,592	768	1,824	$36,591	66.8	$.211	$14.12
Relief.................		2,480	732	1,748	30,444	64.6	.190	12.28
Non-relief.............		112	36	76	6,147	116.4	.472	54.88
Student Aid								
Total all programs......	727	5,756	2,462	3,294	$32,835	24.2	$.236	$ 5.70
School Aid............	692	4,431	1,820	2,611	17,419	19.7	.200	3.93
College Aid...........	35	1,323	642	681	15,385	39.3	.296	11.63
Graduate Aid.........	1	2	—	2	31	31.0	.500	15.50
Total Employment........		8,348	3,230	5,118				

SOUTH DAKOTA

State Youth Director: Mrs. Anna C. Struble
City Hall
Mitchell

Fund Allocations

	Total	Work Projects	Student Aid
1935–1936	$ 509,264.02	$ 257,489.70	$251,774.32
1936–1937	956,740.00	555,270.00	401,470.00
1937–1938	818,837.00	572,152.00	246,685.00
Grand Total.......	$2,284,841.02	$1,384,911.70	$899,929.32

Employment on National Youth Administration Programs for March 1938:

Program	Number Institutions	Number of Persons			Total Earnings	Average Hours Worked	Average Hourly Earnings	Average Monthly Earnings
		Total	Male	Female				
Work Projects								
Total all persons........		3,886	2,023	1,863	$54,787	43.7	$.323	$14.10
Relief............		3,733	1,939	1,794	49,391	42.6	.311	13.23
Non-relief...........		153	84	69	5,396	69.4	.598	35.27
Student Aid								
Total all programs.....	386	5,353	2,352	3,001	$27,660	19.9	$.260	$ 5.17
School Aid...........	370	4,607	1,955	2,652	19,316	16.4	.256	4.19
College Aid..........	16	746	397	349	8,344	41.5	.270	11.18
Graduate Aid.........	—	—	—	—	—	—	—	—
Total Employment........		9,239	4,375	4,864				

TENNESSEE

State Youth Director: Bruce Overton
615 Stahlman Building
Nashville

Fund Allocations

	Total	Work Projects	Student Aid
1935–1936	$ 749,992.33	$ 242,010.54	$ 507,981.79
1936–1937	1,332,603.00	697,190.00	635,413.00
1937–1938	930,996.00	554,586.00	376,410.00
Grand Total.......	$3,013,591.33	$1,493,786.54	$1,519,804.79

Employment on National Youth Administration Programs for March 1938:

Program	Number Institutions	Number of Persons			Total Earnings	Average Hours Worked	Average Hourly Earnings	Average Monthly Earnings
		Total	Male	Female				
Work Projects								
Total all persons........		3,085	1,888	1,197	$38,203	60.0	$.206	$12.38
Relief..............		2,971	1,817	1,154	31,953	58.0	.186	10.75
Non-relief...........		114	71	43	6,250	112.5	.488	54.82
Student Aid								
Total all programs.....	583	7,249	3,394	3,855	$44,435	28.2	$.218	$ 6.13
School Aid...........	538	5,455	2,444	3,011	21,858	22.4	.179	4.01
College Aid..........	45	1,710	892	818	20,551	45.8	.262	12.02
Graduate Aid.........	4	84	58	26	2,026	43.9	.550	24.12
Total Employment........		10,334	5,282	5,052				

TEXAS

State Youth Director: J. C. Kellam
603 Littlefield Building
Austin

Fund Allocations

	Total	Work Projects	Student Aid
1935–1936	$1,761,361.57	$ 654,893.17	$1,106,468.40
1936–1937	2,411,507.00	1,020,843.00	1,390,664.00
1937–1938	1,932,529.00	1,037,359.00	895,170.00
Grand Total.......	$6,105,397.57	$2,713,095.17	$3,392,302.40

Employment on National Youth Administration Programs for March 1938:

Program	Number Institutions	Number of Persons			Total Earnings	Average Hours Worked	Average Hourly Earnings	Average Monthly Earnings
		Total	Male	Female				
Work Projects								
Total all persons........		7,319	3,640	3,679	$84,408	42.6	$.271	$11.53
Relief.................		7,241	3,596	3,645	77,221	41.8	.255	10.66
Non-relief............		78	44	34	7,187	115.3	.799	92.14
Student Aid								
Total all programs.....	2,087	13,895	7,294	6,601	$102,531	28.3	$.261	$ 7.38
School Aid............	2,002	8,929	4,615	4,314	39,810	20.7	.215	4.46
College Aid...........	85	4,940	2,666	2,274	62,323	41.9	.301	12.62
Graduate Aid..........	7	26	13	13	398	37.0	.413	15.31
Total Employment.......		21,214	10,934	10,280				

UTAH

State Youth Director: Wilford G. Frischknecht
519 Newhouse Building
Salt Lake City

Fund Allocations

	Total	Work Projects	Student Aid
1935–1936	$ 310,864.87	$ 92,201.28	$218,463.59
1936–1937	352,941.00	133,555.00	218,986.00
1937–1938	343,603.00	183,808.00	159,795.00
Grand Total........	$1,007,408.87	$410,564.28	$597,244.59

Employment on National Youth Administration Programs for March 1938:

Program	Number Institutions	Number of Persons			Total Earnings	Average Hours Worked	Average Hourly Earnings	Average Monthly Earnings
		Total	Male	Female				
Work Projects								
Total all persons........		936	606	330	$15,537	38.9	$.427	$16.60
Relief............		914	588	326	14,031	37.5	.409	15.35
Non-relief............		22	18	4	1,506	95.9	.714	68.45
Student Aid								
Total all programs......	97	2,987	1,630	1,357	$19,770	22.5	$.294	$ 6.62
School Aid............	87	1,661	805	856	6,983	17.2	.245	4.20
College Aid............	10	1,317	816	501	12,671	29.2	.330	9.62
Graduate Aid........	2	9	9	—	116	30.6	.422	12.89
Total Employment........		3,923	2,236	1,687				

VERMONT

State Youth Director: Allan R. Johnston
State Capitol Building
Montpelier

Fund Allocations

	Total	Work Projects	Student Aid
1935–1936	$ 89,623.85	$ 25,448.47	$ 64,175.38
1936–1937	106,094.00	40,110.00	65,984.00
1937–1938	119,749.00	68,149.00	51,600.00
Grand Total........	$315,466.85	$133,707.47	$181,759.38

Employment on National Youth Administration Programs for March 1938:

Program	Number Institutions	Number of Persons			Total Earnings	Average Hours Worked	Average Hourly Earnings	Average Monthly Earnings
		Total	Male	Female				
Work Projects								
Total all persons........		310	154	156	$5,458	43.7	$.403	$17.61
Relief...............		308	152	156	5,233	42.8	.397	16.99
Non-relief............		2	2	—	225	169.0	.666	112.50
Student Aid								
Total all programs.....	88	726	403	323	$5,791	25.2	$.317	$ 7.98
School Aid...........	76	370	178	192	1,773	17.5	.274	4.79
College Aid..........	12	353	224	129	3,963	33.1	.339	11.23
Graduate Aid.........	1	3	1	2	55	36.7	.500	18.33
Total Employment........		1,036	557	479				

VIRGINIA

State Youth Director: Walter S. Newman
State Office Bldg.
Richmond

Fund Allocations

	Total	Work Projects	Student Aid
1935–1936	$ 616,589.51	$ 204,382.86	$ 412,206.65
1936–1937	891,261.00	450,250.00	441,011.00
1937–1938	821,112.00	485,907.00	335,205.00
Grand Total......	$2,328,962.51	$1,140,539.86	$1,188,422.65

Employment on National Youth Administration Programs for March 1938:

Program	Number Institutions	Number of Persons			Total Earnings	Average Hours Worked	Average Hourly Earnings	Average Monthly Earnings
		Total	Male	Female				
Work Projects								
Total all persons.......		3,054	1,018	2,036	$40,786	61.1	$.219	$13.35
Relief............		2,957	995	1,962	35,803	59.6	.203	12.11
Non-relief...........		97	23	74	4,983	105.3	.488	51.37
Student Aid								
Total all programs.....	691	4,871	2,355	2,516	$39,952	30.9	$.266	$ 8.20
School Aid...........	648	3,075	1,355	1,720	15,827	24.4	.211	5.15
College Aid..........	40	1,760	976	784	23,573	42.1	.318	13.39
Graduate Aid.........	7	36	24	12	552	35.5	.432	15.33
Total Employment........		7,925	3,373	4,552				

State Youth Director: John Binns
Washington Building
Tacoma

WASHINGTON

Fund Allocations

	Total	Work Projects	Student Aid
1935–1936	$ 599,003.80	$195,033.78	$ 403,970.02
1936–1937	744,868.00	333,000.00	411,868.00
1937–1938	721,868.00	401,403.00	320,405.00
Grand Total.......	$2,065,679.80	$929,436.78	$1,136,243.02

Employment on National Youth Administration Programs for March 1938:

Program	Number Institutions	Number of Persons			Total Earnings	Average Hours Worked	Average Hourly Earnings	Average Monthly Earnings
		Total	Male	Female				
Work Projects								
Total all persons........		1,649	811	838	$31,509	42.1	$.453	$19.11
Relief...............		1,585	783	802	28,246	40.4	.442	17.82
Non-relief...........		64	28	36	3,263	86.5	.589	50.98
Student Aid								
Total all programs....	293	4,876	2,590	2,286	$34,703	21.8	$.327	$ 7.12
School Aid...........	270	3,107	1,434	1,673	12,428	15.1	.265	4.00
College Aid..........	23	1,738	1,142	596	21,544	33.3	.373	12.40
Graduate Aid.........	1	31	14	17	731	47.2	.500	23.58
Total Employment........		6,525	3,401	3,124				

WEST VIRGINIA

State Youth Director: Glenn S. Callaghan
607 Great Kanawha Bldg.
Capitol and Kanawha Sts.
Charleston

Fund Allocations

	Total	Work Projects	Student Aid
1935–1936	$ 780,303.20	$ 369,635.54	$ 410,667.66
1936–1937	1,181,315.00	759,340.00	421,975.00
1937–1938	955,584.00	653,259.00	302,325.00
Grand Total	$2,917,202.20	$1,782,234.54	$1,134,967.66

Employment on National Youth Administration Programs for March 1938:

Program	Number Institutions	Number of Persons			Total Earnings	Average Hours Worked	Average Hourly Earnings	Average Monthly Earnings
		Total	Male	Female				
Work Projects								
Total all persons		2,632	1,926	706	$44,322	43.5	$.387	$16.84
Relief		2,549	1,866	683	36,001	40.1	.353	14.12
Non-relief		83	60	23	8,321	149.4	.671	100.25
Student Aid								
Total all programs	366	6,188	3,134	3,054	$33,654	20.1	$.270	$5.44
School Aid	345	5,029	2,479	2,550	22,349	17.4	.256	4.44
College Aid	21	1,152	650	502	11,166	31.9	.303	9.69
Graduate Aid	1	7	5	2	139	39.6	.502	19.86
Total Employment		8,820	5,060	3,760				

WISCONSIN

State Youth Director: John Lasher
149 East Wilson Street
Madison

Fund Allocations

	Total	Work Projects	Student Aid
1935–1936	$1,139,240.82	$ 471,343.90	$ 667,896.92
1936–1937	1,739,186.00	1,003,375.00	735,811.00
1937–1938	1,493,374.00	1,018,411.00	474,963.00
Grand Total......	$4,371,800.82	$2,493,129.90	$1,878,670.92

Employment on National Youth Administration Programs for March 1938:

Program	Number Institutions	Number of Persons			Total Earnings	Average Hours Worked	Average Hourly Earnings	Average Monthly Earnings
		Total	Male	Female				
Work Projects								
Total all persons........		3,242	1,657	1,585	$70,283	44.8	$.484	$21.68
Relief...............		3,086	1,562	1,524	59,157	41.9	.457	19.17
Non-relief...........		156	95	61	11,126	101.9	.700	71.32
Student Aid								
Total all programs.....	616	8,655	4,242	4,413	$54,102	20.3	$.308	$ 6.25
School Aid...........	538	5,890	2,563	3,327	22,447	15.0	.254	3.81
College Aid..........	78	2,715	1,637	1,078	30,822	31.6	.359	11.35
Graduate Aid........	3	50	42	8	833	28.4	.586	16.66
Total Employment.......		11,897	5,899	5,998				

WYOMING

State Youth Director: Ernest Marschall
600 East 25th Street
Cheyenne

Fund Allocations

	Total	Work Projects	Student Aid
1935–1936	$ 73,592.06	$ 31,506.50	$ 42,085.50
1936–1937	116,858.70	59,309.70	57,549.00
1937–1938	114,361.00	79,441.00	34,920.00
Grand Total.	$304,811.76	$170,257.20	$134,554.50

Employment on National Youth Administration Programs for March 1938:

Program	Number Institutions	Number of Persons			Total Earnings	Average Hours Worked	Average Hourly Earnings	Average Monthly Earnings
		Total	Male	Female				
Work Projects								
Total all persons.		324	135	189	$5,313	42.0	$.391	$16.40
Relief.		312	130	182	4,843	40.8	.381	15.52
Non-relief.		12	5	7	470	73.6	.532	39.17
Student Aid								
Total all programs.	84	543	287	256	$4,154	24.6	$.311	$ 7.65
School Aid.	83	359	163	196	1,874	19.1	.273	5.22
College Aid.	1	183	123	60	2,255	35.2	.350	12.32
Graduate Aid.	1	1	1	—	25	70.0	.357	25.00
Total Employment.		867	422	445				

Index

Index

Agricultural demonstration, 51, 52
Agricultural work and training, 90–4, 96, 98
Alabama, 50, 104, 178, 191
Arizona, 32
Arkansas, 4, 19, 22, 32, 42, 57, 58, 78, 90, 91, 92, 103, 119, 191, 194
Automobile mechanics, 72, 90, 103, 104

Baker, W. E., 45
Boy Scouts, 30, 62, 63
Brown, Richard R., 15, 210
Bryan, Dr. Roscoe Floyd, 36
Buildings constructed, 31, 33, 34, 35, 40, 63, 70, 88, 91, 92, 98, 104
Buildings remodeled and repaired, 28–31, 40, 50, 61, 62, 80, 91, 96, 103, 104, 140, 149, 187

California, 38, 104, 116, 194
Campfire Girls, 30
Camps constructed, 29, 33, 93, 94
Canning, 48, 58, 59, 93
Carver, Dr. George W., 179
Casey, Edward L., 75
CCC, 9, 11, 12, 13, 15, 104, 158, 212, 213, 216, 217
Children's Bureau, 13
Civil Works Administration, 11, 12
Clerical and stenographic work, 45–9, 52, 124, 133, 152, 187, 197–9
College aid, 156–84
Colorado, 4, 19, 25, 26, 33, 34, 42, 43, 44, 77
Committees, NYA local, 15, 23, 70, 79, 206
Committees, NYA State, 15, 23, 70, 206
Connecticut, 8, 46, 116, 176, 194
Conservation, 26, 28, 50, 51, 98
Construction, 24–36, 62, 65, 98, 100, 103, 104, 138, 139, 204–6
Co-operating sponsors of work projects, 24, 63, 65, 213

Delaware, 46, 194
Delinquency and NYA, 36, 50, 123, 144, 206

Dent, Albert W., 48
Department of Labor, 14
District of Columbia, 15, 119
Donnelly, Peter E., 71

Edgerton, Prof. A. H., 82
Education, President's Advisory Committee on, 216, 217
Educational background of project workers, 18, 19, 41, 192
Employment, 19, 20, 36, 37, 47, 48, 52, 57, 66, 67, 72, 73, 88, 100, 104, 109–121, 123, 125, 126, 129, 130–3, 137–9, 141, 144, 145, 148, 152, 175, 177, 197–9, 216

Federal Census of Unemployment and Partial Unemployment, 8
Federal Committee on Apprentice Training, 11, 14
Fellows, Perry A., 205
FERA, 11, 12, 13, 14, 15, 158, 160, 175
Fletcher, Dr. J. L., 87
Florida, 33, 62
4-H Clubs, 30, 63, 173
Furniture, 29, 33, 34, 39, 40, 41, 44, 57, 58, 68, 92, 132, 187. See Workshops
Future Farmers of America, 47, 173

Geiger, Phillip G., 28
Georgia, 32, 33, 93, 103, 105, 175, 203, 204, 209
Girl Scouts, 30, 62, 63
Glanders, Ralph, 99
Graduate aid, 156–84
Grannen, Walter A., 99

Haney, Ova, 31
Harrington, Col. F. C., 304
Hayes, Dr. Mary H. S., 115, 117
Health facilities, training, and services, 30–2, 48, 49, 57, 71, 79, 89, 94, 103, 107, 133, 137, 140, 143, 202–4
Hoey, Fred, 77
Home economics, 56, 57, 59, 62, 71, 89, 91, 104, 188

Homemaking, 52, 53, 55–9, 63, 70, 89, 91, 92, 104, 123, 135, 138
Home situations of project workers, 18, 53, 123–8, 131, 134, 136, 140–2
Hopkins, Harry L., 13
Hospital and health aides, 48, 49, 71, 133, 137, 143

Idaho, 96, 97, 103, 161
Illinois, 4, 46, 61, 74, 83, 84, 119, 162, 169, 172, 203
Indiana, 116, 176, 188
Iowa, 4, 104, 116, 161

Junior Placement Divisions, 115–20

Kansas, 4, 28, 29, 50, 83, 104, 177, 188, 194
Kentucky, 4, 19, 22, 31, 40, 53, 54, 70, 74, 116, 130, 149, 154, 181
Kiwanis Club, 30
Kraus, Mrs. Theresa, 46

Laughlin, Anne, 83
Lewis, Travis J., 208
Library work, 43–5, 50, 62, 150, 151, 187
Louisiana, 4, 19, 30, 31, 48, 55, 86–9, 103

Maine, 73, 82, 99–102, 178
Maryland, 4, 180
Massachusetts, 8, 38, 46, 51, 75, 76, 116, 148, 178, 180, 194
McDonough, Mayor John P., 34
Michigan, 45, 51, 77, 82, 188
Minnesota, 4, 11, 27, 28, 62, 78, 83, 104, 116, 166, 171, 174, 197, 204
Mississippi, 74, 82, 104, 173, 174, 191, 194
Missouri, 4, 39, 48, 79, 83, 84, 179, 188
Montana, 180
Moses, Commissioner Robert, 25

Nebraska, 72, 104, 166
Negro youth, 48–50, 61, 62, 93, 94, 104, 119, 159
Nevada, 119, 194
New Hampshire, 80, 104, 116
New Jersey, 174, 194
New Mexico, 51, 64, 77, 104
New York City, 15, 22, 25, 46, 49, 71
New York State, 4, 45, 72, 77, 80, 104, 176, 177, 194, 207
North Carolina, 59, 116, 119

North Dakota, 29, 104, 175
Nursery schools, 47, 57, 92, 140

Occupational studies, 82, 83
Office of Education, 13, 14
Ohio, 49, 72, 81, 103, 164, 167, 170, 203
Oklahoma, 63, 103, 173
Oregon, 75, 194
Overstreet, Pres. Charles A., 91

Park improvement and development, 25–9, 103, 126
Pennsylvania, 4, 8, 46, 51, 104
Playgrounds, 27, 140, 187
PWA, 12

Quoddy, 100–2

Radio, 82, 84
Recreational assistants, 49, 50, 80
Recreational equipment and facilities, 27–31, 34, 39, 42, 50, 62, 103
Red Cross, 70, 106
Reeves, Dr. Floyd W., 99
Related training classes, 56, 57, 62, 69–75, 77, 78, 84, 85, 89, 92–4, 96, 98–100, 103, 104, 133
Resident Projects, 86–107, 123, 147, 150, 161, 196, 200, 203, 208, 212, 215
Rhode Island, 28, 70, 82, 194, 203
Rienow, Dean Robert E., 183
Road work, 26, 27, 28, 30, 97, 103
Roche, Josephine, 14
Rotary Club, 30

Sarré, A. J., 30
Scholarship, student aid, 169–83, 190
School aid, 184–91
School buildings remodeled, 29, 31
School equipment constructed, 27, 39, 40–2, 98
School lunches, 47, 48
Sewing projects, 53–8, 62, 63, 69, 70, 89, 92, 93, 96, 127, 129, 130, 136, 141, 146, 154
South Carolina, 103, 191
South Dakota, 26, 27, 104

Taussig, Charles W., 13, 14
Tennessee, 39, 40, 51, 104, 162, 189
Texas, 50, 80, 103, 104, 116, 208
Turner, Dr. Jennie M., 82

Urban League, 94

U. S. Bureau of Immigration and Naturalization, 46
U. S. Employment Service, 8
Utah, 34, 72, 104, 151, 191

Vegetable raising, 47, 57, 59, 146
Vermont, 177
Virginia, 4, 47, 58, 104
Vocational information, 81, 82, 83, 84

Waite, Col. Henry M., 99
Washington, 104, 176
Weaving, 54, 55, 63, 64, 89
West Virginia, 4, 27, 35, 36, 40, 41, 104, 116, 180
Williams, Aubrey, 14, 15, 209

Wilson, A. T., 94
Wisconsin, 46, 47, 50, 54, 55, 78, 82, 97, 98, 103, 105, 116, 178
Work program, engineers' report on NYA, 204–6
Work projects, student aid, 165–9, 187–190
Workshops, 37–45, 62, 65, 68
WPA, 11, 12, 69, 72, 73–5, 79, 87, 89, 106, 133, 212, 216
Wright, Houston A., 63
Wyoming, 49, 179

YMCA, 30, 70, 76, 80, 83, 94
Youth centers, 34, 35, 60–3, 84
YWCA, 30, 62, 69, 80, 94